THE **COMPLETE** **IDIOT'S** **GUIDE**® TO

World History

Second Edition

by Timothy C. Hall, M.A.

ALPHA

A member of Penguin Group (USA) Inc.

I dedicate this work to my loving and inspiring wife, Debra, and my chess-playing son, Thomas.

ALPHA BOOKS

Published by the Penguin Group

Penguin Group (USA) Inc., 375 Hudson Street, New York, New York 10014, USA

Penguin Group (Canada), 90 Eglinton Avenue East, Suite 700, Toronto, Ontario M4P 2Y3, Canada (a division of Pearson Penguin Canada Inc.)

Penguin Books Ltd., 80 Strand, London WC2R 0RL, England

Penguin Ireland, 25 St. Stephen's Green, Dublin 2, Ireland (a division of Penguin Books Ltd.)

Penguin Group (Australia), 250 Camberwell Road, Camberwell, Victoria 3124, Australia (a division of Pearson Australia Group Pty. Ltd.)

Penguin Books India Pvt. Ltd., 11 Community Centre, Panchsheel Park, New Delhi—110 017, India

Penguin Group (NZ), 67 Apollo Drive, Rosedale, North Shore, Auckland 1311, New Zealand (a division of Pearson New Zealand Ltd.)

Penguin Books (South Africa) (Pty.) Ltd., 24 Sturdee Avenue, Rosebank, Johannesburg 2196, South Africa

Penguin Books Ltd., Registered Offices: 80 Strand, London WC2R 0RL, England

Copyright © 2012 by Timothy C. Hall

International Standard Book Number: 978-1-61564-148-2
Library of Congress Catalog Card Number: 2011910193

14   13   12   8   7   6   5   4   3   2   1

Interpretation of the printing code: The rightmost number of the first series of numbers is the year of the book's printing; the rightmost number of the second series of numbers is the number of the book's printing. For example, a printing code of 12-1 shows that the first printing occurred in 2012.

Printed in the United States of America

Note: This publication contains the opinions and ideas of its author. It is intended to provide helpful and informative material on the subject matter covered. It is sold with the understanding that the author and publisher are not engaged in rendering professional services in the book. If the reader requires personal assistance or advice, a competent professional should be consulted.

The author and publisher specifically disclaim any responsibility for any liability, loss, or risk, personal or otherwise, which is incurred as a consequence, directly or indirectly, of the use and application of any of the contents of this book.

Most Alpha books are available at special quantity discounts for bulk purchases for sales promotions, premiums, fundraising, or educational use. Special books, or book excerpts, can also be created to fit specific needs.

For details, write: Special Markets, Alpha Books, 375 Hudson Street, New York, NY 10014.

Publisher: *Marie Butler-Knight*

Associate Publisher: *Mike Sanders*

Executive Managing Editor: *Billy Fields*

Executive Editor: *Lori Cates Hand*

Development Editor: *Megan Douglass*

Senior Production Editor: *Janette Lynn*

Copy Editor: *Amy Borrelli*

Cover Designer: *William Thomas*

Book Designers: *William Thomas, Rebecca Batchelor*

Indexer: *Joan Green*

Layout: *Brian Massey*

Proofreader: *John Etchison*

Contents

Appendixes

Introduction

Most people assume the study of world history is just the study of an endless series of facts, isolated to certain regions and time periods. This method of studying world history is very limiting: focusing on the details sometimes prevents us from seeing the big picture.

The study of world history is really the study of change. It is about the evolution of civilizations. It is about expansion and decline and about actions and reactions. World history examines the factors of change, including geography, economics, government, culture, science, technology, society, and religion.

The study of world history is also about connections and the themes that connect civilizations over time and space. These themes include …

- The diffusion of culture.

- Interactions of civilizations.

- Changes caused by people and the environment.

- Comparisons of political and social systems.

- Continuity and change in time.

I have not put as much emphasis on providing historical fact upon fact; instead, I have tried to paint the historical picture with broad, sweeping strokes. If you are interested in the fine details, use the further readings found in Appendix D to select an appropriate volume to find out more. This world history is about big pictures and historical themes.

How This Book Is Organized

This book is divided into five parts.

Part 1, The Beginnings and the Foundations of Civilization, starts with the emergence of *homo sapiens*, or humans, as the dominant hominid group in the world. After the beginning of the Neolithic revolution, humans acquired the building blocks of civilization. From there civilizations sprang up around the fertile river valleys of the Tigris and Euphrates rivers, as well as the Nile, Indus, and Huang He rivers. The people created governments, usually monarchies. Many kings rose and fell on the banks of the river valleys.

In time the world witnessed the rise of the classical empires. Classical Greece, Rome, India, and China all made their mark on the history of the world and the present day. The classical period also produced new religions and philosophies. Hinduism, Buddhism, Judaism, and Christianity all originated during this period. Greek and Roman philosophies, as well as the Chinese philosophies of Confucianism, Daoism, and Legalism, emerged, too. All of these religions and philosophies have impacted the history of the world in immeasurable ways.

Part 2, After the Classics, details the fall of the classic regional empires due to the invasions of nomadic tribes. With their collapse, the stability enjoyed by the regions under their influence was lost. People began to rely on decentralized political structures. All appeared to be lost.

Limited trade between the classic regional empires continued along the "Silk Road," which gradually developed into the first interregional trade network. Along this network the ideas and religions of the classical period spread. And there were other impressive developments involving religion—Islam, for example, came into being during this time and became the first global civilization.

As this period came to a close, things were looking up for the civilizations of the world. The decentralization at the beginning of the period began to fall away and centralized nations emerged. Ironically, invasions began this period, and they also ended it. Another nomadic group, the Mongols, staged several invasions. These invasions were disruptive, but it was only temporary. Civilizations continued to centralize and develop. The march of progress would not be stopped.

Part 3, The World Gets Much Smaller, starts modern history. Europe had emerged as number one, so to speak. Once things stabilized after the Mongolian invasions, trade expanded along interregional networks. This trade continued to snowball when European nations, with commerce in mind, began to explore and colonize. The use of technology became a key factor in the expanding empires. The European nations were able to use gunpowder. They ascended to the position of control over most of the world.

In **Part 4, Western Domination,** Europe controls most everything in the world. Things got better for the European nations as they industrialized, which helped to expand the interregional network into a truly global trade network. With industrialization, the European nations started a renewed program of colonization. Most of the significant historical events from this period are the result of other nations' reaction to the West's assertion of power. But just when things were going so well for Europe, the idea of nationalism, belief in the unique superiority of one's nation, caught up with them.

Part 5, The Twentieth Century and Beyond, starts with the beginning of World War I, which was the beginning of the end of European dominance of the world. Although the European nations were able to hold on for a while (to the end of World War II), the nationalism that eventually spread around the world ended their reign as number one. Of course, someone always wants to fill the number one slot. The United States and Soviet Union fought a cold war for that position. The United States came out on top; for how long is another question.

The global trading network that developed in the previous period multiplied. Its influence can be seen in the development of globalization, where distinctions between people and nations start to blur. With globalization have come problems, including substantial environmental and economic issues.

Extras

WHAT IN THE WORLD

This feature will inform you of really interesting historical facts and key points relating world history to the present, making you a hit at most any party.

NOTABLE QUOTABLE

This feature will give you an interesting or important quote from world history related to the topic you are reading about.

DEFINITION

This feature will give you definitions of terms that will make you world-history smart.

Acknowledgments

This volume would not have been possible without the help of some important people in my life. First, I would like to thank my family for their understanding and patience with the long hours I put in on this project. Other thanks go to Jessica Faust for getting me this work. Thank you to the tutors and fellows of Pembroke College, Oxford University, for giving me access to the library and rooms in which to organize this project. Thanks to the faculty and staff at Franklin Academy for their support. And finally, thanks to Dr. Michael Enright of East Carolina University and Dr. Gordon Marino, whose words of encouragement and examples kept me working.

Special Thanks to the Technical Reviewer

The Complete Idiot's Guide to World History, Second Edition, was reviewed by an expert who double-checked the accuracy of what you'll learn here, to help us ensure that this book gives you everything you need to know about world history. Special thanks are extended to Dan McDowell.

Trademarks

All terms mentioned in this book that are known to be or are suspected of being trademarks or service marks have been appropriately capitalized. Alpha Books and Penguin Group (USA) Inc. cannot attest to the accuracy of this information. Use of a term in this book should not be regarded as affecting the validity of any trademark or service mark.

The Beginnings and Foundations of Civilization

With the advent of the Neolithic revolution, humans acquired the building blocks of civilization. From there civilizations sprang up around the fertile river valleys of the Tigris and Euphrates rivers, as well as the Nile, Indus, and Huang He rivers. Many different rulers rose and fell as the civilizations became more and more complex culturally and technologically.

With the increased complexity came many developments. First is the rise of the classical empires. Greece, Rome, India, and China all made their stamp on the history of the world for thousands of years to come. The complexity of the classical period also produced new sophisticated religions and philosophies that have impacted the history of the world in immeasurable ways.

The Building Blocks of Civilization

In This Chapter

- Different hominids
- The origin of humans
- Hunter-gatherer culture
- Neolithic Revolution
- How civilizations are started

Beginning a history of the world is a formidable task. One is tempted to begin with "in the beginning," but that really doesn't help. "In the beginning" suggests the beginning of the earth or possibly even the universe, in which humans have filled only a small portion of time and space. Therefore, to begin the history of the world, we should stick with the history of humans, how they lived and died, and the change that occurred because humans developed a big interest in both living and dying.

You Say You Want an Evolution

The history of human beings begins not with us but with another group of primates known as *Australopithecus*. This group emerged from southern and eastern Africa about 3 to 4 million years ago. *Australopithecus* had an average height of 3½ to 5 feet—definitely not built for basketball—and, with their small brain size, they wouldn't be much good at chess, either. But *Australopithecus* did walk upright on two legs, which distinguishes them as the earliest hominid to walk the planet. They also had a larynx, or voice box, which allowed for the development of primitive verbal communication with all of the understandings and misunderstandings that encompasses. Although *Australopithecus* lived in the luxuriously humid forests of Africa, they were nomadic, constantly moving in search of food and temporary shelter.

Later Hominid Groups

Of course, the reign of *Australopithecus* did not last forever. They were superseded by other "new and improved" hominids. The first hominid group after *Australopithecus* was *homo habilis*, or "person with ability," which emerged from Africa 1½ to 3 million years ago (that date isn't set in stone, so to speak).

Homo habilis were improved over *Australopithecus* because of abilities—such as the creation of crude stone tools—which made their life a bit easier. Socially, *homo habilis* had a limited speech ability. But just like *Australopithecus*, they continued to survive by gathering and scavenging for food.

Homo Erectus

Homo habilis was followed by *homo erectus*, which again came out of Africa about 150,000 to 200,000 years ago. The technological skill of *homo erectus* was decidedly better than that of *homo habilis*. They developed hand axes and other stone tools. *Homo erectus* used caves as a form of shelter and were able to dig pits. They also draped animal skins over themselves as a primitive form of clothing for protection from the elements. *Homo erectus* were the first to control fire for warmth, protection, and the cooking of meat.

All of these big steps in development led to increased life spans with fewer diseases. This group made big leaps socially as well. They developed spoken language, which allowed for the nomadic bands to coordinate small hunting parties to add to the practice of scavenging for dead animals and gathering plant life for food.

Homo Sapiens

Each hominid group that emerged was another step closer to the humans we are. The next group to emerge from Africa was *homo sapiens*, or "person who thinks," around 200,000 years ago. Through the archaeological evidence, they have been divided into two variants.

The first variant was the Neanderthal, which existed approximately from 200,000 to 35,000 years ago. Most people use the word "Neanderthal" to tag someone as not intelligent, but the Neanderthals were very intelligent compared to their predecessors. They developed important technology, including the spear point and hide scraper. Neanderthals needed the scraper because they were sewing hides together to make garments. This hominid group used caves for shelter like *homo erectus*, but also built simple shelters in the form of lean-tos. These shelters weren't architecturally impressive, but they did provide shelter and protection from the harsh environment.

WHAT IN THE WORLD

Cave painters used many different techniques. They used charcoal and other natural pigments to daub, dot, and sketch their cave walls. Cave painters from different time periods often worked on the same cave walls. They simply painted over someone else's work. At the famous cave at Lascaux, France, 13 different time periods of paintings have been identified.

Socially, Neanderthals believed in some type of afterlife, although anthropologists are not sure to what extent. Evidence for this is found in their planned burials for the dead of the community. It also appears that they cared for the disabled members of the community, even though it might have hindered the group in hunting and gathering. This, according to some, suggests a morality in Neanderthals that did not exist in previous hominid groups.

The other group of *homo sapiens* is the Cro-Magnon, which existed from 60,000 to 8,000 years ago, although, again, these dates vary depending on current archaeological findings. They advanced beyond the Neanderthals considerably in technological skill and innovations. The Cro-Magnons developed knives, chisels, spears, and the bow and arrow, making hunting much easier than before. They developed bone tools in the form of needles, fish hooks, and harpoons, as well as fishnets and canoes, bringing about the addition of seafood to their diet. The lines of clothing improved, too! The Cro-Magnons created sewed leather clothing. In the area of food preparation they fashioned sun-hardened pottery, which allowed for better food storage.

The society of the Cro-Magnon advanced greatly, too. They participated in large-scale big-game hunts—*very* big game, like the wooly mammoth! They chose formal leaders, who usually received a special type of burial. Belief in the afterlife progressed into religion, which included magic rituals depicted in cave paintings or sculpted artifacts. The Cro-Magnons were a much more advanced *homo sapiens*, but the story did not end with them.

Almost Human

Some 200,000 to 100,000 years ago, another group of hominids emerged from Africa. This group, *homo sapiens sapiens*, are human beings' direct ancestors. They coexisted to some degree with the Neanderthals and Cro-Magnons, and over time acquired all of the technological skills of both groups of *homo sapiens*.

The time of all of this hominid development and evolution is called the Stone Age, from the very obvious fact that our proto-human ancestors used stone tools. It is divided into three periods: the Paleolithic Age or "Old Stone Age," from 2 million to 12000 B.C.E. The next period is titled the Mesolithic or "Middle Stone Age," which dates from 12000 to 8000 B.C.E. The last is called the Neolithic Age or "New Stone Age," which dates from 8000 to 5000 B.C.E.

DEFINITION

B.C.E. is a newer historical, nonreligious term that replaces B.C. and stands for "Before the Common Era." C.E., meaning "Common Era," replaces A.D.

During the Stone Age there was also an Ice Age, lasting from 2 million to 10,000 years ago, with four long periods of extremely cold and harsh climate. Massive glaciers or sheets of ice spread from the North and South poles, carving and creating much of the landscape of the northern continents as they spread and receded. They also allowed the various roving bands of humans a way to reach continents that would, millennia later, be separated by oceans.

Eventually the Neanderthals and Cro-Magnon became extinct and the *homo sapiens sapiens* were the dominant hominid group. Some 20,000 to 30,000 years ago, the *homo sapiens sapiens* (we can just call them humans now!) migrated from Africa into Asia and Europe, and eventually into North and South America. During this time, humans evolved differently depending on their continent, climate, and environment. This led to modifications in skin color and the evolution of three racial types: African, Asian, and Caucasian. In terms of human biology, racial differences are very slight; the genetic structure of all humans is virtually the same.

Hunter-Gatherer Culture

As the hominid groups progressed through time, so did the development of the hunter-gatherer culture. At first glance, this culture appears to be very simple, but it was and still is quite complex; there are still groups of indigenous people across the globe that continue with this way of life.

First and foremost, it was based on the simple family unit, which expanded into ties of kinship between families. Those ties of kinship eventually combined to create larger connected groups called clans. Clans became interconnected and developed into tribes. The tribes existed through hunting and gathering and in the process created a sophisticated social and political organization that included political leaders (the chief) and religious figures (the priest). There was also a gender division of labor within the hunter-gatherer culture. Males dominated hunting, war, and heavy labor because of their natural upper-body strength. Women became the gatherers and preparers of food, and also tended to the children of the tribe.

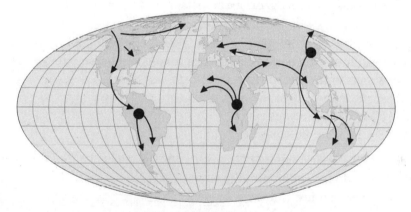

10000 B.C.E.

The tribes of hunter-gatherer culture developed religiously by creating and worshipping many different gods, usually associated with natural forces and features. They practiced a variety of rituals, including, by the Mesolithic Age, sacrifices to the gods—possibly even human sacrifices. As already mentioned, they believed in some kind of afterlife as early as 100,000 years ago, and developed burial practices for the dead. Artistic expression has also been suggested to be a result of religion, with art in cave paintings dating to 32,000 years ago and musical instruments in the form of flutes dating to 30,000 years ago.

NOTABLE QUOTABLE

Archaeology deals with a period limited to a few thousand years and its subject is not the universe, not even the human race, but modern man. We dig, and say of these pots and pans, these beads and weapons, that they date back to 3000 to 4000 B.C., and the onlooker is tempted to exclaim at their age, and to admire them simply because they are old. Their real interest lies in the fact that they are new.

—*Digging Up the Past,* Leonard Woolley, on the significance of archaeology

Neolithic Revolution

The nomadic lifestyle of the hunter-gatherer tribes did eventually change with the Neolithic Revolution. The title comes from the simple fact that all of these changes happened during the Neolithic Age. The revolution happened about 10,000 years ago, but it varies from continent to continent. For example, in the Middle East it occurred around 8000 B.C.E.; in China the revolution occurred around 5000 B.C.E. Regardless of its onset, humans learned to grow certain staple crops on a continual and controlled basis, which led to systematic agriculture.

This agricultural revolution radically changed the hunter-gatherer nature of human culture. At first, with the practice of migratory farming, the nomadic lifestyles of humans continued, but eventually they began to settle down longer with slash-and-burn practices (cutting down and burning forests). Finally humans really settled down with the development of shifting agriculture, which allowed land to be cultivated successfully for centuries. No longer did humans have to roam from place to place in search of food. With this shift to farming mostly performed by males, societies gradually became male dominated.

Permanent dwellings and then villages appeared as tribes stopped their nomadic lifestyle. Certain crops such as wheat, barley, rice, millet, and maize became domesticated for their ease of cultivation. Having a surplus of food meant humans did not have to look for food constantly, leading to more time for other tasks. It is probably no coincidence that fermentation of alcoholic beverages appears at about this time, too!

WHAT IN THE WORLD

An unfortunate effect of civilization and the domestication of animals has been the increase of the number of diseases in humans. Many diseases are the result of humans living near the animals that they tend. The flu originated with ducks and pigs, while anthrax, smallpox, and tuberculosis came from cattle.

Animals were domesticated during this time as well. "Man's best friend" was man's first animal companion and was used to help with the hunting duties that continued throughout this period to some degree. The next animal that was domesticated was the goat, which was used for its milk and meat. Other animals soon followed, including horses, cattle, pigs, sheep, and chickens, all of which provided part of the supply of labor, meat, eggs, and milk for humans in the settlements. This pastoral revolution in the domestication of animals was aided by the steady supply of food created from the agricultural revolution.

How Civilization Develops

With the Neolithic Revolution, most humans began to settle in permanent settlements, villages, and larger cities. Those settlements created complex societies based on advances in the knowledge of farming, trade, government, art, and science.

All of this complexity was possible because of the surplus of food. The surplus of food led to the creation of governmental structures, including powerful leaders to supervise the surplus, soldiers to guard the surplus, and priests to justify the leader's actions (or inaction) with religion.

The surplus also led to a surplus of labor, which allowed for an artisan class that made jewelry, weapons, and pottery. Consequently a merchant class developed to trade the objects that the artisan class created. Furthermore, these artisans, through experimentation, developed bronze, a mixture of copper and tin, which started the Bronze Age. Writing was invented to keep record of the surplus of food, religious offerings, and taxes. (Yes, taxes began that early!) It was also used to record religious myths for the priests and the people. All of this gradually added up to the creation of several civilizations around the world at different times.

Two early cities unearthed by archaeologists appear to be the earliest examples of this process of civilization. The first was Jericho, found on the west bank of the Jordan River in present-day Palestine. The second was Catal Huyuk, found in present-day Turkey. Both cities date from about 8000 to 7000 B.C.E., although these cities did not become the major center of developing civilizations. That award goes to the river valley civilizations.

These civilizations formed in the valleys of the Nile River in Egypt (4000 B.C.E.), the Tigris and Euphrates rivers in the Middle East (3500 B.C.E.), the Indus River in India (2500 B.C.E.), and the Huang He River in China (2000 B.C.E.). The impact of these civilizations cannot be overstated and they are, deservedly, the subject of the next chapters.

The Least You Need to Know

- Paleolithic peoples learned to adapt to their nomadic lifestyle.
- Adaptations led to improved tools and the use of fire, which led to more advances in human culture and society.
- The Neolithic Revolution helped to create even more complex human culture and society. Humans stopped moving from place to place and settled down in agricultural communities.
- These societies developed into the first advanced civilizations.

First Civilizations of Africa and Western Asia

In This Chapter

- The wonders and achievement of Egypt
- The rise of the Tigris and Euphrates River civilizations
- The contributions of the Phoenicians and Lydians
- The kingdom of Israel

Two centers of civilization sprang up amidst the desert sands of northern Africa and western Asia to produce wondrous pyramids and complex urban centers. The civilizations of Mesopotamia and Egypt were soon followed by the other smaller but no less significant civilizations of the Phoenicians, Lydians, and Israelites.

The Nile and Early Egypt

The area around the Nile River has the geographical features to make a great starting point for a civilization. The river itself is 4,160 miles long and empties into the Mediterranean Sea. The advantage the river's length offers the region comes from the rich black soil that covers the banks and the delta of the river. More important, the fertile black soil is replenished frequently by annual and predictable flood waters that allowed for the cultivation of wheat, barley, and papyrus.

Because of the agricultural value of the region, settlements and small kingdoms began to form on the banks of the Nile as early as 5000 B.C.E. By around 4000 B.C.E., two kingdoms—the lower kingdom in the north and the upper kingdom in the south dominated the Nile River valley. They eventually united under the direction of King Menes around 3000 B.C.E. and built a capital city at Memphis. From that point, historians have traditionally divided Egyptian history into three time periods.

The Old Kingdom (2700–2200 B.C.E.)

The Old Kingdom in Egyptian history spanned from about 2700 to 2200 B.C.E. Egypt developed a strong national government that ruled centrally from the capital city of Memphis. The king ruled as a theocrat holding both religious and political power. (Strange, the leadership of early civilizations had this tendency.) With that religious and political power, the kings of Egypt directed large public works. The most famous were (and still are) the Step Pyramid at Saqqara built under King Djoser and the Pyramids at Giza started under King Khufru.

> **NOTABLE QUOTABLE**
>
> The Sun god has placed king N in the land of the living for eternity and all time; for judging mankind, for making the gods content, for creating Truth, for destroying evil. He gives offerings to the gods ....
>
> —"The King as Sun Priest," Anonymous

The Middle Kingdom (2200–1786 B.C.E.)

The Middle Kingdom was not quite as industrious or peaceful as the Old Kingdom. From 2200 to 2050 B.C.E., Egypt experienced a time of internal civil wars and upheaval. Eventually, King Mentuhotep II united the country again under a strong central government and moved the capital to the city of Thebes. This physical and political move was followed by internal peace and prosperity that lasted until about the 1700s B.C.E.

Then trouble began with local nobles who challenged the kings' authority. Those challenges worked to erode the kings' power and Egypt's ability to defend itself. During this time of weakness in Egypt, the Hykos, a nation of people from the region of Syria-Palestine, invaded and conquered Egypt with the use of horse-drawn chariots.

The New Kingdom (1600–945 B.C.E.)

After a short period of outside rule by the Hykos, the Egyptian prince Ahmose drove the invaders from Egypt using the same horse-drawn chariot technology. Eventually Ahmose united and restored Egypt under one central government, and a new leadership role was created called the "pharaoh," which means "great house of the king."

The pharaohs' religious power also expanded as they adopted the view that they were gods on earth. During this period, Ramses the Great ruled Egypt for 67 years. His greatness not only lay in his ability to rule the Egyptian Empire longer than most pharaohs, but also the conquests that he made to expand the empire into the Middle East.

Of course, with expansion comes contraction—what goes up must come down. During the 1100s B.C.E., Ramses III (no direct relation to the great Ramses!) lost several wars in neighboring Syria, which spelled the beginning of the end of the New Kingdom period and the Egyptian Empire. By 945 B.C.E., the Egyptian Empire was sufficiently weakened that the Libyans from the south and the Kushites from the north were able to divide and conquer the territory, ending the glory of the Egyptian Empire.

Egyptian Society and Religion

The Egyptian Empire developed some very sophisticated social and religious systems. There were several classes of people within Egyptian society. At the top were the royal families, nobles, and priests. Below them were the merchants, artisans, scribes, and tax collectors. The lower class, predominantly farmers, made up the majority of the population. Finally, on the very bottom, were the slaves who came from the people conquered by the Egyptians. (You might remember the Israelites were once slaves, according to the Bible.)

Religiously the Egyptians were *polytheistic*, although some gods were more important than others. Some of those important gods included Ra, the sun god; Osiris, the god of life and death; and Isis, the wife of Osiris. As part of Egyptian religion, hieroglyphics were created to cast spells for help in the afterlife—another religious belief the Egyptians held. Hieroglyphs are symbols that stand for objects, ideas, and/or sounds. The Egyptians placed the hieroglyphs in the tombs of the mummified dead to take advantage of the magical powers they felt the hieroglyphs had.

 DEFINITION

Polytheism refers to the societal worship of many different gods.

Belief in the afterlife was also central to the preparation of the body after death because the body was the house of the soul. The process of mummification started because of the perceived need to protect that house. The process itself was very long—sometimes up to 70 days. The dead body was sufficiently dried and wrapped in cloth to be preserved for centuries.

WHAT IN THE WORLD

During the late nineteenth century and early twentieth century there was a huge market for mummies in Europe. Some people even ground up mummy parts for medicinal purposes.

Egyptian Accomplishments

Religion was the engine that pushed the Egyptians to some very important achievements in science. They created the 365-day calendar to track the stars for religious purposes and to predict the flooding of the Nile. Math and engineering were developed to build the various pyramids because they believed the pharaohs' bodies had to be housed in a great monument when their spirits returned to their bodies. The Egyptians detailed the anatomy of the human body—a reference for countless civilizations through the centuries—all because the mummification process was linked to the belief in the afterlife. Those achievements would not be lost in the Egyptian sands of time. Western and world civilization learned from the Egyptians long after their empire had disappeared.

The Tigris and Euphrates Rivers

The Tigris and Euphrates rivers were the location for several other significant human civilizations that appeared in 3500 B.C.E. The Tigris and Euphrates River valley is the geographical area around and between the rivers as they flow from modern-day Turkey into the Persian Gulf, including parts of Iraq, Jordan, Israel, Lebanon, and Syria. It is an excellent area for agriculture and has been justly called the "Fertile Crescent" because of its fruitful soil and its crescent shape. You may also hear it called Mesopotamia, which in Greek means "land between two rivers."

Mesopotamia's advantages are all associated with its agricultural benefits. The Tigris and Euphrates rivers flood often and in an unpredictable fashion. This might appear at first to be a bad thing, but it wasn't. The receding flood waters left deposits of silt, which made great soil for agriculture. Of course, the trick was to control the flood waters, which the early inhabitants of Mesopotamia did by building dams and ditches.

The other benefit of this activity was the advanced restructuring of society to perform the task of controlling the flood waters.

A Summary of the Sumerians

The first group to settle in the Fertile Crescent was the Sumerians in 3500 B.C.E. The word "Sumerians" was derived from the region of the lower Euphrates River called Sumer. They did not think of themselves as "the Sumerian civilization," although historians have referred to them as such. By 3000 B.C.E., the Sumerians had created 12 city-states in the region.

Each city-state ruled itself and the territory immediately around it. The center of the city was dominated by the ziggurat—a massive stone structure topped with a temple dedicated to the god each city-state worshipped. The Sumerians worshipped many gods, who generally ruled over natural forces or human activities. By 2700 B.C.E., most of the city-states had developed a monarchical form of leadership. Those kings also served as the high priest to the god of the city-state, making the king the link between the god and the people. (Hopefully, you can see where that path can lead!) Thus, in Sumerian civilization, religion and politics operated together to maintain a stable city-state.

The stability of the city-states and the relative peace of the region (although the city-states did fight from time to time) allowed for some impressive achievements. In 3100 B.C.E. the Sumerians developed the first form of writing, called cuneiform. Cuneiform writing was created by using a reed to make hundreds of wedge-shaped marks on wet clay tablets. These tablets were later hardened in ovens, making them "set in stone," or unchangeable.

A separate class of people called scribes emerged from the development of cuneiform. The scribes did most of the writing, which included keeping records, recording history, and writing myths. Other Sumerian inventions were generally associated with agricultural production or the prediction and/or control of the flood waters of the Tigris and Euphrates rivers. These include the wagon wheel, arch, potter's wheel, sundial, the metal plow, a 12-month calendar, and a number system based on 60.

Finally, the Sumerians produced a major text of world literature titled *The Epic of Gilgamesh*, which is perhaps the oldest written human story. Written on 12 clay tablets in cuneiform script somewhere around 2500 B.C.E., the epic details the adventures of the historical King of Uruk.

> **WHAT IN THE WORLD**
>
> Our modern system of math has its roots in Mesopotamia. Sumerians began experimenting with numbers as a way to keep records for administration and trade. One mathematical development we continue to use is the number system based on 60—we use it for telling time!

The Action of the Akkadians

Akkad was a typical city-state of the Fertile Crescent until the reign of Sargon I. Born a sheep herder's son, Sargon was abandoned in a reed basket in the Euphrates River by his mother (maybe the story sounds familiar). Despite those obstacles, or perhaps because of them, Sargon ambitiously climbed to the political top as the king of the city-state of Akkad in 2300 B.C.E. Not satisfied with his power as king, Sargon launched an aggressive campaign of conquest against the other city-states of Mesopotamia. He conquered all of the city-states save one and created the Akkadian Empire. Sadly, Sargon I did not prepare well for succession to the throne of his empire—or maybe he was so confident he thought he would not die! The Akkadian Empire fell apart soon after his death, with the help of the one city-state that he hadn't conquered: Ebla.

The city-state of Ebla was powerful enough to resist the attacks of Sargon I. After Sargon's death, Ebla counterattacked, possibly in its own defense, and eventually dominated the Fertile Crescent. Of course, all good things have to come to an end, and this was the case with the Sumerian city-states. The region was very fertile and drew the attention of many potential conquerors. By 2000 B.C.E., the Amorites, outsiders from west Syria who saw the value of the lands of the Fertile Crescent, conquered Ebla. With few natural barriers and the independent nature of the city-states, the rest of the region would soon be conquered as well.

Hammurabi and the Babylonians

After conquering Ebla, the powerhouse of the region, the Amorites continued to expand across the Fertile Crescent and overran most of the city-states, including Babylon. To the Amorites, Babylon looked like a great place to be—or at least a central place from which to oversee a new empire. So Babylon became the capital city for their new empire, and from then on the Amorites were called Babylonians. The Babylonians borrowed much of their culture from the region they conquered. They adopted the Sumerian language and cuneiform writing. Babylonian social structure also retained much of the Sumerian look. Generally there were three classes of people in the society. The kings, priests, and nobles were at the top; the artisans, merchants, and farmers were in the middle (but don't think of them as the middle class—that's a completely different concept); and slaves who came from the conquered peoples were at the bottom of the class structure.

The Babylonians' greatest achievements occurred under the rule of their most powerful and memorable king, Hammurabi, who ruled from 1792 to 1750 B.C.E. He conquered the entire Fertile Crescent and brought order to the region. Hammurabi reorganized the tax structure for easier collection of revenue. He didn't tax the people for selfish intent, but worked to increase the economic prosperity of all the people of Mesopotamia, repairing irrigation canals and increasing the agricultural productivity of the land.

Hammurabi's crowning achievement was the code of laws that he assembled. Hammurabi collected laws from across the Fertile Crescent to create one unified law code for the entire Babylonian Empire. The Code of Hammurabi was stricter than old Sumerian laws by exacting an "eye for an eye, and a tooth for a tooth." Although it did not treat different classes equally, the code was a movement toward equality under the law.

Of course, like the other empires of the Fertile Crescent, the Babylonian Empire eventually went into decline. This decline began with the death of Hammurabi and lasted until the empire fell to the Hittites in the 1600s B.C.E.

More Civilizations

After the Babylonian Empire, the Hittites, Assyrians, Chaldeans, and Persians in succession ruled over the Fertile Crescent. The Hittites migrated to Mesopotamia from the area of the Black Sea, and by 2000 B.C.E. they dominated most of Asia Minor. In 1650 B.C.E., the Hittites built a capital city at Hattusas from which to launch campaigns of conquest. By 1595 B.C.E., with the use of light chariots and iron weapons, the Hittites conquered the Babylonian Empire and the region. But their rule did not last long, ending around 1200 B.C.E.

The Hated Assyrians

Following the Hittites were the Assyrians, who originated in the northern regions of Mesopotamia. Around 900 B.C.E. they migrated and conquered the entire Fertile Crescent. The Assyrians used a variety of military technologies and techniques to gain success at warfare. During battle they used men on horses to intimidate opposing foot soldiers, as well as chariots, iron weapons, and battering rams to break down city-state doors and walls.

NOTABLE QUOTABLE

I slew their warriors with the sword …. In the moat I piled them up, I covered the wide plain with the corpses of their fighting men, I dyed the mountains with their blood like red wool.

—*Royal Annul,* Assyrian king Shalmaneser III

After battle, the Assyrians were notorious for treating people who resisted them very cruelly (the movie *Texas Chainsaw Massacre* would be tame entertainment to the Assyrians!). This reputation, so to speak, preceded their armies, which caused many opposing forces to surrender without a fight. By 650 B.C.E., the Assyrian Empire reached its height, with Nineveh as its capital.

During its existence, the empire created a very efficient central government and improved the network of roads in the region. But like others before, their rule came to an abrupt end in 612 B.C.E., when the Chaldeans from the city-state of Babylon successfully rose up against the Assyrians.

The New and Improved Babylonians

The Chaldeans from Babylon (sometimes called Neo-Babylonians or New Babylonians) knew something about controlling Mesopotamia; they were descendants from Hammurabi's Babylonian Empire. They were able to not only regain control of their own city-state from the Assyrians, but to extend control over the Fertile Crescent.

WHAT IN THE WORLD

King Nebuchadnezzar created the Hanging Gardens of Babylon—one of the Seven Wonders of the Ancient World—for his wife to remind her of her home in the mountains of Media in northwestern Iran.

The greatest ruler to come out of the Neo-Babylonian Empire was King Nebuchadnezzar, who ruled from 605 to 562 B.C.E. He added to the might and power of Babylon with new building projects and worked to extend and maintain the borders of the empire.

The Neo-Babylonians are noted for their fascination with the stars, which resulted in the practice of astrology and even early charting of the movements of the night heavens. The Neo-Babylonians were conquered by the Persians in 539 B.C.E.

The Pretty Persians

The Persians emerged from central Asia around 2000 B.C.E. and migrated into present-day Iran. After some time the Persians became powerful and ambitious enough to conquer most of the Middle East under the leadership of King Cyrus. In addition to the Middle East, in 525 B.C.E., King Cambyses, Cyrus's son, conquered Egypt.

But neither of these men is considered by most historians to be the greatest ruler of the Persians. That title is reserved for King Darius I, who ruled the Persian Empire from 522 to 486 B.C.E. During his reign he divided up the empire into provinces called "satraps," which were ruled by governors, or "satrapies." This made the empire more manageable. King Darius also built the city of Persepolis into the most magnificent city of the empire, and created the Royal Road, which spanned 1,500 miles and aided communication across the whole of the empire. In addition, Darius created a common currency for trade, which expanded the role of commerce in the empire a great deal. But most importantly, Darius was very tolerant of the divergent views of his subjects, allowing them to practice their own customs and religions. This tolerance attracted many of the best and brightest of the ancient world to Persia while creating a sense of loyalty to the empire.

All of this advancement slipped into decline beginning with King Xerxes, the son of Darius, who was not tolerant of the divergent views of his subjects. This lack of tolerance made the Persian Empire less appealing. Many did not have the same kind of loyalty to the empire. This was evident during Xerxes' effort to expand the empire further, in which he tried and failed to conquer the Greek city-states in 480 B.C.E.

The Z-Man and His Religion

During the stable time of the Persian Empire, a new religion took shape that would influence other religions of Western civilization. Zoroastrianism was a religion that developed from the teachings of a prophet named Zoroaster and a collection of texts based on his teachings called the *Avestas*.

In the *Avestas*, Zoroaster taught that there was only one god to be worshipped: Ahura Mazda, or the "wise lord." There was also another god, Ahriman, the god of darkness, who existed but should not be worshipped. The events (good or bad) of the world were the result of the cosmic struggle between these gods.

Although Zoroastrianism was only a partial commitment to monotheism, historians have argued that it had a decisive influence on the monotheism found in Judaism and Christianity. Regardless, Zoroaster's teachings gained widespread appeal in the Persian Empire, eventually outliving it.

Other Civilizations of Note

A few other civilizations emerged out of western Asia and Africa that also contributed to Western civilization and world civilization.

The Phoenicians

Although historians are not exactly sure of the Phoenicians' origin, it is known that they settled in Canaan around 3000 B.C.E. Canaan is located in parts of present-day Lebanon, Israel, and Jordan. The Phoenicians created a network of trade around the Mediterranean Sea with the use of strong, fast ships that were made of cedar and used sails. In addition, they built large trading cities on the Mediterranean coast of Canaan at Tyre, Byblos, Sidon, and Berytus.

These cities and expanded trade network brought the Phoenicians to the peak of their power from 1200 to 1100 B.C.E. Also with this expansion of trade the Phoenicians colonized the Mediterranean Sea rim. Their most famous colony was Carthage. (Its importance will be discussed in Chapter 6.)

The lasting contribution of the Phoenicians to world civilization originated in commerce—an *alphabetic script* for trading developed around 1000 B.C.E. The script had 22 letters and was later adopted by the Greeks and modified by the Romans. From there it became the alphabet that most of the world still uses.

DEFINITION

An **alphabetic script** is a type of written communication in which symbols represent speech, sounds, and/or letters.

The Lydians

Another civilization of note was the Lydians, who migrated into Asia Minor and by the 600s B.C.E. developed into a wealthy civilization. Like the Phoenicians before them, the Lydians depended on trade and commerce to acquire their wealth and power. To become more efficient at their livelihood, the Lydians dismantled the barter system (trading goods for goods) and created a system based on currency or coins. This system made a lasting impression on world civilization and is used by most countries today.

The Israelites

The last notable civilization was the Israelites, who, like the Phoenicians, were located in the region of Canaan. Most of the history of the civilization of Israel has come from the Bible and archaeological records.

Around 1900 B.C.E., Abraham, the father of the nation of Israel, left the city-state of Ur in the Fertile Crescent and settled in Canaan. The Israelites believed that their god, a monotheistic god, made a covenant, or promise, with Abraham at this time to sustain his descendants in the land of Canaan.

Later, Jacob, Abraham's son, raised 12 sons, who become the leaders of the 12 tribes of Israel. During a period of drought in Canaan, the tribes of Israel migrated to Egypt and later were enslaved by the Egyptians.

Sometime after the 1200s B.C.E., a leader named Moses (who was also, oddly enough, found in a basket floating in a river, like Sargon of the Akkadians) led the Israelites out of Egypt into the desert of Sinai. While in the desert, Moses introduced a moral code of conduct for the tribes of Israel called the Ten Commandments. This code became one of the foundational law codes of Western civilization. By the 1000s B.C.E., the Israelites returned to Canaan, displacing the Philistines and the Canaanites.

 NOTABLE QUOTABLE

I am the Lord thy God .... Thou shalt have no other gods before me.

—Exodus 20:2–3

Davidic Monarchy

During a period of 100 years called the Davidic monarchy, the Israelites reached the height of their power. In 1020 B.C.E., the 12 tribes of Israel united under one king named Saul. This united kingdom was strengthened by the next king, David, who made Jerusalem the capital, organized the central government further, and enlarged the kingdom of Israel.

By 961 B.C.E., King Solomon, the son of David, constructed a temple for the Israelite god in Jerusalem, which became the focal point of the Israelite religion, called Judaism.

The decline of the kingdom of Israel began in 922 B.C.E. when it broke into two kingdoms: Israel in the north and Judah in the south.

In 722 B.C.E., the Israelites (sometimes called the Jewish people), divided and weakened, were conquered by the Assyrians of the Fertile Crescent. Eventually the Assyrians relinquished control of the region, but in 586 B.C.E. the Neo-Babylonians invaded a still weak region and enslaved the Jewish people. Their enslavement ended when, in 539 B.C.E., the Persians conquered the Neo-Babylonians and permitted the Israelites to return to Canaan. Still unable to catch a break, the Jewish people were conquered by the forces of Alexander the Great and later the Roman Empire.

The Jewish Legacy

Although it appears that the Israelites were one of the least powerful civilizations we have examined to this point, their impact on Western and world civilization was immense.

First and foremost, the Israelites developed a truly monotheistic religion—a first for humankind. This monotheistic belief in the god Yahweh, or Jehovah, who formed a covenant with a chosen people, the Israelites, was another unique human development. The covenant, and the law code found in the Ten Commandments and the *Torah*, the Jewish holy writings, made the Israelites accountable for their actions. They also introduced a better sense of equality for all people because, in Yahweh's eyes, every human being had infinite worth. All of these ideas became a key part of Western civilization's ethical, intellectual, and cultural foundation.

The Least You Need to Know

- Civilizations developed in western Asia and Africa along the river valleys of the Nile and the Tigris and Euphrates.
- The people of Mesopotamia and Egypt organized their civilizations to center around religious architecture and ritual.
- The Phoenicians and Lydians contributed to civilization with an alphabet and coinage.
- The Israelites developed a new monotheistic religion called Judaism, which continues to impact world civilization.

Ancient and Classic China

In This Chapter

- China's geography
- Early civilizations of China
- The Zhou, Qin, and Han dynasties
- Chinese achievements

Civilization in China developed along the fertile Huang He, or Yellow, River over 4,000 years ago. The Shang dynasty emerged from this early civilization to rule China in the eighteenth century B.C.E. After the decline of the Shang, three more dynasties—the Zhou, Qin, and Han—provided governmental and cultural stability to China.

As a result of this cultural stability, three philosophical traditions developed during this period of classical China: Confucianism, Daoism, and Legalism. In addition to these philosophical traditions, other important Chinese cultural and technological achievements include gunpowder, paper, the compass, and, perhaps most impressive—visible even from space—the Great Wall of China.

The Benefits of China's Geography

The geography of east Asia (known to us today as China) was, like the previous civilizations you have read about, an ideal place for a civilization to develop. First, China benefits from three major rivers: the Huang He, Chang Jiang, and Xi Jang. The Huang He River, sometimes referred to as the Yellow River, dominates the region, running 2,400 miles from the interior of China to the Yellow Sea, leaving deposits of loess, a rich, yellow soil fertile for agriculture. The region also has a good climate without extremes in weather. Finally, a third of China is mountainous, which, although it does hinder transportation and cultural diffusion, also helps prevent damaging migrations and invasions.

Early Civilizations of China

Very little is known about the early civilizations that developed around the Huang He River. Settlements around the river started around 5000 B.C.E. Later, two distinct cultures emerged and disappeared: the Yang-shoo culture flourished from 3000 to 1500 B.C.E., and the Lungshan culture appeared in the 2500s B.C.E. and disappeared from archaeological records by 2000 B.C.E.

Not until the 1700s B.C.E. and the introduction of writing with the Shang dynasty does more information become available about the civilization that developed on the banks of the Huang He River.

The Shang

The Shang dynasty represents the first true civilization that emerged on the banks of the Huang He River. Ruling from their capital city of Anyang, the Shang kings wielded tremendous political and religious power over the people.

The people of the Shang were polytheistic, worshipping many gods as well as their ancestors. To learn the will of the gods, the Shang used oracle bones—animal bones inscribed with various questions the people wanted answered by the gods. In a religious ceremony, a heated rod was inserted in the oracle bone, resulting in many different cracks. Then a priest or king would interpret the meaning of the cracks, giving people the answers they sought.

During the Shang dynasty there was much advancement that made a lasting impression on the culture of China. The Shang developed an *ideographic* written script, which became the Chinese script. Shang craftsmen cast bronze metal, carved ivory, produced silk garments, and shaped white clay into pottery.

DEFINITION

Ideographic is a type of written script in which a graphic symbol represents an idea, concept, or object without expressing the sound that forms its name.

The Shang dynasty, of course, did not last forever. In 1028 B.C.E., an ambitious lieutenant named Wu took advantage of weak Shang leadership to march on the capital of Anyang with a loyal army. At the capital, Wu killed the Shang king and established the Zhou dynasty.

WHAT IN THE WORLD

According to Chinese legend, an early Chinese king ordered his wife to investigate what was killing his mulberry trees. She found some white worms spinning cocoons on the leaves. Accidentally she dropped one of the cocoons into hot water. When she removed it, thread unwound from the cocoon. She had discovered the wonderfully soft silk!

The Zhou

The Zhou dynasty was able to centralize power, stabilize the region, and expand its territory during its time. This was partly because of the new principle of kingship that the Zhou dynasty introduced. The principle, called the Mandate of Heaven, stated that if rulers were just, they had the authority to rule from heaven. Because of this principle, Zhou kings were called sons of heaven, which gave the Zhou kings extra authority to accomplish things politically and religiously.

The people of the Zhou Empire made impressive technological strides. In warfare, the Zhou armies invented the crossbow and began to use cavalry in battle. Agriculturally, the Zhou people used iron plows and developed better irrigation systems to use the water of the Huang He River. Finally, the Zhou built better roads, which allowed the empire to make more contact with outside groups through foreign trade.

Around 771 B.C.E., the Zhou dynasty's expansions were halted with a loss in war to enemies from the north. The dynasty then began a slow decline, when a series of civil wars sparked the Period of Warring States. Finally, in 256 B.C.E., the Zhou dynasty's empire broke into many small city-states ruled by local lords who had once served the sons of heaven.

WHAT IN THE WORLD

Only foreigners use the term "China" in reference to the nation. The Chinese use the name "Zhongguo" for their nation. It means "Middle Kingdom" and refers to the early Chinese belief that the nation was the center of the world.

The Qin

The Qin dynasty was a short-lived dynasty established by one very ambitious and cruel man, Qin Shihuangdi. In 221 B.C.E., with the help of an able army, Qin conquered the remnants of the Zhou dynasty. Not wanting to be just a king, Qin took the title First Emperor, or Shihuangdi, and became the Qin dynasty's first and last emperor. Qin put all of the government under his direct control. Government officials who resisted were put to work or death—or worked to death. Many were sent to the northern parts of the territory to help begin building the Great Wall of China, which Qin felt was needed to protect his northern border from invaders. Most of the workers died during construction and are entombed in the wall itself. The majority of the Qin wall is north of the Great Wall that most tourists see today, which was mostly constructed during the much later Ming dynasty.

Qin tried to aid the commerce of his empire by enforcing a standard system of weights and measures and building more canals and roads. Despite these positive achievements, Qin would be considered by most a cruel tyrant. Not a man to accept criticism, he once buried alive some of his detractors, mostly Confucian scholars who disagreed with his strong-arm tactics. Qin died in 210 B.C.E., and his dynasty died shortly thereafter. Over 2,000 years later, in 1974, Qin's burial tomb was discovered untouched by grave robbers. One of the more interesting finds at this fascinating archaeological site was its 6,000 life-size terra cotta soldiers, all of whom had different faces, suggesting a realism not previously exhibited in Chinese culture.

The Han

By 207 B.C.E., the people of China had had enough of the Qin dynasty. Qin's son was an ineffective ruler, which made Liu Bang's move to seize power much easier. By 202 B.C.E., Liu Bang had successfully ended the Qin dynasty, restored order to the empire, and declared himself first emperor of the Han dynasty, which ruled for over 400 years.

The most renowned emperor of the Han dynasty was Wudi, who ruled from 141 to 87 B.C.E. His ambition and power allowed him to conquer a great deal of territory in the north and expand trade routes to the West, which became the Silk Road. To make a more efficient government bureaucracy, he instituted a civil service examination that lasted centuries beyond the Han dynasty. During the time that Wudi ruled and immediately after, China enjoyed a period of peace and prosperity that is sometimes called the Pax Sinica, or Chinese Peace.

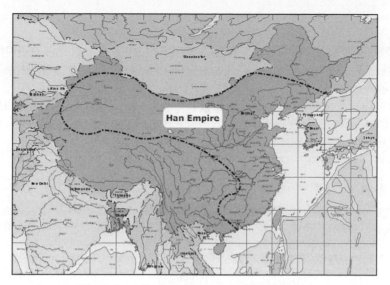

China from the late Ahou to the Han Dynasty.

Three Great Philosophical Traditions

During the period of classical China (the Zhou, Qin, and Han dynasties), three great Chinese philosophical traditions emerged that would influence south Asia for centuries to come. Confucianism and Daoism developed in response to the disorder during the decline of the Zhou dynasty (Period of Warring States). The other philosophy, Legalism, gained favor during the Qin dynasty.

Confucianism

The philosophical tradition of Confucianism was started by the teacher K'ung Fu-tzu, better known by his Latinized name, Confucius. Confucius was born around 551 B.C.E. and lived during the chaotic time of the decline of the Zhou dynasty.

Working as a government official, Confucius saw up close and personal how a state did and did not work. After his retirement, he began to think about the interaction between the individual and state. Eventually Confucius traveled across China, sharing his ideas with an ever-growing group of followers. These followers, or disciples, gathered his thoughts on paper in the *Analects*, the "selected sayings."

Confucius felt that order and hierarchy should be of primary importance. People should live by a principle of ethics in which the well-being of the group comes before that of the individual. He believed good government was the responsibility of the ruler, just as being good subjects was the responsibility of the people. Everyone must perform the duty of his or her station for society to work effectively. The ideas of Confucius were very appealing to the people of China during the turbulent times of the Zhou dynasty, and continued to be very influential in Chinese culture throughout the centuries—even under the present Communist regime.

NOTABLE QUOTABLE

If there is righteousness in the heart, there will be beauty in the character. If there is beauty in the character, there will be harmony in the home. If there is harmony in the home, there will be order in the nation. If there is order in the nation, there will be peace in the world.

—*Analects,* Confucius, on order and harmony

Daoism

Like Confucianism, Daoism appeared in response to the turbulent times of the Zhou dynasty. The founder of the Daoist movement is considered by most to be Laozi, or "Old Master." Little is really known about Laozi, partially because he shunned public life. But his ideas were recorded by some of his followers in the *Dao De Jing (The Classic Way and the Virtue).*

Laozi believed that people attained wisdom and happiness by seeking the dao, or "path," in all things. That path is aided by seeking harmony with nature, which included rejecting social structures and renouncing worldly ambitions.

The yin and yang symbol represents the Daoist theory of harmony. The yin is the cool, dark, feminine, and submissive side of people, while the yang is the warm, light, masculine, and aggressive side of people. All people have both elements, and harmony is obtained when people have the elements in balance.

The slightly mystical nature of the Daoist philosophical tradition made it an attractive alternative to Confucianism, and it quickly spread throughout China and later had a strong cultural influence on Japan and Korea.

Legalism

The last philosophical tradition that developed during classical China was Legalism, led by two men, Han Fei Zu and Li Si. Legalism had a few tenets that struck a chord in the Qin dynasty, when it gained widespread acceptance.

First, according to Legalist thought, human nature is essentially evil. A ruler must provide strict discipline to overcome the evil of human nature and maintain order. Legalists also believed that education was unnecessary; most people should be put to work to produce for the state. (After reading the tenets, you can see why the Qin dynasty loved Legalism!)

After the Qin dynasty, Legalism fell out of fashion, mostly because of its association with the tyrant Qin. Its influence has been minimal in Chinese history in comparison to Confucianism and Daoism.

Chinese Society

In addition to the philosophical traditions of Confucianism, Daoism, and Legalism, Chinese society was influenced by the concepts of family and social class. Like the philosophical traditions, both stressed a need for order and harmony.

The Family

The Chinese family structure during the classical period revolved around what we call the nuclear family: parents and children. It was also based on a hierarchical structure, with the father on top, followed by the oldest son, younger sons, the mother, and finally the daughters. Strict rules and expectations maintained the hierarchy, with a focus on duty, respect for ancestors, and *filial piety*.

 DEFINITION

Filial piety means the duty of family members to subjugate their needs and desires to those of the male head of the family or ruler.

Regrettably, the status of women suffered in this family hierarchy. Women in the family were subservient to fathers and brothers, regardless of age or ability. And partly because of this subservient status, few women were able to receive an education.

Social Classes

Social class in classical China was also based on the desire for order and harmony. At the top of the social structure were the landowners. In most civilizations, peasants generally make the lower class, but that was not the case in classical China. The peasants, who made up about 90 percent of the population, formed the class below the landowners. The lower classes were the merchants, which consisted of shopkeepers, bankers, and traders. Movement between the classes wasn't prohibited, but with the Chinese emphasis on order, harmony, and duty, most of the population remained in the class in which they were born.

NOTABLE QUOTABLE

These Seres (Chinese) … study to pass their lives in peace … and so free are they from wants that, though ready to dispose of their own products, they purchase none from abroad.

—Ammianus Marcellinus, Roman statesman on China and the Silk Road (380 C.E.)

Achievements of Classical China

The classical period of China was a time of unprecedented advancement in science and technology. In the field of astronomy, the Chinese calculated the solar year as $365\frac{1}{4}$ days, and recorded and predicted solar and lunar eclipses—even Halley's Comet in 240 B.C.E.

In agriculture they improved irrigation systems, fertilized their crops, and practiced veterinary medicine on their livestock. During this period the Chinese also developed many key inventions, including gunpowder, the wheelbarrow, suspension bridges, the compass, and paper. All of these achievements clearly put China ahead as a civilization and made life in China easier than anywhere in the world to that point.

WHAT IN THE WORLD

Paper was so valued in China that it was against the law to step on a piece of paper that had writing on it.

The Silk Road was also an impressive achievement of classical China. The peace and prosperity of the efficient Han dynasty allowed for the growth of large-scale trade, resulting in a continuous network of roads starting in China with the Han dynasty, to northern India and the Kushan Empire, to the Parthians of Persia, and finally to the Roman Empire.

For 2,000 years the Silk Road formed the world's longest road. In addition to being a route to export the luxury items of silks and spices from China, it provided the way for the positive influence of Buddhism to eventually spread into China.

The Least You Need to Know

- Civilization in China developed along the Huang He River.
- The Zhou, Qin, and Han dynasties provided stability to the region.
- Three philosophical traditions—Confucianism, Daoism, and Legalism—were developed during the period of classical China.
- Many of the Chinese cultural and technological achievements came during the classical period, including the use of gunpowder, paper, and the compass.

Ancient and Classic India

In This Chapter

- The geography of India
- The Indus River valley civilization
- The Aryans
- Hinduism and Buddhism
- The Mauryan and Gupta Empires

Several culturally strong civilizations arose in the Indian subcontinent. First to develop was the Indus River valley civilization, of which little is known. They were followed by the Aryans, who formed the foundations of later empires of the Indian subcontinent, the Mauryan and Gupta. During this period in India, several important religions came into being, including Hinduism, Buddhism, and Jainism.

The Safety of the Indian Subcontinent

Several civilizations were rooted in the Indus River valley, located in modern-day India, Pakistan, and Bangladesh. But what made this region and the area around it, sometimes referred to as the subcontinent of India, so central to civilizations of south Asia?

In part, like the early civilizations of western Asia and Africa, it was because of a river or rivers. In the western region of the Indian subcontinent, the Indus River begins in the Hindu Kush Mountains and drains into the Arabian Sea, providing fertile land along the banks and a steady supply of water. The Ganges and Brahmaputra rivers, which start in the Himalaya Mountains and empty into the Bay of Bengal, also provide fertile farmland and a supply of water.

But it wasn't all about the rivers. The Indian subcontinent has some natural barriers that helped to protect civilizations from outsiders. The Himalaya and Hindu Kush Mountains in the north are the home to some of the largest mountains in the world (Mount Everest comes to mind). In the south is the Indian Ocean, with its tricky wind and ocean currents created in part by the monsoons, or seasonal winds, which bring rain and drought to India. All of these factors made the Indian subcontinent an excellent region for civilizations to start.

Early Indus River Valley Civilization

Little is truly known about the first Indus River valley civilization. Groups of humans settled in the region in the 2500s B.C.E., eventually developing two major cities, Harappa and Mohenjo-Daro. Historians sometimes refer to this as the Harappan civilization, after the larger city.

Harappa and Mohenjo-Daro

Archaeologists have excavated and examined the ruins of both cities, but the ruins of Harappa best demonstrate the sophistication of the civilization's urban planning. All of the streets were perfectly straight and intersected throughout the city at right angles. The city had a sewer system, because each house had at least one indoor bathroom. (Indoor plumbing wasn't universal in the United States until the mid-twentieth century!) The houses themselves were sturdy and, making use of the natural resources in the region, were constructed of oven-baked bricks. Finally, a citadel or fortress built on a brick platform overlooked the city to protect the inhabitants.

Harappan Culture and Collapse

The clues left of the Harappan way of life also provide the sense that this civilization was very advanced. Most of the people were farmers who developed the cultivation of a wide variety of crops, including wheat, barley, and rice for food and cotton for clothing. The artisan class made elaborate jewelry that has been found as far away as the Fertile Crescent. The Harappans also created writing in the form of ideographic pictograms, but historians have not yet been able to decipher their meaning because there are few examples. The writings do show that the Indus River valley civilization worshipped many gods associated with natural forces.

For all that historians do not know about Harappan civilization, they have concluded that it declined and then collapsed during the 1500s B.C.E. But most historians cannot agree on why. Some have argued that invaders destroyed the Harappans; others have argued that it may have been environmental problems associated with flooding from the Indus River.

The Aryans

The Aryans were the next group to take advantage of the Indus River valley. They migrated to the Indian subcontinent from the Black and Caspian Sea regions, perhaps destroying the Harappans during the 1500s B.C.E.

The Aryans were a male-dominated, nomadic, tribal society, usually led by a rajah or chief, but once they settled into the Indus River valley, the Aryans adopted an agricultural way of life. Politically, the Aryans never consolidated beyond small petty kingdoms ruled by princes. These independent, small kingdoms warred with each other constantly, causing a great deal of instability, but the Aryan cultural influence upon the Indian subcontinent has lasted through modern times.

WHAT IN THE WORLD

Hitler used the word "Aryan" to justify his aggressive racist policies toward minorities in Germany. He interpreted the Aryan race as ancient Greeks and Romans and modern-day Germans and Scandinavians. Hitler wrongly believed that the Aryans were a superior race that once ruled the world and were destined to do so again.

Language and Traditions

The Aryan language, called Sanskrit, was very important to their culture. First developed by warriors during their nomadic period to recite epic poems celebrating Aryan heroes, Sanskrit later became a written language. From 1200 B.C.E. to 500 B.C.E., the epic poems that were once recited were collected into holy books called vedas. The oldest of the vedas, called the *Rig-Veda*, was compiled around 1000 B.C.E. The vedas also included legends and religious rituals that the Aryans knew and practiced, all of which made them an important teaching tool. The vedas were so important, in fact, that this period is called the Vedic Age.

Darkness was hidden by darkness in the beginning; with no distinguishing sign, all this was water. The life force was covered with emptiness.

—*Rig-Veda*

The Caste System

The Aryans developed a strict social system based on caste. In a caste system, people were born into the class of their birth parents and could not change their caste or class through any means.

At the top of the Aryan caste system were the brahmans (or priests), followed by the *kshatriyas* (or rulers), and the warriors. Other important groups of the system were the *vaisyas*, or common people; and the pariahs, or slaves. The system was reinforced with a set of strict rules and the concept of dharma, in which each class was encouraged to perform only its set of duties.

The Aryan Religion

The Aryan religion was very typical of early civilizations. Only later did it develop into one of the largest religions in the world today. The Aryans were polytheistic, like many other early civilizations. They believed in several gods, including Agni, god of fire; Indra, god of thunder and war; and Usha, goddess of the dawn or rebirth. These gods controlled the natural forces. The Aryan vedas detail some of the rituals that were performed to appease the gods.

Some Aryan religious thinkers became discontented with this religion of appeasement. They eventually wrote their ideas and beliefs down in the religious writings called the *Upanishads*.

Hinduism

The *Upanishads* advanced the religious belief that there is one eternal spirit called Brahman Nerguna. To become part of the eternal spirit, a person needs to have a pure soul. If someone dies before his or her soul is pure, it will be reincarnated. Into what living thing or caste of Aryan society a person's soul is reincarnated depends on the person's *karma* in the previous life. Through self-denial, including fasting and meditation such as yoga, a person can be released from reincarnation, or *moksa*.

Hinduism's cycle of reincarnation created a society that tried to practice nonviolence toward all living things, or *ahimsa*. But the religious ideas that grew from the original Aryan belief system did not end with Hinduism.

DEFINITION

Karma is a Hindu belief that actions performed in one stage of a person's existence determine the fate of the next stage of existence.

Yoga is a system of physical and mental exercises that separate the soul from the mind and body and help to bring it union with the universal spirit. Yoga translates into the word "discipline" in Sanskrit.

Buddha and Buddhism

The transformation of Aryan religious beliefs started with the birth of a prince and member of the *kshatriya* caste named Siddhartha Gautama, in 566 B.C.E. Siddhartha became disenchanted with the world and the suffering he witnessed among people. At the age of 29, the prince left his wife and title and wandered for seven years throughout India to look for the meaning of life and suffering. At the end of this time, Siddhartha discovered the meaning of life and began to share his "enlightenment" with a group of followers. His followers then called him Buddha, or the "Enlightened One."

So what was the meaning of life according to Buddha? Buddha taught that there were four Noble Truths:

> First, all people suffer and know sorrow.
>
> Second, people suffer because of their desires.
>
> Third, they can end their suffering by eliminating these desires.
>
> And fourth, to eliminate those desires, people should follow the Buddha's Eightfold Path.

The Eightfold Path includes knowing the truth, resisting evil, saying nothing to hurt others, respecting life, working for the good of others, freeing the mind from evil, controlling thoughts, and practicing meditation. Following the Eightfold Path, a person can reach nirvana, a state of freedom from the cycle of rebirth or the state of extinction. Buddha also taught his followers to reject the caste system of India because of its inequalities.

Buddha traveled and taught across India for 45 years, converting thousands of students into disciples who helped spread his teachings throughout Asia. Buddhism later split into two different sects. The Theravada sect regards Buddha to be a great teacher to be read and understood. The Mahayana sect worships Buddha as a savior of the people and believes he is a god.

Regardless of the split, the religion Buddha founded did not fare so well in his country of birth. Probably his rejection of the caste system made him unpopular with the priests and ruling castes who could have promoted Buddhism. Today a majority of Indians follow the religion of Hinduism.

NOTABLE QUOTABLE

Let a man overcome anger by love, let him overcome evil by good; let him overcome the greedy by liberality, the liar by truth ….

—Buddha

Another Religion?

Buddha was not the only one who was dissatisfied with the injustice of the caste system and the pessimism of the cycle of death and reincarnation found in Hinduism. Mahavira, who lived from 540 to 468 B.C.E., also developed an alternative religious view. Mahavira taught that the universe was composed of souls and matter. The way for the soul to achieve oneness with Brahama Nerguna was to rid oneself of matter in order to be able to rise to the top of the universe.

Mahavira's doctrine of Jainism, as it is called, taught that all life has a soul, so all life is sacred and should not be destroyed. To do this, one must be a vegetarian and disavow material possessions in a form of extreme self-denial. These extreme practices did not make it very popular with the people, so it became more of a religion of the fringe.

In spite of its fringe status, Jainism influenced many proponents of nonviolent protest, including the twentieth-century leaders Mahatma Gandhi and Martin Luther King Jr.

After the Vedic Age

At the close of the Vedic Age, the kingdom of Magadha, under the leadership of King Bimbisara from 542 to 495 B.C.E., consolidated power and expanded its territory through marriage and conquest. His kingdom became the center of India's first true empire.

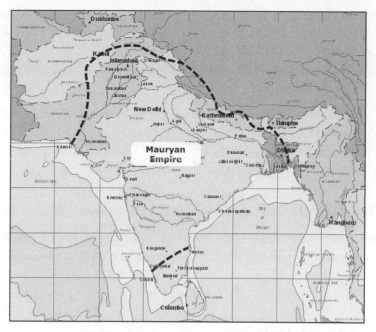

The Mauryan and Gupta empires in India.

The Mauryan Empire

In 321 B.C.E., an ambitious man named Chandragupta Maurya overthrew the king of the declining kingdom of Magadha. Once in power, King Maurya created a strong kingdom with the use of a tough and efficient army and administrative structures. Some historians believe that he was strongly influenced by another contemporary, Alexander the Great. In legend, Maurya inspected a Greek army to compare with his own armies. After his death, the Mauryan Empire continued to gain power, territory, and influence in the Indian subcontinent.

The strongest ruler of the empire was King Asoka, who came into power in 274 B.C.E. Oddly, his rule was not punctuated entirely with war and conquest. Like most kings of the Mauryan Empire, he conquered many territories. But after one particularly brutal battle, Asoka became a pacifist, very concerned with the value of human life and the problem of human suffering.

WHAT IN THE WORLD

The people of India admire and revere the leadership of Asoka to this day, so much so that the official Indian governmental seal features one of the pillars that Asoka erected.

His concerns led him to the Buddhist religion, which he promoted through his laws and government administration. To promote peace in the empire, Asoka created the High Commissioners of Equity. This group traveled throughout the empire, investigating the complaints and needs of minority groups. Despite being an ardent follower of Buddha, Asoka also allowed its rival religion, Hinduism, to be practiced in the empire.

But with Asoka's death, the Mauryan Empire began to decline; the rule of the last Mauryan ended in 184 B.C.E.

Between the end of the Mauryan Empire and 310 C.E., the subcontinent fell into disarray as various kingdoms fought to gain political control and different invaders migrated into India. The invaders were generally assimilated into Indian culture.

The first invaders were the remnants of a Hellenistic Greek army led by King Demetrius. His army pushed into northwestern India during the 200s B.C.E. King Demetrius transformed his capital city of Gandhara into a Hellenistic city that also blended with Indian culture.

The Greek hold on India did not last long. A new group of invaders, named the Kushans, migrated into India in the 100s B.C.E. The Kushans were absorbed into Indian society and eventually became the *kshatriya* caste, or warrior class. Their most influential ruler was Kanishka, who was a convert to Buddhism. He assembled a great council of Buddhist monks to help regulate the teachings of Buddha. Mahayana Buddhism, discussed earlier in this chapter, originated from this council and was exported through missionaries along trade routes to China.

The Gupta Empire

In 310 C.E., Chandragupta I, a determined ruler from the kingdom of Magadha who was tired of the rule of outsiders, centralized power and started to expand his kingdom, beginning the Gupta Empire. This empire reached the height of its power and influence over the Indian subcontinent under Chandragupta II, who ruled from 375 to 415 C.E. Although the empire only lasted for about 200 years, it was considered India's golden age.

WHAT IN THE WORLD

The Gupta Empire was the home of several universities. One, the university at Nalanda, had eight colleges and three libraries and attracted students from across the Asian continent.

The society of India thrived under the short-lived Gupta Empire. Hinduism was the dominant religion of India and also the official religion of the empire. The stability provided by the Gupta Empire allowed Hinduism to flourish. Many new temples were built to the different subgods of the religion. The empire also gave the people many freedoms, which permitted the growth of learning.

As a result, it was during the Gupta Empire that most of the concepts of algebra were created, the concept of zero explained, and the numerals one through nine were identified. Interestingly enough, Muslim traders began using these numbers from India, and later Europeans started to use the numbers because of trade with the Muslims in the Mediterranean. But by that time, the numbers were known as "Arabic numerals" by the Europeans, not giving India due credit.

Astronomers of the Gupta Empire knew the world was round. Their doctors reset broken bones in their patients. The stability of the empire brought prosperity. The Gupta Empire's trade expanded to the far-off regions of Arabia, central Asia, China, and Rome.

Eventually India's golden age did come to an end. The prosperity of the empire attracted more invaders, the White Huns of Asia for one, which weakened the administration and army. By 600 C.E., the Gupta Empire dissolved into many small petty kingdoms, which again fought for control of the Indian subcontinent. But the culture of the Gupta Empire survived to influence India for centuries to come.

The Least You Need to Know

- Several culturally strong civilizations arose in the Indian subcontinent.
- The Aryans formed the foundations of the empires that emerged in India.
- The Hindu religion developed from discontentment with the Aryan religion.
- The teachings of Buddhism and Jainism grew out of unhappiness with tenets of Hinduism.
- Many of the cultural achievements of India came during the rules of the Mauryan and Gupta empires.

Classic Greece

In This Chapter

- What is so special about Greece?
- Many cities on many hills
- Greek philosophy
- Greek art
- Alexander the Great
- Hellenistic culture

The civilization of Greece rivaled the other classic civilizations of India and China in cultural richness and effect on history. Its institutions, literature, art, and philosophy reverberate into the later history of the Middle East and Europe, and extend into the Americas. But our understanding of classic Greek civilization and culture is sometimes complicated by its expansion into the Middle East through Persia and the development of Hellenistic culture.

The Geography of Greece

The area in which the Greek civilization emerged is in the southernmost part of the Balkan Peninsula. Unlike most of the civilizations we have previously examined, Greece did not benefit agriculturally from a great river and valley. However, it *was* surrounded by water: the Aegean, Mediterranean, and Ionian seas. Of course, sea water has limited agricultural benefit.

Furthermore, three quarters of the region in which the Greek civilization developed was covered by mountains. These factors did not make the development of Greek civilization easy—but one factor did. The land had a very mild climate, which led to more agricultural production.

WHAT IN THE WORLD

The Greeks called themselves Hellenes for a good reason. They believed that they were descendants of the goddess Helen, whom they worshipped.

Aegean Civilizations

Before the classic Greek civilization that we think of, two other civilizations existed on the Greek Peninsula. Together, the Minos and Myceneae are called the Aegean civilizations. They were the early ancestors and the foundation of Greek civilization.

The Minoans

The Minoan civilization centered on the island of Crete from 2000 to 1450 B.C.E. Much of what we know about the Minoans has come from the discoveries of Sir Arthur Evans, an archaeologist who in the early twentieth century excavated the capital city of the Minoans, Knossos, found at Crete.

Although little is known for certain even today about the Minoans, some basic facts have been deduced. First, because of their geographic location on an island, the Minoans depended on trade around the Mediterranean Sea basin for their wealth and power. They apparently reached the height of their power around 1600 B.C.E. But around 1450 B.C.E., the Minoan civilization collapsed, oddly and quite suddenly.

Historians from antiquity to modern times have speculated that a catastrophic tidal wave flooded and destroyed the civilization. It is possible that this gave rise to the myth of Atlantis. But such speculation should be taken with a grain of salt.

The Mycenaean Civilization

The Mycenaean civilization took over in Greece where the Minoans left off, but in contrast, it was centered on the Greek mainland and used conquest for its wealth and power. Unfortunately for the Mycenaeans, their reign over the Greek Peninsula did not last long. They moved into the Balkan Peninsula around 2000 B.C.E. but were unable to organize sufficiently to control Greece until around the 1450s B.C.E. By the 1100s B.C.E., the Mycenaeans were warring amongst themselves, which left them very weak.

In their weakened state, a group of upstart, Greek-speaking Indo-Europeans invaded from the north, plunging the land into what are called the Greek Dark Ages from about 1150 to 800 B.C.E. Although politically divided, the Dorians formed a single culture based on common language and religion, eventually calling themselves Greeks or sometimes Hellenes.

The Greek City-States

Eventually the Greeks began to get it together, turn on the lights, and end the Dark Ages. During the Archaic period (800–500 B.C.E.) they moved forward socially, culturally, and politically. The political advancements were to some degree affected by the hilly, mountainous geography of Greece.

The Greeks settled and lived on the top of the hills because it was, and still is, much easier to keep an eye on suspicious people from the top of a hill rather than the bottom. These large and small settlements formed protected cities that ruled the surrounding countryside. The end result was that hundreds of Greek city-states grew up politically independent of each other.

The Polis

The city-state, or polis, included the Greek city itself and the surrounding countryside, which it controlled and used for farming. The word "politics" is derived from polis; despite what most people think, politics means to participate in the development of the polis.

Many of the citizens of the Greek city-states—generally the free, landowning males (sorry, ladies, equality has always been a difficult road)—took part in the process of government. They could vote, hold public office, own property, and speak in court. With that participation came rights and responsibilities, which the citizens of the polis took very seriously. The famous philosopher Socrates died an unjust death honoring those rights and responsibilities! (More on Socrates later in the chapter.)

thens

...re a few leaders of the hundreds of city-states in ancient Greece. Corinth ...d Thebes were largest and were very politically powerful. But Sparta and Athens truly led the pack. Not only did they have the honor of being the leaders of classical Greek civilization, they were also the death of classical Greek civilization.

The Spartans, who descended from the original Dorian invaders and claimed descent from Hercules (remember him, the big strong guy?), inhabited a landlocked city-state. They depended on a large slave-holding population gained through wars and agriculture for their wealth. This created a measure of paranoia in the Spartans (a huge slave revolt in 650 B.C.E. didn't help) —so much so that they were very strict and maintained a dictatorship.

It also led the Spartans to put a lot of time (and I mean *a lot*) into the training of a large and effective army, which became one of the most feared in the ancient world. Spartan boys entered the military at age 7, did not leave the military barracks until age 30, and did not fully retire from the military until age 60.

NOTABLE QUOTABLE

At seven years old they were to be enrolled in … classes, where they all lived under the same order and discipline …. He who showed the most courage was made captain; they had their eyes always upon him, obeyed his orders, and underwent patiently whatsoever punishment he inflicted.

—*The Lives of the Noble Grecians and Romans,* Plutarch, on the beginning of Spartan military training

The Athenian way was the opposite of the Spartan way on almost every point. First, Athens had access to the Aegean Sea, which allowed it to depend on trade for its wealth. To protect that trade, the Athenians became a naval power. That trade brought a steady flow of new culture and learning into the city on which Athenians prided themselves. Athens also developed a new, more liberal form of government called democracy.

Democracy began in Athens in 508 B.C.E., when the dictator of Athens, Cleisthenes, gave Athenian male citizens a voice in governing with the Council of 500 and the Athenian Assembly, made up of all the citizens of Athens. The Athenian Assembly made and passed laws for the city-state, while the Council of 500 administered those laws and performed the everyday business of government. The Assembly also chose 10 generals each year to command the army and navy. Athenian democracy even provided for a jury system to try cases in court. This democratic form of government reached its high point in Athens under the direction of Pericles (461–429 B.C.E.), and at that time was the most representative form of government yet created.

All of that democratic practice and freedom in the city-state of Athens was an exception rather than a rule in Greece. In general, the majority of the city-states were ruled by an oligarchy, or an elite group of wealthy and powerful men. All of the city-states in some form or fashion used slaves from other regions as laborers, teachers, or servants. Finally, women were treated as inferiors in Greek society (most ironically in Athens) and not given any kind of status equal to that of the male citizens.

All Greek to Me

During the time of the city-states, the Greek culture advanced by leaps and bounds, and laid the first bricks of Western culture. Greek religion with its myths, although not practiced today, is taught to students across the world. The philosophy of the Greeks remains the foundation of Western thinking. Greek drama and literature still provide inspiration for movies and books. And the art and architecture of the Greeks has been copied in the buildings of Washington, D.C., and elsewhere.

Greek Religion

Greek religion developed in response to the sometimes scary mysteries of the natural world. The gods became connected to the elements of nature. For example, Poseidon was the god of the oceans and Apollo was the god of the sun. Eventually the gods and goddesses took on human form and characteristics. The stories that the Greeks told about the gods and goddesses became mythology. Most of the myths taught a lesson (don't mess with the gods because they're a dysfunctional lot!).

The gods became the center of social and civic life, with each polis dedicating itself to one particular god or goddess. Athens, for instance, was dedicated to its namesake, Athena, the goddess of wisdom (although she apparently wasn't much help during the Peloponnesian Wars). Each city-state built temples and celebrated festivals to honor its particular god or goddess.

...Games

...o B.C.E., the Greek city-states assembled every four years at Olympia
...estival to honor Zeus, father of the gods. At first the Olympic Games
...re made up of only footraces, but later they included wrestling, boxing, javelin
throwing, discus throwing, long jumping, and chariot racing.

In 393 C.E., a very pious Christian Roman emperor objected to the games because
of their pagan origin, so they ceased to be played. The Olympic Games were later
revived by the French baron Pierre de Coubertin, who was inspired by the Greek
ideals he found in the games. In 1896, the first modern Olympic Games were held in
Athens with competitors from nations around the world. Of course, the tradition of
the Olympic Games continues to this day and includes all of the countries around the
world, as well as winter events.

Great Greek Philosophy

The Greeks created new ways of thinking based on humanism and rationalism,
starting the discipline of philosophy. Humanism is the focus on man as the center of
intellectual and artistic endeavors, while rationalism is the doctrine that knowledge
comes from reason without the aid of the senses. The new discipline of philosophy
was most exemplified in three great Greek philosophers: Socrates, Plato, and
Aristotle.

Socrates

Socrates (470–399 B.C.E.) studied human behavior and ethics. He was famous for his
ability to argue and challenge ideas through question after question, which became
known as the "Socratic method."

Socrates believed in an absolute truth, not a relative truth. His questioning focused
on the search for the truth, which he thought was the most important thing a person
could do. Of course, questioning everything all of the time can sometimes get one
into trouble. Socrates was a case in point.

After Athens lost the Peloponnesian War, Socrates was set up as the scapegoat
because of his questioning of the decisions of the Athenian government. He was
put on trial for corrupting the youth and sentenced to death by drinking hemlock.
Socrates could have easily escaped but refused, because he thought a citizen should
not defy the decisions of the city-state.

Plato

Plato (427–347 B.C.E.) was a student of Socrates and it's through him that most historians get their knowledge of Socrates. Plato loved the concept of government, and put most of his thinking and writing talents into examining the politics of the city-state. Although Plato wrote a great deal, his volume on politics titled *The Republic* is his most enduring work.

In *The Republic*, Plato stressed the importance of ideals and truths. The ideal ruler of a city-state, according to Plato, would be a philosopher-king, who would have greater knowledge of the truth and the state's ideals—and plenty of experience. The ideal polis would be a place where the individuals of the city-state would place the welfare of the polis above their own welfare.

Plato's influence extended beyond his writing when he opened an educational center for young men to learn and discuss philosophy, called the Academy. In this setting, he taught Aristotle for 20 years.

Aristotle

Aristotle (384–322 B.C.E.) was more interested in the meaning of life than politics. He taught and practiced a life of moderation, or the "Golden Mean," but Aristotle was also a master of logic. He argued against his former teacher Plato and Plato's forms in the volume *Metaphysics*, writing that all matter is form and substance or ideal and reality. He also argued with logic and reason for the concept of a single god.

In another book, *Organan* (he produced over 200 different volumes), Aristotle explored how humans learned and divided learning into two groups—deductive and inductive. Aristotle thought that people have to individually decide which type of learning best suited them to ensure a good education. In the volume *Politics*, Aristotle described a good government as one that should serve all citizens, very similar to Athenian democracy. Like his teacher Plato, Aristotle's influence went beyond his writing when he opened up his own school, called the Lyceum, for young men to learn. One young man who learned from him was the famous world conqueror Alexander the Great.

Classical Greek Achievements

The Greeks didn't just think great thoughts. They also wrote entertaining literature, drama, and history, all of which has made a lasting impression on world civilization.

Homer (not the Simpson)

Homer was possibly (there is still debate about whether he even existed) a blind poet who lived during the 700s B.C.E. He has been named as the author of two epic poems, *The Iliad* and *The Odyssey*, which greatly influenced Greek and Western civilization.

The Iliad is an epic tale about the Trojan War, which was possibly (there is also debate about whether this war actually happened) waged between the city-states of Greece and the nation of Troy. The war began when the beautiful Spartan princess Helen left her husband the king of Sparta for the love of Paris, a Trojan prince. The Trojans decided to shelter Helen, and they were successful defending the walls against the Greeks' greatest warrior, Achilles. The war ended very badly for the Trojans, however; the trickery of Greek prince Odysseus and the Trojan horse allowed the Greek forces to enter Troy and destroy it.

The Odyssey picks up where *The Iliad* ends, detailing the adventures of Odysseus as he tries for 10 years to return to his beloved wife and Greece. Beyond being a great yarn, the Greeks used the epics to teach the values of Hellenic culture—excellence, loyalty, dignity, and the importance of heritage—to their youth.

Drama

At first, plays were written to be presented at religious festivals of the gods, but later snowballed into events of their own. The plays were emotional and entertaining but also instructive, much like the Greek myths and Homer's works. Usually the dramas revolved around the idea of fate and character flaws that lead someone to greatness and then ruin.

Sophocles wrote one of the more memorable examples of this dramatic use of success, flaw, and ruin with *Oedipus Rex*, a play about a king who unwittingly kills his father and marries his mother. Once this is discovered, it all ends rather badly, with Oedipus's mother hanging herself and Oedipus stabbing his eyes out.

WHAT IN THE WORLD

As bizarre as the story of *Oedipus Rex* appears, twentieth-century psychoanalyst Sigmund Freud based much of his approach to understanding unconscious desires on it. In Freud's mind, men unconsciously want to be with their mother and kill their rival—that is, their father—for her attention!

Other important tragic playwrights include Aeschylus, one of the earliest writers, who wrote *Orestia*, and Euripides, who wrote *Trojan Women*. But it wasn't all tragic. Aristophanes wrote popular satires and social comedies like *Knights*, which poked fun at government officials, and *Clouds*, which ridiculed the seriousness of philosophers.

Historians and History

In addition to literature and drama, Greek civilization produced some of the first historians and histories. Herodotus produced one of the first books on the subject, *The History of the Persian Wars*. Although the account of the Persian Wars has some accurate facts, Herodotus also colored some facts in an epic way to add to the story. He also included the Greek gods as part of the narrative, making the history even more epic than historical.

Thucydides, the father of history (a title I wish I could get), wrote the first true historical work, *The History of the Peloponnesian Wars*. Thucydides tried to be accurate and objective with the facts in his history of the war between Athens and Sparta, even traveling to the places where the events took place and interviewing participants. Thucydides' approach influenced historians of Western and world civilization through the centuries—including this author!

NOTABLE QUOTABLE

Our constitution is called a democracy because power is in the hands not of a minority but the whole people. When it is a question of settling private disputes, everyone is equal before the law.

—*History of the Peloponnesian Wars,* Thucydides' account of Pericles' description of Athenian democracy

Math and Science

The Greeks also made substantial strides in the human understanding of math and science. Thales (ca. 600 B.C.E.), considered a philosopher by most, was said to have predicted a solar eclipse. By today's standards, he would be considered a scientist with his development of theories about the nature of the world. He formulated a theory that water was the most basic substance of the world. (He got an A for effort; humans are made mostly of water.)

Pythagoras (ca. 530 B.C.E.) also tried to explain the nature of the world, but in mathematical terms. His Pythagorean Theorem ($a^2+b^2=c^2$) demonstrates his influence today—and that of classical Greece—in the field of geometry.

Art and Architecture

When the Greeks were not thinking great thoughts or writing entertaining literature, they were building really big, beautiful buildings. The Parthenon on the Acropolis in Athens was the crown jewel of Greek architecture and art. Built as a temple to Athena from 447 to 432 B.C.E., it was perfectly balanced in form and surrounded by beautiful marble columns. The frieze displayed at the top of the Parthenon and the statue of Athena in the temple was created by the sculptor Phidias, who used balance and restraint in his realistic depictions of gods, humans, and animals. He also created the great statue of Zeus found in the Olympia, one of the Seven Wonders of the Ancient World.

Other great Greek sculptors who defined the art of the age were Myron, who portrayed more idealized versions of people—in other words, what they *should* look like, rather than their actual looks. And Praxiteles favored grace in the subject rather than power.

A Little Persian with Your Greek

Eventually the Greeks began to rub elbows with other big civilizations, namely the Persian Empire. This contact allowed the Greeks to go global, so to speak. In the end, the contact created an interesting mixture of east and west, or Persian and Greek, civilizations.

The Persian Wars

Around 500 B.C.E., the Ionian Greek colonies, which were under the control of the Persian Empire, revolted. The Greek city-states, naturally, wanted to help their oppressed brothers and sisters, so they created an army and sent some very strong words to King Darius of Persia. King Darius was not too impressed with the Greeks or their strong words, so in 492 B.C.E. he invaded Greece to teach them a lesson.

The Persian army was larger but not as unified as that of the Greeks, and King Darius and his army were defeated at the Battle of Marathon by an Athenian army in 490 B.C.E. This sent King Darius back to the Persian Empire with his proverbial tail between his legs and ended the First Persian War.

The next king of Persia, Xerxes, did not forget the Greek victory. In 480 B.C.E., he invaded Greece, this time with a superior army and navy. The Spartans were able to hold off the Persian army at the Battle of Thermopylae to give the other Greek city-states a chance to prepare. Later, at the Battle of Salamis Bay, the Athenian navy, with the use of ship rams, was able to destroy the Persian navy as King Xerxes helplessly watched from a nearby cliff. Finally, in 479 B.C.E. at the Battle of Platea, Sparta and Athens joined forces and sent King Xerxes and the Persians packing for home.

WHAT IN THE WORLD

The modern marathon was inspired by the story of the Athenian runner who ran 26 miles from the Marathon plain to Athens to deliver the news of victory at the Battle of Marathon to Athens. What modern marathoners don't know (or seem to forget) is that the runner died of exhaustion after delivering the news.

The Beginning of the End

The teamwork between Athens and Sparta quickly dissolved in the years following the Persian Wars. Athens, fearful of another Persian invasion, formed a defensive alliance of Greek city-states called the Delian League in 478 B.C.E. The Athenians didn't invite the Spartans because they wanted to lead it.

The Spartans were understandably hurt and worried about a new powerful alliance of Greek city-states. So Sparta created a defensive league of Greek city-states called the Peloponnesian League. Eventually the interests of both leagues clashed and the resulting armed conflicts were called the Peloponnesian Wars (432–404 B.C.E.). Sparta and the Peloponnesian League were victorious over Athens and the Delian League, but the wars devastated the whole of Greece, leaving all of the city-states weakened.

The Rise of Macedonia and Alexander the Great

The weakened state of Greece left the door wide open for a conqueror, and the man to do it was King Philip of Macedon, whose kingdom was located north of the Greek city-states. The Macedonians were related to the Greeks but were not as socially or politically advanced. But at the end of the Peloponnesian Wars, King Philip saw his chance to make Macedon a first-rate Greek kingdom and, by 338 B.C.E., he conquered all of the Greek city-states. His success fueled his confidence, and King Philip prepared for an invasion of the Persian Empire, but he was murdered (probably arranged through his wife) before he could start.

WHAT IN THE WORLD

In his *The History of Alexander,* Roman historian Curtius Rufus said that when Alexander the Great was born there "was a flash of lightning" and "thunder resounded." Apparently Aristotle recognized this flash of brilliance. When asked by Philip of Macedon to tutor Alexander, the philosopher jumped at the chance.

Philip's son, Alexander the Great (r. 336–323 B.C.E.), took over where his father left off. At 20 years of age, Alexander began a 12-year campaign of conquest through the Persian Empire and Egypt. With only 50,000 soldiers, he accomplished his mission and conquered over 2 million square miles of territory. Marching over 20,000 miles with his Greek soldiers, Alexander crossed the Indus River into India to conquer more territory. At this point his Greek soldiers refused to march any more and demanded that Alexander turn back to Greece.

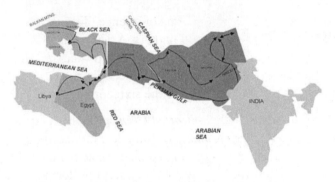

The empire of Alexander the Great.

On the return march, Alexander died at age 33, probably from a combination of exhaustion, fever, and too much drink. After his death his quickly conquered and created empire was divided into three large administrative kingdoms ruled by his former generals.

Hellenistic Culture

From the death of Alexander to 30 B.C.E., Hellenistic culture combined the best of Greek and Persian cultures, growing out of the trade that flourished with the protection of the kingdoms of Alexander the Great's former empire. This trade benefited from the use of the same Greek language and methods of buying and selling goods. It eventually produced sufficient wealth to allow new cities and inventions to be built and new ideas to flourish.

A prime example of this combination of trade and wealth in action was found at the city of Alexandria in Egypt, which became the place to be if you wanted to be on top of Hellenistic culture. Alexandria also was the home of the Library of Alexandria, the official repository for all that was known (a pretty tall order).

New philosophies and ideas spread across the Hellenistic kingdoms. Cynicism, advocated by Diogenes (412–323 B.C.E.), taught that humans should live in harmony with nature and forgo luxuries. Epicureanism, created by Epicures (340–270 B.C.E.), taught that human pleasure equals the good life—the "eat, drink, and be merry" attitude. And the philosopher Zeno (335–262 B.C.E.) wrote that humans must participate in society in their assigned role with virtue and duty as their guides.

There were also many leaps in the realms of science. Thales was one of the first to record the movements of the stars and planets. Aristarchus (310–230 B.C.E.) theorized that the earth orbited the sun, while Ptolemy argued that the sun and stars orbited the earth. He was wrong, but Ptolemy's earth-centric theory remained the accepted one until Copernicus proved it wrong in the sixteenth century.

Euclid (ca. 300 B.C.E.) wrote *The Elements of Geometry*, which still provides some of the most fundamental proofs of geometry. Archimedes, Greek inventor and mathematician, wrote in his book *Plane Equilibrium* some of basic principles of mechanics, including the lever. He even invented the compound pulley and the Archimedean screw, used to pump water. Finally, Eratosthenes (285–204 B.C.E.) calculated the circumference of the earth to be 24,675 miles. He was only off by 185 miles, which is pretty good considering he didn't have a pocket calculator!

The Least You Need to Know

- Athens and Sparta became the leading city-states politically and economically.
- The Greek cultural contributions to philosophy, literature, architecture, and art formed the foundation of Western civilization.
- The Greek city-states reached their apex shortly after the Persian Wars, but were weakened by the Peloponnesian Wars.
- Alexander the Great launched an ambitious conquest of the Persian Empire. He died after his troops reached India, but Hellenistic culture flourished as a result of his conquests.

When in Rome

In This Chapter

- The geography of Rome
- The rise of the Roman Republic
- The Roman Empire and its achievements
- Jesus and the rise of Christianity
- The decline and fall of the Roman Empire

During the first half of Roman history, the Roman Republic, influenced by the Greeks, developed legal traditions and government to a higher and more advanced level than had been seen before in the Mediterranean region. Later, during the second half of Roman history, the Roman Empire spread those traditions all over Europe to become a foundation of Western civilization.

The Boot of Europe

The Italian Peninsula, which most people recognize from its bootlike shape, was where the Roman civilization began and also ended. This boot in southern Europe extends into the Mediterranean Sea, which gives it a very mild and sometimes damp climate, excellent for farming. Of course, the nutrient-rich soil doesn't hurt, either. And isn't it odd that most great civilizations are founded on the sweat and dirt of a farmer's brow?

The Italian Peninsula is also protected by natural barriers that prevented migrations and invasions (with the exception of Hannibal). There are the Alpine Mountains, or Alps, in the north, and the surrounding waters of the Tyrrhenian, Adriatic, and Ionian seas, all part of the much larger Mediterranean Sea. All of these factors made the Italian Peninsula an excellent spot to start a civilization.

Early People of the Italian Peninsula

Roman history and legends have it that in about 753 B.C.E. the twin brothers, Romulus and Remus, founded the city of Rome. This historical fact shouldn't be taken too seriously. The legend also says the orphaned twins were suckled by a she-wolf that took in the abandoned boys.

The archaeological and historical records indicate that from 2000 to 1000 B.C.E., Latium and Oscan tribes migrated and settled in the Italian Peninsula. From 900 B.C.E. to 500 B.C.E., the Etruscans invaded the peninsula and conquered the Latium and Oscan tribes, by that time called the Romans after their major population center, the city of Rome.

WHAT IN THE WORLD

Oddly, another part of the legend of Romulus and Remus has the boys' great-uncle setting the infants adrift in a basket on the Tiber River. Variations of this legend have been found in the Bible as well as Mesopotamian lore.

Rome If You Want To

Little is known about the Etruscans, and what historians do know comes from the conquered Romans. With that in mind, the following events are said to have taken place during the period of Etruscan rule.

Around 620 B.C.E. the Etruscans gained control of the city of Rome. A wealthy Etruscan family, the Tarquins, provided Rome with kings to rule over the city. These kings tended to treat the Romans rather harshly, especially Tarquin the Proud, who came to the throne in 534 B.C.E. By 509 B.C.E., the Romans had had enough of Tarquin the Proud, overthrew him quickly and violently, and declared Rome a republic ruled by the people. Around 270 B.C.E., the Roman city and republic had control of the entire Italian Peninsula—and were poised for something much bigger.

The Roman Republic

The Roman Republic was not the first representative form of government; you'll remember that Athens holds that honor. But the Roman government did represent more people and territory than ever before. To govern well, the Romans had to develop an efficient government. This was a constant struggle, and one that they ultimately lost.

At first the Roman government was organized into two branches, the executive and the legislative. The Office of the Consul took care of the day-to-day operations as the executive branch. The legislative branch was made of the Senate and the Assembly of Centuries. The 300 members of the Senate were elected men who served for life; the Assembly of Centuries was made up of only 100 men who were elected on a regular basis.

Generally the legislative branch was dominated by the patricians, the wealthy aristocratic class. The plebeians, the middle class, resented their lack of political power and were continually locked in a struggle with the patricians. Eventually the plebeians were able to gain a measure of political equality by threatening to strike from service in the armed forces. The patricians created the Office of Tribune for the plebeians. It had veto power over any law passed by the Senate, a sizeable check on the powers of the legislative branch.

Roman Law

The Roman Republic created an impressive law code beginning with the Twelve Tables in 451 B.C.E. Twelve bronze tablets engraved with Roman law were placed throughout the republic so the law could be fairly applied to all. Of course, fairness and equality are sometimes subjective, and the Romans created the position of *praetor*, or judge, to act as moderator.

As the republic developed, so did the law codes. Gradually, three types of laws were created. The first was *jus civile*, or civil laws, which were the laws for the citizens of the Roman Republic. Another was *jus gentium*, the law of the gentiles, which governed noncitizens of the republic. And the Romans debated the idea of *jus naturale*, the natural laws that governed all humans.

This legal advancement by the Roman Republic created some conceptions of law that have endured into modern times. In the Roman legal mind, a state should be made of laws, not men; in other words, no man should be above the law. Another Roman concept was the idea of guilt based on verifiable evidence, which was closely related to the Roman concept of legal rights. Finally, the Romans advocated a respect for law and justice in the citizenry.

Roman Culture

The Roman Republic was not only made of government and laws but also people whose culture was becoming distinct as they assimilated and then modified cultures with which they came into contact.

At first, the Romans worshipped different spirits they believed were found in nature. Under Etruscan influence, the Romans saw these spirits as gods and goddesses. As the republic expanded and took control of Greece, they borrowed Greek deities and myths, giving them Roman names. Finally they stamped Roman structure and organization upon religion, creating the office of Pontifex Maximus, in charge of the prayers and sacrifices for the entire Roman Republic.

Rome Around the World

The Roman form of democracy and law spread across the Italian Peninsula and began to expand into other regions. Part of the catalyst for this expansion was the Punic Wars, a series of three conflicts with the city-state of Carthage in north Africa. The Carthaginians' wealth and power were based in trade and commerce. The city-state was originally a colony of the great trading empire of the Phoenicians.

NOTABLE QUOTABLE

Let us relieve the Romans of the fear which has so long afflicted them, since it seems to tax their patience too hard to wait for an old man's death.

—Hannibal, on being forced to drink poison when the Romans caught him long after the Punic Wars

The Punic Wars

The conflict between the two powers began over trading interests in the island of Sicily. The Romans had considerable territory and interest in the island; the Carthaginians wanted it to expand their commerce into the Mediterranean Sea.

The war lasted 23 years, from 264 to 241 B.C.E. In the end the Romans won, making Carthage pay a huge indemnity for the inconvenience of the war.

But this was not the end of the conflict. The Second Punic War began in 221 B.C.E., when Carthage, led by the brilliant general Hannibal, took Roman territory located in Spain. Knowing about Roman military weakness on the Italian Peninsula, Hannibal brought the war to them by leading an army across the Alps. Once on the peninsula, Hannibal defeated several Roman armies and terrorized the Italian countryside. Finally the Roman general Scipio formulated a plan to advance on Carthage, forcing Hannibal's army to return to its defense. In 202 B.C.E. at the Battle of Zama, Scipio defeated the Carthaginian army, forcing the city-state of Carthage to sue for peace.

The Carthaginians thus sufficiently humbled, the Romans felt confident enough to expand eastward. For 45 years, from 214 to 169 B.C.E., the Romans defeated forces in Greece, the Balkans, and modern-day Turkey, then returned to the Carthaginians, perhaps from a deep-seated fear of their return to power. In 146 B.C.E., the Romans went to war with Carthage over some imagined offense. By the time they left, Carthage was burnt to the ground and the soil around the city was sowed with salt to prevent the growth of plant life. The Romans also sold all of the Carthaginians—men, women, and children—into slavery. The message this sent to the Mediterranean rim people was "don't mess with the Romans." This reputation allowed the Romans to conquer more territory in western Asia, Egypt, and Europe.

WHAT IN THE WORLD

The Roman army did not defeat every foe. In 9 C.E., three Roman legions, approximately 15,000 men, were slaughtered to the man in the Teutoburg Forest by Germanic tribes led by a former Roman ally, Arminius. After that, Rome's policy of aggressive expansion ceased and the empire focused on border defense.

The Roman Army

It wasn't just their reputation that allowed the Romans to expand their territory and interests around the Mediterranean rim. It was also their military discipline and organization. Roman troops were organized into legions of 5,000 men trained to fight with a short sword and shield.

In battle, the legion moved as a unit with their tall shields up. Once upon the enemy, they used their short swords in a stabbing motion while constantly moving forward.

As men fell, the disciplined Roman soldiers filled in the ranks and pressed forward, with none of the fancy sword play of later medieval knights! With these tactics, the legions literally pushed other armies from the battlefield. Of course, it became more complex as the years progressed with archers and cavalry, but the common denominator was the discipline of the legion, which won many battles for the Romans.

Problems with Expansion

The expansion of the Roman Republic brought many benefits, including commerce and wealth, but it also caused problems. The exploitation of the newly conquered provinces brought resentment and armed resistance, which required an ever-larger Roman army. A steady supply of slaves created a labor problem, as many Romans became unemployed.

In addition, people flocked to other cities within the empire as they became centers of the new commerce and wealth. The Roman farmer, the backbone of the early republic, began to disappear from the landscape. Food production went to the hands of wealthy landowners.

Finally, the ranks of the military, once populated with small farmers who volunteered for short periods, became populated with professional soldiers who could fight long campaigns. In times of peace, however, these professional soldiers grew restless and troublesome.

> **WHAT IN THE WORLD**
>
> One unusual ruler of the Roman Republic was Cincinnatus. He was called to lead Rome when his military services were needed to defend the borders. When the invaders were defeated, he returned to his farm, allowing for an orderly change of power. George Washington was said to have thought of himself as an American Cincinnatus; following his example, Washington only served two terms as president of the United States.

The Beginning of the End of the Republic

With the problems came solution-minded men, two brothers and two generals. The first reformers were two brothers, Tiberius Gracchus and Gaius, the grandsons of the great general Scipio. Tiberius Gracchus came to power after he won the office of tribune in 133 B.C.E. He gained support by representing the plebeians and their economic and political struggles. This did not sit very well with the patricians. They organized a riot, in which Gracchus was killed.

Apparently Gaius, his brother, did not learn very well from his brother's fate. Gaius suggested a redistribution of land to help poor farmers, and wanted to help Rome's urban poor. Again the patricians organized a riot, killing Gaius in 121 B.C.E.

The generals, Marius and Sulla, tried different strategies to end the economic inequalities and acquire political power in the Roman Republic. General Marius was the first to try a new strategy when he was elected consul in 107 B.C.E., giving the poor jobs as soldiers in the army. This created an army loyal to him, but combined military and political power—generally a dangerous combination.

By 88 B.C.E. General Sulla, using Marius' example, recruited an army to defeat Marius' army; Sulla was victorious and became dictator for a short period before the republic was restored. These men did little to solve the problems of the republic, but these small episodes in the history of the Roman Republic were not forgotten. Marius and Sulla gave political leaders who followed them a template for acquiring power in the Roman Republic.

The First Triumvirate and the Rise and Fall of Julius Caesar

The men who learned most from Marius and Sulla were the so-called First *Triumvirate:* Pompey, Crassus, and Julius Caesar. They combined their respective political and military powers in 60 B.C.E. to gain control of the Roman government. Afterward, Julius Caesar, always the general, went to the territory of Gaul to defeat the Celtic and Germanic barbarian tribes and protect the north European borders of the Roman territory. He probably also sought to gain Rome's popular support through his military victories. Everybody loves a winner!

DEFINITION

A **triumvirate** designates a group of three rulers who ruled ancient Rome with equal authority.

Crassus also tried this method to gain the support of the Roman people, but was killed in battle in 53 B.C.E. At that point Pompey, who had stayed in Rome and the Senate, feared that Caesar might use his army in Gaul to seize power in Rome.

When Caesar marched south into the Italian Peninsula, they sent word to him to stay north of the Rubicon River. Legend has it that Caesar crossed the Rubicon and announced, "The die is cast," meaning that whatever his fate, he was ready.

At first Caesar's prospects were good. He cornered and defeated Pompey and his forces, and the Roman people loved him and supported the reforms he advocated to solve the republic's ills. But the Roman Senate feared Caesar and his popular appeal—with good reason. In 45 B.C.E., Caesar took the position of dictator for life, weakening the power of the Senate considerably. In response, a group of senators, some of them once friends of Caesar, cornered and stabbed him to death on the floor of the Senate. Caesar's fate was the beginning of the end of representative government in Rome.

NOTABLE QUOTABLE

As soon as Caesar took his seat the conspirators crowded around him … one of the Casca brothers with a sweep of his dagger stabbed him just below the throat …. Confronted by a ring of drawn daggers, he drew the top of his gown over his face and did not utter a sound … though some say that when he saw Marcus Brutus … he reproached him in Greek with: "You, too, my child?"

—*The Twelve Caesars,* Gaius Suetonius Tranquillus

The Real End of the Republic

The end of the republic began with revenge and ended with an emperor. Octavian, grandnephew and adopted son of Caesar, formed the Second Triumvirate with Marc Anthony and Lepidus to exact revenge on Caesar's enemies in the senate. The three men then divided the large Roman Empire into three parts.

Of course, that arrangement did not last long. Octavian wanted more power and, in 31 B.C.E., reached his goal of total control of the empire with the defeat of Marc Anthony in Egypt. Once in Rome, Octavian took the name Augustus Caesar, by which most people remember him. Augustus ruled Rome from 27 B.C.E. to 14 C.E. During his rule he systemically took power away from the Senate and became the sole lawmaker and law executor, ending the representative government of the republic. Although most would consider the end of the representative government a bad thing, it did provide stability for an expanded empire for which the republican form of government was unsuited. This began a period of 200 years of relative peace in Roman history, called the Pax Romana, or Roman Peace.

The Roman Empire

The new Roman Empire that Augustus established wasn't all roses. There were some interesting episodes of intrigue among the first four emperors who ruled from 14 to 68 C.E., called the Julian emperors because they were all related to Julius Caesar.

Tiberius Caesar was paranoid of treachery within his administration (could you blame him?) and accused innocent people of treason. The emperor Caligula was mentally disturbed, and it showed. Claudius was old and frail and could not focus on affairs of the state. And Nero was cruel and as mentally disturbed as Caligula. It was even rumored that in order to have a palace built in a section of Rome that was already settled, Nero set fire to it and that while "Rome burned, Nero fiddled."

WHAT IN THE WORLD

Gaius Julius Caesar Germanicus, Roman emperor from 37 to 41 C.E., was born and raised in Roman military camps. There he gained his nickname, Caligula, meaning "little boots," on account of the little military boots he wore as an infant. Apparently the name did not contribute to his mental stability. Caligula was said to be mad and participated in many wild exploits of debauchery during his reign. His madness became evident to the Roman public when he tried to name his favorite horse as a Roman consul.

The Good Emperors

After Nero, things were put back on track by the senate, which in 96 C.E. began to elect emperors. What followed were five good emperors who have been aptly named … the "Five Good Emperors." Nerva was the first, ruling with justice and temperance. Emperor Trajan followed and expanded the empire to its greatest size. Hadrian then strengthened the empire's frontier defenses with fortresses and walls—one of which is Hadrian's Wall, found in north England. Antoninus Pius maintained a steady hand on the rudder of prosperity that the empire produced. Finally, Marcus Aurelius, Stoic philosopher, brought order and stability and even more wealth to the empire.

Pax Romana

Early in the Roman Empire and Pax Romana, there were several significant improvements in Roman rule. The emperors learned to carefully choose the governors of the provinces to keep them under control. The emperors also ended the office of

Pontifex Maximus and themselves became chief priest of the Roman state religion. In fact, starting with Augustus, the emperors were considered divine gods on earth, and as such, worthy of worship. The emperors also made all conquered peoples citizens of Rome, with all the rights and privileges, which created loyalty in the provinces. Conquered peoples were even allowed to join the Roman legions.

The Roman Empire enjoyed unprecedented wealth and prosperity, most of which came from imports and exports that extended from England to China. The prosperity allowed the Roman people to enjoy over 130 holidays to partake in festivals, races at the *Circus Maximus*, or the gladiatorial contests at the Coliseum.

The Romans made cultural advancements during Pax Romana, too. In architecture, the Romans constructed many impressive projects, such as the Pantheon, finished in 128 c.e. The Romans also built one of the first major roadways, the Appian Way, portions of which still survive to this day.

Roman education advanced as well. The Romans borrowed a great deal of knowledge from the conquered Greeks, but, unlike the Greeks, who generally focused on theory, the Romans looked to the practical. The theories of the Greek physician Galen were systemized, forming the basis of Roman medical science. The work of the Egyptian astronomer Ptolemy was perfected and formed the basis of Roman astronomy. With Latin as the official language of the Roman Empire, literature flourished. *The Aeneid*, written by the Roman poet Virgil, compares to Homer's *Iliad* in beauty, style, form, and epic dimensions. Other Romans, most notably Livy and Tacitus, wrote accurate histories (by the day's standards) of Rome.

NOTABLE QUOTABLE

The study of history is the best medicine for a sick mind; for in history you have a record of the infinite variety of human experience plainly set out for all to see; and in that record you can find yourself.

—*History of Rome,* Livy

Roman Religion and Christianity

During the Pax Romana, a new religion was established that would eventually conquer the empire via the very roads and trading networks the empire had established and protected with Roman legions. This new religious force was Christianity, and it changed the face of Rome and, of course, all of Western civilization.

The Roman State Religion

Officially, Romans had to worship the emperor and various gods and goddesses of the Roman pantheon. Romans believed that observing certain rituals made them right with the gods. This meant it was a Roman citizen's duty to perform the appropriate rituals to ensure the peace and tranquility of the empire.

That did not make Romans intolerant of other religions. In fact, worshippers of other religions from Persia, Greece, and Africa flooded Rome after their conquest. To be accepted by the Romans, these people needed only to perform the prescribed rituals at the appropriate times—they didn't have to believe in them.

The Jewish People Under Rome

Under Roman rule the Jewish people of Judea were given certain freedoms, including a degree of religious freedom and self-rule. By 6 B.C.E., the Romans sent a *procurator* to rule the nation of Judea, and self-rule was revoked. This caused widespread unrest, and three groups emerged. The Sadducees favored cooperation with the Romans. The Essenes preferred to wait on a Messiah or savior to save them from Rome. And the Zealots thought, "Why wait?" They wanted a violent overthrow of Roman rule, and they wanted it now.

DEFINITION

A **procurator** was a Roman official who was in charge of the financial affairs of a province or who was governor of a lesser province.

Jesus of Nazareth

During this period, Jesus of Nazareth was born. Although little of Jesus can be found in historical records, his disciples provided many details of his life and teachings in the four Gospels that make up the New Testament of the Bible. A carpenter by trade, Jesus preached for a short period, probably no more than three years. During that time he spread a new message to the Jewish people. That message was not about the importance of Jewish law, but the importance of transforming the inner person. To Jesus, the greatest commandment was to love your neighbor as yourself.

Jesus was well received by the Jewish people, but the Jewish priests saw him as a rival to be silenced. So when he brought his message to the capital, Jerusalem, he was detained and denounced for his teachings by a Jewish court, and crucified by Roman authorities. The Jewish court convicted Jesus most likely in response to the real or imagined threat to the political and social order of Jerusalem, yet under Roman law, Jesus had committed no crime. Long-standing interpretation of Jesus' trial and execution found in the four Gospels of the New Testament placed a majority of the blame for Jesus' death on the Jewish community, and helped to poison Christian-Jewish relations for 2,000 years.

The Spread of a New Religion

Jesus' death did not stop his teachings from spreading. Many of Jesus' followers believed that he rose from the dead and was the Messiah, the Savior of Israel. Inspired by this belief, now called Christianity, his followers spread Jesus' teachings across the Mediterranean rim along Roman roads and trade routes.

Two leaders emerged during this early Christian movement. Simon Peter was one of the leaders and the first bishop of Rome, who focused on teaching that Jesus was the son of God, or Christ. Paul of Tarsus was the other leader of the early Christians who arguably had the most impact. He cleared the way for gentiles, or non-Jews, to be converted to Christianity, setting the stage for the conversion of the Roman Empire. His letters also form a major portion of the New Testament of the Bible.

The Romans did not tolerate the new religion, and it spread underground at first. The Romans viewed Christianity as a threat to the state religion, because Christians refused to perform the Roman state religious rituals. Christians were persecuted and suffered death by crucifixion or sport. Yes, throwing Christians to the lions in the Coliseum really was once a favorite Roman pastime. The persecutions reached their peak under the emperors Nero and Diocletian, but the Christian church grew despite this violent opposition. It has been said that the Christian church grew because it was watered by the blood of Christian martyrs.

Why was Christianity so popular? It gave some Romans meaning and purpose in their lives. In addition, Christianity fulfilled the need to belong, which was sometimes hard to find in the vastness and the cosmopolitan nature of the empire. Finally, the teachings of Jesus were attractive to the poor and powerless.

> **NOTABLE QUOTABLE**
>
> Blessed are the poor in spirit for theirs is the kingdom of heaven.
>
> —Mark 5:3, Jesus on the poor

The Conversion of Rome

By the fourth century C.E., a majority of citizens in the Roman Empire had converted to Christianity. This became apparent when pagan Emperor Constantine issued the Edict of Milan in 313 C.E., which granted official tolerance for the religion. Constantine later converted to Christianity himself.

Once given official tolerance, the Christian religion became an unstoppable force in the empire. In 395 C.E., Emperor Theodosius the Great adopted Christianity as the official religion of the Roman Empire, putting an end to the pagan traditions of Rome that had endured for 800 years. Some historians have pointed to this historical moment as the beginning of the decline of the empire.

Roman Chaos and Decline

In reality, the decline of the Roman Empire, which began around 180 C.E., can't be attributed to one factor. Between 235 and 284 C.E., there was a great deal of political upheaval, as evidenced by the list of 22 emperors who ruled during that 49-year period. It was also after the third century C.E. that the Germanic tribes that had been kept outside the borders of the empire began to make incursions into Roman territory. The Germanic problem forced higher and higher taxes, as it cost more money to fund and equip a large army to protect the borders. Trade and small industry also declined, and the wealth of the empire started to dry up.

Diocletian and Constantine

Two emperors tried to stop this decline. Diocletian ruled the empire from 285 to 305 C.E.—quite long compared to the preceding 22 emperors. He made his rule more efficient by dividing it into four administrative units. Diocletian also pushed economic reforms, including price and wage freezes, to fight inflation.

His successor, Emperor Constantine, enjoyed a long rule, too. He consolidated his rule over the empire and constructed a new capital city in the eastern Roman Empire named after himself: Constantinople. Constantine was able to make both economic and military reforms to help slow the decline of the empire. But slowing the decline was all Diocletian or Constantine could do. Their administrative reforms were only a quick and temporary patch.

This Is the End

The fall of the Roman Empire is traditionally thought to have started in the fifth century. The fall was started by tribes united under Attila the Hun, who migrated from the plains of Asia in the east and pushed a Germanic tribe, the Visigoths, into Roman territory. By 410, the Visigoths had invaded the Italian Peninsula and sacked Rome, an act that sent shockwaves throughout the Roman world.

Later, a Germanic tribe called the Vandals (from whom the word *vandal* originates) invaded the Roman Empire from the west and sacked the city of Rome in 455. Finally, in 476, a Germanic chieftain deposed the last emperor of the remnants of the western Roman Empire. Because of this, 476 is traditionally considered the date of the fall of the Roman Empire, but the eastern portion of the Roman Empire, under the capital city of Constantinople, continued for another 1,000 years as the Byzantine Empire.

> **DEFINITION**
>
> The term **vandal,** which means one who intentionally destroys something, originated with the Germanic tribe named the Vandals, who destroyed the beauty of the Roman Empire during their invasions.

Reasons for the Fall

Over the ages, historians have speculated over the exact reason for the fall of the Roman Empire. No single cause can be established, but several factors are possible contributors. The first was the conversion of the empire to Christianity. Some historians have suggested that this led the Romans to spend more time thinking about the afterlife rather than the here and now of the empire. In addition, the cohesive power of the Roman state religion was lost.

Other historians have thought that a decline in traditional Roman values associated with the simple, humble, agrarian lifestyle of the Roman Republic was the reason for the fall. Other factors include successive plagues that weakened the empire, slavery that made the Romans lazy and unemployed, and even poisoning from the lead pipes that provided their indoor plumbing.

Finally, one factor that has carried a lot of credence with historians is the fact that the Romans struggled to find a workable political system to control such a vast empire for an extended period. Regardless of the reason, the Roman Empire fell and left a void in western Europe … but its legacy remained.

> **NOTABLE QUOTABLE**
>
> The union of the Roman Empire was dissolved; its genius was humbled in the dust; and armies of unknown barbarians, issuing from the frozen regions of the North, had established their victorious reign over the fairest provinces of Europe and Africa.
>
> —*The Decline and Fall of the Roman Empire,* Edward Gibbon

The Least You Need to Know

- The Roman Republic originated in the city of Rome, inhabited by the Latium people.
- After winning the Punic Wars, the Romans dominated the Mediterranean Sea rim.
- With expansion came political strife, and the Roman Republic was replaced by an empire ruled by an emperor.
- The Christian religion was founded during the period of Pax Romana, or Roman Peace, and spread throughout the Roman Empire and became its official religion.
- The Roman Empire fell into political and cultural decline during the fifth century C.E., and by 476 C.E. the empire fell after a series of invasions by Germanic tribes.

After the Classics

The classic regional empires that flourished had all fallen partly due to nomadic invaders. With their fall, the stability enjoyed by the regions under their influence was lost. People began to rely on local political structures.

The limited trade between the classic regional empires continued along the "Silk Road" connecting China, India, and the Middle East and developed into the first interregional trade network. This interregional network spread ideas and religion of the classical period.

Invasions began this period, and they also ended it. Another nomadic group, the Mongols, migrated along the interregional trade network. Although these migrations were disruptive, they were only a temporary condition. Civilizations continued to centralize and develop. The march of progress would not be stopped.

Islam and Africa

In This Chapter

- The geography and culture of the Arabian Peninsula
- Muhammad and the origin of Islam
- Islamic empires
- Early African civilizations
- Africa and Islam

Of all the civilizations that have been described to this point, none truly could be called a global civilization. Arguably, though, that distinction could be given to the Islamic culture that rose out of the hot sands of the Arabian Peninsula.

Arabian Peninsula and the Bedouin

The Arabian Peninsula is 1 million square miles of arid desert and scarcely populated hot plains between the Red Sea on the west and the Persian Gulf on the east. The people who chose to live in this hostile climate on the peninsula were called the Bedouin. They were typically nomadic and herded sheep, camels, and goats from vegetated area to area. Like most nomadic cultures, the Bedouin lived in tribes of related families led by a sheikh or chief. Their culture was simple in most respects, but eventually it developed its own written language, Arabic, and also a trade network that spanned the peninsula.

Mecca

As the commerce network developed, connecting all of the points of the peninsula, the area became a crossroads for the trade of luxury goods between the western and the eastern trading settlements. As a result, the Bedouin towns grew in population and strength. Mecca (sometimes spelled Makkah) was such a town. It developed quickly in the 500s C.E. because it was a commercial crossroads.

Mecca was also a place of religious pilgrimage for the Bedouins and Arabs. A shrine had been constructed for the mysterious stone of Kaaba and other statues of Arabic gods. The Bedouin religion during this time had grown into an eclectic mix of polytheism and *animism*. As trade connections increased in Mecca, so did contacts with monotheistic religions like Judaism and Christianity. This would arguably have a major influence on the Bedouin and Arabic religion.

DEFINITION

Animism is the conviction that life is produced by a spiritual force that is separate from matter, sometimes incorporating the belief that spirits and demons may inhabit particular objects. For example, some people have traditionally knocked on wood to avoid bad luck. This tradition comes from European animist beliefs in which knocking on wood scared the evil spirit of the tree away.

Muhammad

It was within this cultural background that Muhammad was born in Mecca around 570 C.E. His parents died early in his life and he was raised by his closest relative, an uncle. Muhammad was involved in the practice that made Mecca what it was: commerce. After trading for several years, Muhammad married a wealthy older widow, and, at the age of 25, he was financially set.

But the life of luxury did not suit Muhammad. In his spare time he walked the city of Mecca and saw many problems. He worried about the greed of people and the mistreatment of the poor. He spent many hours alone in the desert pondering the meaning of life and suffering. Around 610 C.E. he heard a voice in his head instructing him to recite its words and warn the people. Muhammad came to the conclusion that it was Allah (the Arabic word for god) speaking to him, but not until 613 C.E., after reassurances from a relative that he wasn't crazy, did Muhammad share with others what Allah told him.

Muhammad's Message

Like the Bedouin culture itself, Muhammad's message was simple: there is only one god, Allah, and everyone is equal in his eyes, so everyone should be treated equally. (Not a bad message at any rate.)

NOTABLE QUOTABLE

They stirred up against him [Muhammad] foolish men who called him a liar, insulted him, and accused him …. However, the Messenger continued to proclaim what God ordered him to proclaim.

—*The Life of Muhammad,* Ibn Ishaq

This message was not well received by the merchants of Mecca, who perceived economic inequalities as a natural condition. In addition, Muhammad's new religion, now called Islam (meaning "submit"), was a threat to the economic livelihood of the city, which came from the pilgrims who visited the Shrine of Kaaba. According to Muhammad, the stone was part of the pagan past. If Islam was accepted by the population of Arabia, the revenues received from pilgrims might dry up. So in response, the merchants of Mecca persecuted Muhammad and his first followers, called Muslims.

Exile and Return

The persecutions did not stop Muhammad, but instead inspired him to create an Islamic state. In 622 c.e., Muhammad left Mecca to travel to nearby Medina at the request of the people of that city who wanted him to settle a dispute. His journey to Medina is known as the Hijrah, and it now marks the first year of the Muslim calendar. Once in Medina, Muhammad formed the beginnings of an Islamic state out of the city.

In 630 c.e. he returned to Mecca with an army of followers to conquer the city for Islam. When he arrived, however, the city gates swung open to him and he was accepted as Mecca's rightful ruler. Muhammad then cleared the Shrine of Kaaba of all pagan idols and rededicated it as an Islamic house of worship. Very rapidly, Muhammad took his forces and his appeal to the Arabic people and consolidated the whole Arabian Peninsula under Islamic rule.

Islamic Teachings

During this period the practices of Islam solidified into what they are today. At the foundation of Islam is the Quran (sometimes spelled Koran). The story has it that the angel Gabriel revealed the content of the Quran to Muhammad over a 22-year period. The text was written in Arabic and, according to tradition, should only be read in Arabic to understand the truth of its revelation. In the end, Muhammad's revelations became the holy book of Islam and the final authority in matters of faith and lifestyle for the Islamic people.

The Five Pillars of Islam

The Five Pillars of Islam found in the Quran represent the core of the practices of Islam:

- The first pillar is faith, professed in the recited creed, "There is no God but Allah; Muhammad is His prophet."

- The second pillar is prayer five times daily, which is announced or called by the *muezzin*, or reciter.

- The third pillar is almsgiving, or *zakat*, which means simply giving to the poor.

- The fourth pillar is the required fasting during the holy month of Ramadan.

- The fifth and final pillar is the undertaking, if possible, of a pilgrimage to Mecca, or *hajj*, once during one's lifetime.

In addition to the practices found in the Quran, Islamic social teachings can be found in the Hadith, a collection of sayings and acts of Muhammad. There is also Sharia, or Islamic law, derived from both the Quran and Hadith.

The "People of the Book" and the "Seal of the Prophets"

Another fundamental belief of Islam is that Allah sent many other prophets, including Moses in the Old Testament and Jesus in the New Testament of the Bible, to instruct the people. Because of that belief, Muslims accept Christians and Jews as people who worship the same God, sometimes referred to as "People of the Book."

However, in the Islamic view, Muhammad was the last prophet, and through him the full and perfect religion was revealed. Muhammad was the "Seal of the Prophets," so although there is some kinship with the "People of the Book," there is also friction because they have not accepted the "Seal of the Prophets."

After Muhammad

Muhammad passed away in 632 c.e., and leadership of the Islamic state passed to men called caliphs, meaning "successor," who were elected for life. The first of these men was Abu Bakr, Muhammad's best friend and right-hand man. He was followed by Umar and Uthman, two other early converts and close companions of Muhammad.

These men were named the "Rightly Guided Caliphs" because of their exceptional leadership abilities and religious devotion. During their rule, the Islamic state of the Arabian Peninsula expanded to the rest of the Middle East, including North Africa, Egypt, Persia, and Levant (part of Palestine). But after the "Rightly Guided Caliphs," questions of succession of caliphs caused a major rift in the unity of Islam.

Division

When Uthman died in 656 c.e., a dispute over who would succeed him led to civil war between members of Muhammad's family, including Muhammad's son-in-law and wife. Finally, after several years of struggle, another leader named Muawiyah, not related to Muhammad's family, announced that he was the new caliph and established his rule of the expanded Islamic state.

A majority of the Muslims accepted his rule, which marked the beginning of the Umayyad dynasty. These Muslims refer to themselves as Sunni, or the "People of Tradition and Community." Today this group makes up about 80 percent of the Islamic community. But there were members of the Islamic community who did not accept Muawiyah's rule because he was not related to Muhammad. This group is known as the Shiites from Shi'at Ali, or "Party of Ali," referring to their belief that Ali was Muhammad's rightful successor.

The Umayyad Dynasty

The Umayyad dynasty founded by Muawiyah did not retain power long, but it did spread the Islamic faith through conquest. The first major change initiated by the dynasty was that the capital was moved from Mecca to Damascus in present-day Syria. From this strategic vantage point, the Umayyad dynasty was able to add even more territory to the Islamic state, including all of North Africa and the Middle East.

More important, Islamic faith spread to the continent of Europe through the conquest of Spain. Islamic forces were only stopped from entering and conquering the region of France by the Merovingian ruler Charles Martel at the Battle of Tours. The Umayyad dynasty also harassed the borders of the Byzantine Empire. Only the high and thick walls of Constantinople protected eastern Europe from falling to Islamic rule.

The underlying political philosophy of the Umayyad dynasty spelled its defeat. Unlike the "Rightly Guided Caliphs," the dynasty's government was politically based rather than religiously. This did not sit well with many Muslims. In addition, some felt that Muhammad's original intent was to spread Islam through conversion. The Umayyads preferred to be religiously tolerant and accepting of other religions. Nonconverts in conquered territories were allowed to keep their legal systems and worship as they pleased. This policy made ruling conquered territories for the Umayyads much easier. However, oddly enough, converts to Islam were actually taxed in an effort to maintain the old Islamic aristocracy. A change in rule was in the works.

WHAT IN THE WORLD

Most historians think that the defeat of the Muslim army at the Battle of Tours in 732 C.E. marked a turning point in European history. As one historian put it, if Charles Martel had not won the battle, the Islamic call to pray would be heard in Oxford rather than church bells.

The Rise of the Abbasids

By 747 C.E., Muslims and Muslim converts had become disenchanted with the Umayyad rule. These men, numbering 50,000, had started to settle in eastern Iran. The Abbasid family, whose ancestor had been a cousin of Muhammad, allied themselves with this group to overthrow the Umayyad dynasty in 750 C.E. From there the capital of the Islamic state was moved to Baghdad, once the site of Babylon and a major cultural center of the old Persian Empire. This gave the Abbasid dynasty a distinctly cosmopolitan outlook during its reign, which lasted until 1258 c.e., when it was sacked by the Mongols.

During the Abbasid dynasty, specifically during the rule of Harun al-Rashid (786–809 c.e.), Islamic culture experienced its golden age. The empire became a truly global civilization, incorporating a variety of religions and cultures within its large borders.

Islamic Culture

It almost goes without saying that the culture of both the Umayyad and Abbasid Islamic empires was influenced heavily by the teachings of Islam. But oddly, the Islamic culture retained much of its male-dominated nature despite the Quran's teachings on the equality of women, taking many of the cultural traits of the Persians who previously controlled the territories of the Middle East. Persian males had traditionally secluded and covered Persian women.

Muslim men could have up to four wives and many slave women with which to form a harem. In addition, women were considered property; they stayed at home and were not to be seen or heard. This, of course, also meant that women received little education. Muslim males, on the other hand, entered school at the age of 7. Once completing their required education, some continued their studies at *madrasas*, or theological schools, where they learned to become political or religious leaders in Islamic society.

WHAT IN THE WORLD

The Arab surgeon Abu al-Qasim (936–1013 c.e.) developed surgical techniques that he wrote down in the first illustrated surgical textbook. His textbook was used for hundreds of years in Europe and the Middle East.

Art

Despite the inequalities, the culture did flourish in the areas of art, literature, and philosophy. Calligraphy, the art of elegant handwriting, developed in response to the desire for religious decoration, which in Islam did not involve human images. (The Islamic people were iconoclasts to the extreme. Images of Muhammad, for example, were severely prohibited. This extremism would be felt in the Christian Byzantine Empire!) So, too, they developed the art of arabesque, in which intricate geometric designs were created for religious decoration.

Philosophy and Literature

During the Abbasid period in which Islamic culture reached its zenith, many libraries were created and stocked across the empire. This expansion can be compared with the spread of libraries and learning during the Greek Hellenistic period. Because of this, there was much advancement in the areas of philosophy and literature.

Muslim philosophers, most notably Ibn-Rushd, Ibn Sina, Al-Kindi, and Moses Maimonides, tried to combine the teaching of the Quran with those of Greek philosophy, the teachings of Aristotle in particular. Others, like Tabari, Ibn al-Athir, and Ibn Khaldun, wrote histories in which, for the first time, events were arranged in the order that they occurred. Ibn Khaldun even went so far as to examine history scientifically by looking for cause-and-effect relationships in events. In literature, Muslim writers produced many influential works, including the *Rubaiyat* by Omar Khayyam and *A Thousand and One Arabian Nights*.

NOTABLE QUOTABLE

How beautiful is that which [Aristotle] said in this matter! We ought not to be ashamed of appreciating the truth and of acquiring it wherever it comes from, even if it comes from races distant and nations different from us.

—*On First Philosophy,* Al-Kindi

Africa and Islam

The Islamic faith not only spread throughout the Middle East, it also spread deep into the continent of Africa. But to understand how that expansion occurred, we need to examine the geography of Africa and some of the earlier civilizations that emerged on the continent.

The Geography of Africa

The climate of Africa is divided into four zones. The desert zone is found in the region of North Africa and includes the area of the Sahara and Kalahari deserts. The mild zone has a Mediterranean climate and temperate weather and is located across the very northern tip of Africa. The rain forest zone stretches along the equator; despite what most people imagine about African climate, it only makes up about 10 percent of Africa. And finally, the savanna just north and south of the equator is made up of broad grasslands with small trees and shrubs.

In this land of geographic diversity, several early African civilizations developed before the Common Era and during the early centuries of the Common Era. The civilizations of Nubia, Kush, Axum, and the Nok all served as the basis for later civilizations that formed Islamic Africa.

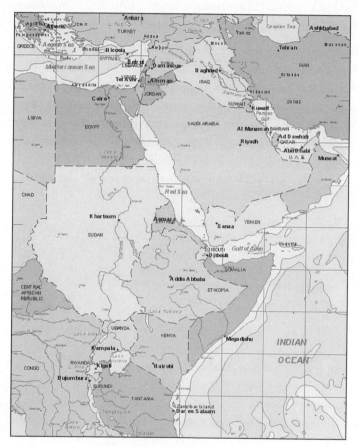

The Middle East and East Africa.

The Kingdom of Nubia

One of the first civilizations to develop in Africa emerged in the southern Nile Valley around 3000 B.C.E. The Nubians were heavily influenced by Egyptian culture because of their close proximity to the land of the pharaohs. But archaeological evidence has shown that the influence also went the other way. The kingdom of Nubia existed for close to 1,000 years, but eventually fell into decline.

The Kingdom of Kush

Around 2000 B.C.E., the kingdom of Kush emerged from the ashes of the kingdom of Nubia, but they were dependent on the Egyptian kingdom. The kingdom of Kush did not attain cultural or political independence from their neighbor to the north until 1000 B.C.E. In an odd twist, the Kushites later conquered their one-time oppressors when in 724 B.C.E. King Piankhi led the kingdom in the conquest of Egypt.

Their control over the lands of the Nile did not last for long. The Assyrians drove the Kushites out of Egypt in 663 B.C.E. Although this was a setback, it did not spell decline for the kingdom of Kush, which continued to develop into a major trading empire. They engaged in commerce with some of the major civilizations of the classical world, including the Roman Empire, India, and Arabia. The city of Meröe became their major trading and population center, attracting goods from across the continent of Africa. The zenith of the kingdom of Kush was from 250 B.C.E. to 150 C.E., but during this peak of power and influence it was conquered by the civilization of Axum.

The Axum

The civilization of Axum started as an Arab trading colony along the Red Sea. It eventually came to dominate the region of East Africa for over 500 years. In part because of its geographic location, the Axum civilization combined the best of African and Arabic cultures.

Like the Kushites they had conquered, the Axum depended on trade and commerce for their power. The Axum civilization also had far-reaching trade connections with the Roman Empire, India, and Arabia. It was probably because of its trading connections with the Roman Empire that the Axum people gradually converted to the Christian religion. In 330 C.E., King Ezana made Christianity the official religion of the Axum. Christianity probably served as a cohesive force in Axum, but like all civilizations, they began a slow decline around 600 C.E.

The Nok

The last early civilization of Africa was the sub-Saharan civilization of the Nok. The Nok civilization emerged from the fertile river valleys of West Africa from 700 to 200 B.C.E. As the Nok population increased, food grew scarce and the civilization began a slow decline. The decline of the Nok caused a great migration to the east and south of Africa, sometimes referred to as the Bantu migrations after the Bantu language which these people spoke.

The Bantu Migrations

By 1000 C.E., as the Bantu migration progressed, different ethnic groups formed. These groups became close-knit communities that settled in small villages across eastern and southern Africa. Rather oddly, considering the track record of male domination in previous civilizations, the villages traced their ancestry through the mother of the family, making the culture matrilineal rather than patrilineal.

During this Bantu period, religious beliefs also solidified. To most Africans there was a single supreme god who created the universe. This god also made marriage customs and all other laws and traditions that the society practiced. In addition, many of the Africans of the Bantu migrations believed that the spirits of the dead lived among the villages and served as guides for the people.

The early Africans of the Bantu migration period developed important cultural traditions in the areas of art, music, and literature. They sculpted masks and figures to represent the spirits of the dead in the villages. The Africans created music for religious ceremonies and also for everyday work, using a variety of instruments, including drums, harps, flutes, and horns. Finally, the Africans of the Bantu migrations passed down from generation to generation an impressive oral literary tradition.

WHAT IN THE WORLD

The language of Swahili, spoken in Africa today, is a combination of the Bantu, Arabic, and Persian languages.

The Kingdoms of the Niger River Valley

Not all of the African people of the Niger River valley region migrated during the Bantu migrations. Three kingdoms later developed along the fertile banks of the Niger River: Ghana, Mali, and Songhai.

The Kingdom of Ghana

Ghana was the first kingdom of the Niger River valley, emerging on the banks of the river around 400 C.E. The name of the kingdom itself came from the word for the king, or *ghana*, who ruled over the kingdom. As the kingdom developed, commerce focused on the export of iron and animal products, as well as the gold and salt mined at the Saharan salt mines.

This commercial activity led to the development of several trading centers, including the key city of Saleh. These trading centers eventually proved too rich and attractive to outside groups, such as the Almoravids, a Muslim group that invaded from North Africa. These attacks led to the decline of the kingdom by 1200 c.e.

The Kingdom of Mali

Mali was the next kingdom to grow along the banks of the Niger River, beginning around 1250 c.e. Like Ghana, it depended on trade for its wealth, including the trade of salt and gold. Timbuktu emerged as the largest city of the kingdom and the focus of cultural and political activity.

The kingdom of Mali holds the distinction of producing one of the most notable Islamic rulers of Africa, Mansa Musa. He ruled the kingdom from 1312 to 1332 c.e., doubling its size. In addition, he created a Muslim center of learning in Timbuktu that attracted students and scholars from across Africa and even the Mediterranean Sea basin. After his rule, the kingdom began a slow decline, and by 1450 c.e. it was divided up into many different small states.

The Kingdom of Songhai

The final kingdom to originate in the Niger River valley was Songhai, which emerged in West Africa around 1000 c.e., with its key city located at Gao. Eventually with the decline of Mali and the conquest of the cities of Timbuktu and Jenne, Songhai gained control of the salt and gold trade of West Africa.

Under the Islamic king Askia Muhammad, who ruled from 1493 to 1528 c.e., the kingdom reached the height of its commercial and political power. To help standardize justice, Askia introduced laws based on the Quran.

Sadly, the decline of the kingdom of Songhai started at the peak of its power and influence. Askia Muhammad's son, who was dissatisfied with his father's rule, staged a violent rebellion and in 1529 c.e. Askia Muhammad was overthrown. Shortly after the change in power, a Moroccan army attracted by the wealth of the region invaded the kingdom of Songhai and ended its reign of West Africa.

Coastal City-States and Central Empires

Beyond the fertile banks of the Niger River, other powerful city-states and kingdoms rose to prominence in the regions of eastern and central Africa. In East Africa there were the Arabic coastal city-states, and in central Africa was the kingdom of Karanga, as well as the Changamire and Monomotapa empires.

The city-states of East Africa developed over a long period of time. As early as the 500s B.C.E., the coastal areas of East Africa traded with the Arabian Peninsula. This trade allowed for the slow emergence of Arabic-influenced city-states along the shores of East Africa.

In the 900s C.E., as trade and commerce spanned across Eurasia, Arab and Persian merchants settled in the cities of East Africa in an effort to extend existing trade connections. By the 1200s C.E., the city-states of Kilwa, Malindi, Mombassa, Sofala, and the island of Zanzibar surfaced as the most important trade centers of the region. During the 1300s, these cities reached the height of their power and influence, which extended into the Arabian Peninsula and central Africa. But the city-states of East Africa did not dominate central Africa. That was reserved for the kingdom of Karanga and the Changamire and Monomotapa empires.

WHAT IN THE WORLD

As early as the 1200s C.E., the city-states of East Africa had developed trade connections with India and China! They exported gold and ivory to Indian Ocean ports in India and China in exchange for cotton and porcelain.

The kingdom of Karanga grew up in the region of central Africa around 1000 C.E. To protect their territory, the people of Karanga built over 300 stone-wall fortresses. The largest and greatest of these fortresses was called the Great Zimbabwe. But despite its defensive measures, the kingdom of Karanga did not control central Africa long. Rival factions split the kingdom apart in the 1400s C.E. These rival factions eventually became the Changamire and Monomotapa empires, both of which ruled the region for a short period before falling under Arabic and Portuguese spheres of influence by the 1800s.

The Least You Need to Know

- The Islamic religion originated in the Arabian Peninsula.
- Muhammad and his followers, Muslims, established the beliefs and practices of the Islamic faith.
- At its height, the Islamic Empire encompassed all of the Middle East, North Africa, and modern-day Spain.
- During the seventh century, the Islamic faith split into two groups, the Shiite and the Sunni, over the issue of succession.
- Trade led to not only the exchange of goods but of cultural ideas that affected the way African civilizations developed.

The Byzantine Empire and Russia

In This Chapter

- The origins of the Byzantine Empire
- The Byzantine culture
- The Slavs and the origin of Russia
- The third Rome

The Byzantine Empire emerged at first as part of the Roman Empire. As the Roman Empire declined, it took on a life and form of its own, which continued for a thousand years after the fall of the Roman Empire. Finally, as it declined, some of the Byzantine traditions of government and religion spread into southeastern Europe and Russia.

The End of Rome?

The Byzantine Empire, or Byzantium as it is sometimes called, was the eastern half of the Roman Empire, which had been divided administratively in 395 c.e. Its capital and cultural center was Constantinople (modern-day Istanbul), built by the Roman emperor Constantine, who favored the site and the eastern territories of the Roman Empire. The city itself is located on the narrow Bosporus Strait overlooking the Black Sea, making it a natural crossroads for trade between Europe and Asia. Constantinople is geographically located in Europe, but across the Bosporus Strait 12 miles away is the continent of Asia. This, in effect, gives the city a unique position of almost being of two worlds, the West and the East.

Maybe because of its unique position, Byzantium was able to survive long after the barbarian invaders killed the last Roman emperor of the Western Roman Empire. Or maybe it was the combination of Latin and Greek heritage that it took on. The emperors still spoke Latin, but the people of the empire spoke Greek. The emperors did look to its Western Roman past, but also stressed the Greek heritage of the territories of Byzantium. Regardless of its dualistic nature—West and East or Latin and Greek—the Byzantine Empire, after the fall of the Roman Empire in 476 C.E., was considered by most people of the classical period to be the "New Rome." To many, Rome did not fall, but continued on in another location. But eventually the Roman nature of the empire changed into something different, the Byzantine Empire. This empire was founded on Roman traditions but developed with Greek and Persian influences.

The Byzantine Empire

The territory of the Byzantine Empire consisted of more than just the city of Constantinople and its immediate area. During various times the empire held territory in Asia Minor, North Africa, the Balkans, and Italy, including the city of Rome itself. But as Islam expanded and the Germanic barbarians consolidated power and established rule under a monarch, the empire lost its territory in North Africa and in Italy. Although the walls of Constantinople were besieged several times, the empire retained its possessions in Asia Minor and the Balkans for most of its existence.

WHAT IN THE WORLD

Greek fire was a weapon used by the Byzantines similar to a modern-day flame thrower. It was an incendiary material that could burn on most materials, even on water. The Byzantine Empire was able to win many battles expanding and defending the empire using this substance. What Greek fire was and how to make it was a closely guarded state secret.

The Byzantine Emperors

During the Byzantine Empire's reign, there were many different dynasties and interesting characters as emperors. It would be pointless to evaluate the merits of each dynasty and its emperors, but some generalizations can be made.

First, there were many periods of political peace and prosperity, but there were also many times of instability caused by issues of imperial succession. During these periods, however, the imperial bureaucracy saved the day by continuing with the daily business of the empire.

Some dynasties did stand out as being exceptionally able at ruling an empire. These were the dynasties of Justin (518–610 C.E.), Heraclius (610–717 C.E.), the Syrian dynasty (717–820 C.E.) and the Macedonian dynasty (867–1059 C.E.). Within those dynasties, some emperors truly stood out as exceptional rulers who put their stamp on the imperial office, including Justinian the Great, Heraclius, and Leo III.

NOTABLE QUOTABLE

Justice is the constant and perpetual wish to render every one his due. The maxims of law are these: to live honestly, to hurt no one and to give every man his due.

—*Corpus Juris Civilis*

Justinian the Great

Justinian the Great ruled the Byzantine Empire during the dynasty of Justin from 527 to 565 C.E. He was sometimes called the "Emperor Who Never Sleeps" because of the long hours he dedicated to the empire at the height of its power.

Militarily, Justinian was able to defeat the Persians and secure the eastern borders of the empire. He also tried, with some success, to expand the empire's border to include former territories of the Western Roman Empire, including territories in Italy, Sicily, and the city of Rome itself.

Domestically, Justinian reinitiated the Roman legal tradition by compiling the laws of the empire into the *Corpus Juris Civilis*, or *The Body of Civil Law*, which remained a legal standard in Europe well into the nineteenth century. He also spent time revitalizing Constantinople, including overseeing the additions to the Hagia Sophia. This large and beautiful Christian church became a central point of the city and inspired many people with its magnificent art and architecture. When a mission of pagan Russians came to the Hagia Sophia in the tenth century to witness the Orthodox Christian religion, they were so impressed with the church that one of the members of the delegation reportedly said, "There God dwells among men."

Heraclius and Leo III

During the reign of Heraclius, from 610 to 641 C.E., the empire took a more eastern direction. Unlike previous emperors, Heraclius spoke Greek (not Latin). His entire reign was preoccupied with resisting several Islamic and Persian invasions. Although he was unable to completely stop the Islamic expansion into the Levant and Egypt, he did break Persian power and influence in Asia Minor.

Leo III, or Leo the Isaurian, who ruled from 717 to 740 C.E., was the first emperor of the Syrian dynasty. Unlike his predecessor Heraclius, he was able to defeat the Islamic armies and reclaim much of the territory of the Levant. Leo III also added more territory from Asia Minor to the Byzantine Empire. Interestingly, Leo III pursued a controversial iconoclastic policy that offended Western Christians. This started the slow division in the Christian church that still exists to this day. It has been speculated that Leo III, despite being a devout enemy of Islam, was heavily influenced by Islam's theology, which resulted in his policy of *iconoclasm*.

DEFINITION

Iconoclasm or iconoclastic refers to policies or people who oppose the religious use of images and advocate the destruction of such images.

Byzantine Religion

Byzantine culture and religion were almost entirely inseparable, just as the empire and the Christian church were. There was no separation of church and state. Christianity, culture, and empire were intertwined to produce the grandeur and ceremony that was the Byzantine Empire. Emperors led the Christian church, just as they led the empire and the people.

This authoritative stance made relations difficult with the Christian church in the West and its leader, the bishop of Rome (also known as the pope). The iconoclastic controversy during Leo III's reign was just one of many of the periods of disagreement between the Western and Eastern Christian churches. Eventually the friction between East and West led to a schism or separation of the church in 1054 C.E., with the Roman Catholic Church in the West and the Eastern Orthodox Church in the East.

The Economy of Byzantium

The Byzantine Empire lasted for almost a millennium because of the strength of its economy. The base of this economy was agriculture, which was continually protected by the emperors' governmental polices. Perhaps learning from the decline of the Western Roman Empire, the emperors appeared to have recognized the importance of an agricultural base.

In addition, because of the geographic location of the empire, commerce and trade fueled the economy. Using the well-developed Silk Road (a trading route that links China, India, and the Middle East together), goods from China and India poured into Constantinople before making their way into Europe. This made Byzantium and Constantinople one of the richest civilizations and cities of the late antiquity. Lastly, silk weaving developed as an industry in the empire as early as 550 C.E., again adding fuel to the massive economy of Byzantium.

NOTABLE QUOTABLE

Great stir and bustle prevails at Constantinople in consequence of the great conflux of merchants who resort thither from all parts of the world.

—*Itinerary,* Benjamin of Tudela

Byzantine Art and Learning

Supported by the strength of the Byzantine economy, the arts and learning flourished within the borders of the empire. In art, the subject of the Christian religion was dominant. Despite the iconoclastic tendencies of the empire, icons and mosaics depicted Jesus, Mary, the apostles, saints, and martyrs. Intricate illuminated manuscripts of the Bible were made.

Just as art was heavily influenced by religion, so was education and learning. The Eastern Orthodox Church provided schools for parishes to train priests and the laity (only men at this point in history) in medicine, law, philosophy, math, geometry, astronomy, grammar, and music. Of course, all of the subjects were taught with a decidedly religious perspective. Higher education was also available at the University of Constantinople, founded in 850, which trained scholars and lawyers for service in the Byzantine imperial bureaucracy.

Some of those scholars spent their time copying the classical writing of the Greeks and Romans for the Byzantine libraries. Literary achievements of the empire were once again dominated by Christianity. Byzantine literature focused on the salvation of the soul and obedience to God's will. Hymns and poems were written in honor of Jesus Christ and his mother, Mary. Books detailed the lives of the various saints for the people to learn from and imitate. Byzantine art, architecture, and scholarship were heavily studied and imitated in Europe by the Germanic and Slavic people. It even influenced the culture of Islam to the east.

The Spread of Eastern Orthodox Christianity

With the amazing amount of energy spent pursuing religious ends, it only seems fitting that the Byzantine Empire sought to spread the message of Christianity. Many monasteries and religious communities were founded throughout the Byzantine Empire during the 300s and 400s C.E. Later these monasteries sent missionaries to the northern lands to convert the pagan Slavs and Germanic tribes.

The missionaries St. Cyril and St. Methodius were the most successful at this type of dangerous missionary work. Around 863, Cyril developed an alphabet loosely based on the Greek alphabet to help in his conversion of pagan tribes. Known as the Cyrillic alphabet, it formed the basis for the Russian and other Slavic languages. This missionary work and subsequent spread of Christianity is arguably the most enduring legacy of the Byzantine Empire because, as it declined, it was the converted Christian Slavs who carried on its traditions.

The Decline and Fall of Byzantium

The decline of Byzantium occurred over an extended period of time. In general, the never-ending struggle to maintain its borders on the east and the west put the empire at a disadvantage. In addition, the economic trading interests of Byzantium came into conflict with later Italian city-states such as Venice and Genoa. This led to several economic, political, and military conflicts that peaked during the period of the fourth Crusade (1202–1204 C.E.), when the Venetians convinced or possibly coerced crusading European knights to sack Constantinople.

NOTABLE QUOTABLE

Sometimes [the cannon] demolished a whole section of a tower or turret. No part of the wall was strong enough to resist it …. Such was the unbelievable and inconceivable nature of the power of the implement. Such a thing the ancients neither had nor knew about.

—*History of Mehmed the Conqueror,* Michael Kritovoulos

After that, the Byzantine Empire existed as a faded image of its former self until the walls of Constantinople were again breached and conquered by the invading army and cannons of the Ottoman Turks in 1453 C.E. Although it looked like the end of Byzantium, the leadership and traditions of the empire and Eastern Orthodox Church that was so much a part of it passed on to the Slavic people, whom missionaries had begun to convert hundreds of years before.

WHAT IN THE WORLD

One of the problems with tracing Slavic ancestry is that the name "Slav" was not used until the mid-sixth century. Before that time, the people were referred to as the Venedi or the Antes.

The Slavs and the Origins of Russia

Historians and anthropologists have been uncertain as to the exact origin of the Slavic people for some time, but in general a few facts can be agreed upon. The Slavs originally lived in the steppes of Asia north of the Black Sea. In the second half of the first millennium, the Slavic people separated into three distinct groups. The West Slavs migrated from the steppes and settled in east-central Europe. The South Slavs preferred to migrate and settled closer to the Byzantine Empire's border in the Balkan Peninsula. The Eastern Slavs stayed put and continued to inhabit the area north of the Black Sea, in what is now Russia.

The Slavic people were, in a word, primitive. They spent their time hunting, fishing, and gathering their food, mostly because the areas in which they settled had rich soil for farming but not a good climate.

The Slavic people engaged in some primitive forms of trade and waited for foreign merchants to come to them. Following a combination of land and river routes, Byzantine merchants reached the Slavs to peddle their wares (silk was probably one of the fastest sellers, as it is very soft compared to fur and wool). The Slavic people were very impressed with the goods and culture of Byzantium, so much that on several occasions they invaded Byzantine territory. Of course, the professional Byzantine army knew how to deal with these untrained and primitive armies, but when they could not, the empire gave the Slavs some token tribute (probably lots of silk).

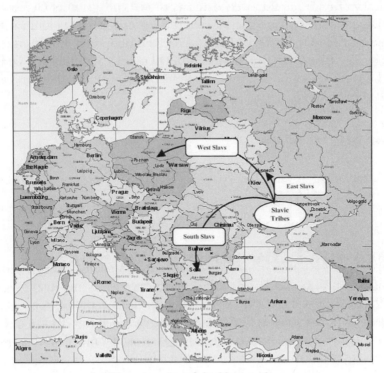

The migration of the Slavic tribes.

The Rise of Kievan Rus

The Eastern Slavic people also began to encounter different Viking groups out of Scandinavia, part of a larger Viking movement that lasted from 800 to 1100 C.E. The Vikings journeyed from their Scandinavian lands in search of plunder and new trade routes. By the late 800s they came to dominate the Eastern Slavs. The Viking rulers of the Slavs were called Rus, from which the name Russia comes. A Viking leader named Oleg founded the principality of Kiev at the beginning of the tenth century, and took control of the territory between the Baltic and Black seas and the Danube and Volga rivers.

NOTABLE QUOTABLE

[In the year 882] Oleg set himself up as a prince in Kiev and declared: "May this be the mother of Russian cities."

—*Primary Chronicle,* Anonymous

The territory of Kiev developed into an organized collection of city-states or principalities. Each city-state had its own self-government—as long as it paid taxes and respect to the grand prince of Kiev. Democratic forms of government were also adopted in the city-states. Some city-states had councils of nobles called *boyars* who assisted the prince of the principality. Others had assemblies that represented all free adult male citizens.

The Conversion of Kiev

The growth of the principality of Kiev and its governmental structures attracted the attention of the Byzantine Empire, which saw the new, organized Slavs as a bit more troublesome than the old, unorganized Slavs. In response, the Byzantine Empire sent missionaries to convert the Slavs to Orthodox Christianity, which was inseparable in some respects from the empire itself.

Olga, a princess of Kiev, was one of the first nobles to convert to the new religion. Later, in 989 C.E., when Prince Vladimir wanted to marry the Byzantine emperor's sister for political purposes, he had to accept Eastern Orthodox Christianity for himself and his people. Thus, Eastern Orthodox Christianity became the religion of the principality of Kiev, and Kiev in a sense became a cultural and political satellite of the Byzantine Empire.

The Golden Age of Kiev

With the development of a strong governmental system and the addition of the cohesive force of the Christian religion, the principality of Kiev enjoyed a golden age during the tenth and eleventh centuries.

Two rulers were also in part responsible for this peak in the Kievan Rus. Vladimir the Great, who ruled Kiev from 980 to 1015, was responsible for converting the principality to Eastern Orthodox Christianity by proclamation. Vladimir also expanded the western borders of Kiev.

Yaroslav the Wise ruled from 1019 to 1054. and improved the culture and education of Kiev. More important, Yaroslav organized the Kievan legal system under the title Pravda Russkia (Russian Justice). This action also gave him the nickname "The Wise," an Old Testament reference to the wisdom and justice of the judgments of King Solomon.

The Decline of Kiev

Kiev's cultural, commercial, and, to some degree, political dependence on the Byzantine Empire led to its decline. When the Byzantine Empire experienced economic, military, and political instability, Kiev also suffered, at least economically. So as the Byzantine Empire and trade declined, Kiev declined, too, until it was conquered in 1240 C.E. by Mongol invaders from the plains of central Asia.

> **NOTABLE QUOTABLE**
>
> They [the Mongols] attacked Russia, where they made great havoc, destroying cities and fortresses and killing men; and they laid siege to Kiev, the capital of Russia; after they had besieged the city for a long time, they took it and put the inhabitants to death.
>
> —*History of the Mongols,* John of Plano

The Rise of the Third Rome

However, the story does not end there. The Mongols were able to conquer all of the city-states of the principality except one, the city-state of Moscow, which remained free by cooperating with the invading Mongol armies. By 1350, this cooperation was paying huge dividends, and Moscow was the most powerful city-state in the region of Russia. Of course, the yoke of outside rule had to be thrown off eventually, and in 1380 the Muscovite forces defeated the Mongols and claimed independence.

Gradually the principality of Moscow acquired more territory from the Mongols. It also freed other Russian city-states from Mongol rule, which gratefully accepted the supremacy of Moscow. Finally, in 1480 Ivan III, also known as the Great, pushed the last of the Mongols from Russian territories.

Ivan the Great earned his name for several very good reasons. He was, of course, an Eastern Orthodox Christian, which still indicated a strong relationship with the Byzantine Empire regardless of its stature or lack thereof. (Remember, Ottoman Turks had conquered Constantinople in 1453.)

In 1472, Ivan III married Sophia, the niece of the last Byzantine emperor, which made Russia, to some, an extension of the Roman imperial tradition. Ivan III and all the subsequent rulers took the title of czar, meaning "Caesar," in reference to the power of the Roman imperial tradition. If the Byzantine Empire was an extension of the old Roman Empire, then Russia was now an extension of Byzantium, and thus the third Rome. That mentality influenced the Russian state and its political philosophy until early in the twentieth century, when revolution toppled the last czar.

NOTABLE QUOTABLE

[The czar] is on earth the sole emperor of the Christians, the leader of the Apostolic church which stands no longer in Rome or Constantinople, but in the blessed city of Moscow. She alone shines in the whole world brighter than the sun .... Two Romes have fallen, but the third stands.

—Letter from Philotheus of Pskov to Czar Basil III

The Least You Need to Know

- When the Western Roman Empire fell, the eastern Roman territories kept Roman imperial tradition alive as the Byzantine Empire.
- The Byzantine Empire was a crossroads of trade and a center of cultural diffusion between the East and the West.
- Byzantine missionaries spread Orthodox Christianity to the Slavic and Germanic tribes.
- The East Slavs migrated to the area of Kiev to form a principality of independent city-states, which was later conquered by the Mongols.
- The principality of Moscow overthrew the Mongols and maintained a strong tie with Byzantine culture, identifying itself by extension with the tradition of imperial Rome.

Rebirth in China

In This Chapter

- The end of strife and the Sui dynasty
- The Tang dynasty
- The Song dynasty
- The golden age of Chinese culture
- The emergence of Neo-Confucianism

The surfacing at the end of the sixth century of the Sui dynasty from the long and chaotic warring states period brought China again under the rule of a strong dynasty. Later, during the seventh century, the Tang dynasty revived the bureaucratic traditions of the Han dynasty, including the civil service examination. This revival helped the later Song dynasty consolidate rule over Chinese territory.

During this time of relative political stability, Neo-Confucian philosophy developed, providing the ideological basis for centralized rule under later imperial dynasties. The result of these strong dynasties and Neo-Confucian philosophies was a golden age of art, literature, and culture that lasted 700 years.

Out of the Chaos: The Sui Dynasty

After the collapse of the Han dynasty in 200 c.e., China suffered from more than 300 years of civil war, chaos, strife, and instability. The people needed a savior to bring them out of their cycle of suffering. The Sui dynasty that emerged did not actually qualify as a savior, but it did bring stability to the region. The Sui dynasty was able to consolidate power among the warring three kingdoms and gain some control over eastern Asia by 581. The dynasty was named after the second—and last—emperor of the dynasty.

Sui Yangdi was the reason for the strength of the dynasty, and also its collapse. The second emperor took on a massive public works project, the Grand Canal, which linked northern and southern China through the Huang He and Chang Jiang rivers and a series of canals. Sui believed, justifiably, that this type of link would increase trade and unity in the region. He was a visionary; but like most visionaries, he was not a practical man.

Sui was a cruel ruler and forced the peasant population of China to build the Grand Canal. In addition, he raised taxes to unbearable heights to fund the materials to build the canal. To make matters worse, Sui led an extravagant and expensive court life and engaged his armies in several military expeditions that turned out to be disastrous. Eventually the people of China had had enough and a rebellion overthrew the Sui dynasty. Sui himself was promptly killed.

Although things ended rather poorly for the Sui dynasty, it did serve two very important purposes. First, it consolidated power and brought about stability in China. Second, the Grand Canal provided China with improved communication and trade. Thus the Sui dynasty served as a bridge to the much more enduring Tang dynasty.

> **WHAT IN THE WORLD**
>
> During the twentieth century, with the development of roads and railroads, the importance of the Grand Canal faded and it fell into disrepair, used only by small boats. The Communist Chinese government took on the Grand Canal as a new public works project in the late 1950s and modernized it over a period of five years. Today, the canal again is used as a way to transport goods to market.

The Tang Dynasty

The Tang dynasty seized power and ruled China after the overthrow and murder of Sui in 618, remaining in power until 907. The Tang rulers built on the new unity created by the Grand Canal and brought years of peace and stability to China.

Reformers and Pencil Pushers

The Tang rulers were reform-minded. They saw that if they increased the government's ability to administrate, they would increase their power. The Tang dynasty restored the civil service examinations, which had been out of use since the Han dynasty.

This gave the Tang a pool of competent bureaucrats to administrate the government, which was needed because Chinese control had been extended to new regions of southern Asia, including Tibet. The Tang also established diplomatic relations with southeastern Asia in an effort to expand trade. Finally, the Tang took on the awesome task of breaking up the powerful landed aristocracy and redistributing land to the peasant population.

The Problem with Pencil Pushers

Despite all of the reforms that were instituted, problems arose in the Tang dynasty. As with any bureaucracy, the Tang government became large and corrupt as members entered politics for self-interest, and the extension of Chinese control to new territories created additional problems.

The Tang had developed a well-trained pencil-pushing army to administer the empire, but did not balance that with a well-trained military army to protect the empire. (Sometimes the sword works better than the pencil.) So the Tang hired soldiers: the Uighurs, a group of Turkic-speaking people from central Asia. Eventually, the hired Uighurs saw the weakness of the Tang dynasty (too many pencils and not enough swords!) and overthrew the dynasty in 907.

The Rise and Fall of the Song

The Song dynasty rose to power around 960 by wresting power away from the Uighurs who, due to their nomadic nature, couldn't be expected to remain in power long. The Song dynasty retained power over China until 1279, when they made a major strategic error. Fearing that the generals might overthrow the dynasty, the Song emperors forced their veteran generals to retire. In the place of the generals, the Song emperors put scholars in charge. This maneuver, which helped to strengthen the power of the emperors who could dictate to the inexperienced scholars, served to weaken the empire.

During the Song dynasty, China enjoyed a period of economic and cultural prosperity and achievement, but not without problems. The Song dynasty lost control of the territory of Tibet, and the Uighurs did not simply disappear from the Chinese political and military landscape. They continued to harass the borders, forcing the Song to move the capital from Changan to Hangzhou in the southern region.

When the harassment continued, the Song dynasty made a very bad decision. Like the Tang dynasty before, the Song rulers invited a nomadic, warrior group to protect them: the up-and-coming Mongols. The Mongols overthrew the dynasty in 1279, but, unlike the Uighurs, the Mongols planned to stay and created a Yuan dynasty to rule China.

The Golden Age of Chinese Culture

Beginning with the stability of the Sui dynasty and ending with the Tang dynasty, China experienced a 700-year period of cultural achievement considered by some historians to be the golden age of China. However, as with any golden age, there were highs and lows throughout.

The Chinese Government and Economy

The Chinese government experienced a proverbial "shot in the arm" starting with the Sui dynasty and the reinstitution of the civil service examination. The government was rooted in the principles of the Qin and the Han dynasties, which meant China was ruled by a monarch who used a large and fairly efficient bureaucracy.

To make this rule even more effective, the Chinese empire was divided into provinces, districts, and villages administered by bureaucrats using Confucian principles. In spite of a few bumps in the road (the Uighurs and the Mongols), the Chinese emperor retained relatively successful control over a large amount of territory.

Trade and Technology

With a stable government, trade flourished within the Chinese boundaries. There was renewed trade on the Silk Road, with exports of tea, silk, and porcelain going toward central, western, and southeast Asia. In exchange for these exports, Chinese merchants imported exotic woods, precious stones, and tropical goods.

With the expansion of trade, China developed technologically as well. Steel was invented for the manufacture of swords and sickles, and gunpowder was used in the creation of explosives and flame throwers (known as the "fire lance"). Finally, cotton was grown in limited quantities for the production of cotton garments.

WHAT IN THE WORLD

During the Song period of China, the barter system was replaced with a cash system using copper coins. When these ran short in 1024, the Chinese started to print paper money, the first documented use of today's most common medium of exchange.

A Prosperous Society

The prosperity of the region during the golden age led to changes in the social structure. Of course, at the top of this societal structure were the emperor and the emperor's family. They were followed by a new group of prosperous city dwellers who benefited from the riches that trade provided, spending their leisure time playing games like cards and chess (the classic strategy game imported from India) and reading the new literature that was blossoming during this period.

After this group, a new class called the scholar-gentry was developing, replacing the landed aristocracy that had been broken during the Tang dynasty. It controlled most of the countryside and produced the civil servants and bureaucratic corps that became the political and economic elite of China. The rest of Chinese society was a mixture of landowners, free peasants, sharecroppers, and landless laborers.

Of course, this is only half of the story of the Chinese social structure. Women, who made up the other half of the population, had little status. Most families had to provide a dowry for a daughter to be married and, because women were undesirable, poor families often sold their daughters to wealthy villagers for menial labor.

The Golden Age of Literature and Art

Beyond the renewal of trade, development of technology, and societal transformations, the prosperity and stability of the Chinese dynasties allowed for the peaking of Chinese literature and art. During the Tang dynasty, the invention of block printing allowed for the production and proliferation of many works of literature, including poetry.

Over 48,000 poems were written and published by over 2,000 authors, the most popular of which were Li Bo and Duo Fo. Li Bo wrote poems about nature, while Duo Fo created poems using Confucian principles to highlight social inequalities and the poor.

NOTABLE QUOTABLE

In 1041–1049 a commoner named Bi Sheng also devised moveable type. His method was to cut the ideographs in sticky clay to the depth of the edge of a copper coin, each one constituting a separate piece of type. These were then baked to make them hard.

—Shen Gua, writer during China's Song period

Chinese culture also blossomed artistically with the development of what are now considered traditional Chinese landscape paintings during the Song and even Mongol dynastic periods. These paintings were influenced by Daoist religious philosophy. The artists weren't seeking realism; it was their intention to discover through the painting the hidden form of the landscape. Humans appeared in some of these paintings, but usually as tiny figures to show their insignificance in comparison to nature.

Religious Revival and Change

Before the collapse of the Han dynasty, several religions/philosophies were practiced within China's territories. These were native religious/philosophical traditions of Daoism and Confucianism, as well as Buddhism, which had come to China during the first century C.E. with the help of Buddhist missionaries from India.

During the troubled times between the Han and Sui dynasties, when there were civil wars, instability, and hardship, the Chinese people embraced the religious and spiritual ideas found in Buddhism and Daoism. Confucian philosophy lost its grip on Chinese culture as order and stability disappeared. Buddhist monasteries were built across the Chinese territories and, by the time of the Tang dynasty, had become quite powerful religiously and politically. The Tang rulers, who had started to reinstitute the civil service examinations based on Confucian principles, saw Buddhism as a threat to Confucianism and the dynasty. Buddhism was also criticized as a foreign religion with too much wealth and power. Daoism was also considered a threat, with what the Tang rulers thought to be primitive beliefs. So the Tang dynasty worked to eradicate both religious traditions by confiscating lands and destroying many Buddhist temples and monasteries.

New Confucianism

The Tang rulers did not completely end Buddhism or Daoism, nor did they stop the Chinese culture from acquiring a spiritual tradition. Religions within cultures always evolve as they interact with the progression of society and history. Such was the case in China.

Neo-Confucianism was a philosophical revival and, more importantly, a spiritual birth that occurred in reaction to the growing popularity of Daoism and Buddhism. Neo-Confucianists seemed to understand that traditional Confucianism was not addressing the spiritual needs of Chinese culture, and that the Chinese government had a structural need for Confucian principles. So Neo-Confucianists combined the philosophical elements of Confucianism with spiritual elements of Buddhism and Daoism.

The tenets to Neo-Confucianism make it much different from earlier Confucian philosophy. First and foremost was the acknowledgment of a god, or Supreme Ultimate. The other important points of belief in Neo-Confucian are as follows:

- The world is real, not illusory.

- Personal fulfillment is gained by full participation in the world, not withdrawal from it.

- The world is divided into two worlds: material and spiritual.

- The goal of everyone should be to unify with the Supreme Ultimate.

With the development of Neo-Confucianism, there was little backlash with the Tang rulers' purging of Buddhism and Daoism from Chinese culture. The people got the spiritual contentment they needed from Neo-Confucianism, while the Tang government got rid of rival religions that didn't support the philosophical underpinnings of its rule. Neo-Confucianism was in China to stay, and its impact was much more pronounced than Buddhism or Daoism.

The Least You Need to Know

- Although the Sui dynasty was not in power long, it ended a period of strife in China and began a period of stability and prosperity.
- The Tang dynasty renewed trade and culture with its reinstitution of the civil service examination and subsequent bureaucracy.
- The Song dynasty presided over the final years of a golden age of Chinese culture and accomplishment.
- Buddhism and Daoism had made successful inroads in China, but their impact was later minimized by efforts of the Tang dynasty and the emergence of Neo-Confucianism.
- Neo-Confucianism combined the philosophy of Confucianism with spiritual elements to create a new religious tradition in China.

Chinese Culture Spreads in East Asia

In This Chapter

- Feudalism in Japan
- Japanese culture
- China's little brother—Korea
- The states of Southeast Asia
- The culture of Southeast Asia

As the Chinese Empire developed and grew culturally and politically, so did its influence on the surrounding regions of Japan and Southeast Asia. But these regions later grew up rapidly and pulled away from China's political and cultural influence.

The Rise of the Island Nation of Japan

Japan is unique compared to the empires and kingdoms that we have examined so far. It is an island nation that, although from all appearances is close to the Asian continent, was quite isolated from other peoples and cultures of east Asia.

Japan is a chain of islands that total about 146,000 square miles of land. The population is concentrated on four main islands: Hokkaido, the main island of Honshu, and the two smaller islands of Kyushu and Shikkohu. The land is very mountainous, with only about 20 percent of it suitable for agriculture. But what might appear to be limitations turned out to unify its people. The people of Japan believed that they had a separate identity and destiny from the rest of Asia.

The Beginning of the Japanese State

Early settlers first arrived to Japan from east Asia in the first century C.E. These settlers formed many different clans that developed a simple social structure, with an aristocratic class at the top and farmers, artisans, and servants at the bottom. Eventually, the ruler of the Yamato clan from the central island of Honshu was able to unite all the clans to become the sole ruler of Japan, although this rule was somewhat unstable.

Shotoku Taishi

Shotoku Taishi of the Yamato clan made the most strides in stabilizing the government and controlling the other clans. Shotoku became ruler of the Yamato clan and Japan in the early seventh century. Taking the Tang dynasty as his model, Shotoku centralized the government of Japan by limiting the powers of the aristocrats and increasing his own power, taking the title of emperor. In addition, Shotoku made the personage of the emperor divine and a symbol of the Japanese nation. Shotoku divided the island into administrative districts that paid taxes to the central government. The Japanese state took over the farmland to ensure that all the people of Japan would be fed.

After Shotoku died in 622, the Yamato family's power declined. In order to maintain his stable centralized government, the Fujiwara family seized power and retained the figurehead of the emperor from the Yamato clan. A new capital for the central government was built in Nara in 710.

The Nara and Heian Period

The Nara and Heian periods mark a period of decentralization in Japanese history. Although the emperor began to use the title "son of Heaven" during this time, the aristocracy grew more powerful and mostly ignored the emperor and his title. In 794, the emperor moved the capital of the Japanese government to Heian. With this action, the decentralization of the government grew exponentially.

At first, the aristocrats began to dominate the rural areas of the island. Later, the systems of law and justice were also placed in aristocratic hands because the central government was unable to administrate the island districts it had created. The aristocrats hired warriors to protect the people and the lands. These warriors were called samurai, or "those who serve." Much like the chivalric code of medieval European knights, the samurai developed a code of conduct called *bushido*, or "the way of the warrior," to guide samurai interactions in Japanese society.

> **WHAT IN THE WORLD**
>
> The warrior code dictated that a samurai had to endure strict training in a variety of fields. Beyond swordplay, he had to learn the proper way to conduct a tea ceremony and how to write poetry.

The people depended on local aristocrats and their samurais as protectors and a *feudal society*, again much like medieval Europe, emerged in Japan. Once entrenched, Japanese society remained in this feudalistic state for the next 400 years.

> **DEFINITION**
>
> A **feudal society,** or feudalism, is an economic, political, and social system in which land, worked by peasants who are bound to it, is held by a lord in exchange for military service to an overlord. The peasants receive protective services provided by the lord of the land. The lord benefits from the work of the peasants. The overlord benefits from the military service of the lord and work of the peasants.

The Kamakura Shogunate

At the end of the twelfth century, an aristocratic noble named Minamoto Yoritomo defeated several local aristocratic rivals and centralized Japanese government around the city of Kamakura. This government kept the emperor and his powerful divine status as a figurehead whom the Japanese people revered. The real power rested in the hands of the shogun, a powerful military leader who ruled by the sword.

Yoritomo's system of government was called the Kamakura Shogunate for its centralization around the city of Kamakura, and it controlled the island of Japan from 1192 until 1333. Strangely enough, a failed Mongolian invasion in 1281 that the Kamakura Shogunate was able to defeat put a strain on the shogunate's power and began Japan's return to a more decentralized government.

The Final Collapse of Central Rule

As the Kamakura Shogunate slipped from power during the fourteenth and fifteenth centuries, local aristocrats and their samurais rose again in power and prominence. The aristocrats, called daimyo, controlled large estates of farmland while relying on the samurai for protection. Eventually, daimyo rivalries surfaced as each competed for power and land with their armies of samurais. This competition led to the Onin War, an islandwide civil war that lasted from 1467 to 1477. During this period Japanese central government collapsed. Kyoto, the capital of Japan at the time, was destroyed and depopulated. The whole island of Japan fell into a state of internal and constant warfare.

Life in Early Japan

The economy of Japan during the rise of the Japanese state was based on farming, and the staple crop was wet rice. Wet rice is grown in flooded fields for a majority of its lifecycle. Foreign trade was virtually nonexistent until the eleventh century, and even after that it was very limited. The imports that did reach Japanese markets from China included silk, porcelain, books, and copper—but again, these items were few and far between.

Compared to other cultures we have examined, women shared a measure of equality in Japanese society. They could inherit property, divorce, and remarry. Women were even able to have an active role in Japanese society. Some were prominent in aristocratic courts and known for their literary and artistic talents.

Religion played a major role in Japanese culture. Two religions were practiced by the Japanese during this early period: Shinto and Buddhism. Shinto, or the "sacred way," started as the worship of *kami*, or spirits, living in trees, rivers, and mountains. Later the worship included that of the ancestors of the Japanese people. Eventually, Shinto became the state religion, incorporating the divinity of the emperor and the sacredness of the Japanese nation.

Buddhism arrived in Japan during the sixth century from China. The Zen sect of Buddhism became the most popular, although there were many sects of Buddhism with monasteries and shrines across Japan.

Japanese literature developed in a rather unique fashion. Unlike most cultures, where literature was primarily dominated by men, Japanese literature was a female occupation. This was partially because of the Japanese belief that writing was vulgar gossip and beneath men. Between the ninth and twelfth centuries, Japanese literature flourished. *The Tale of the Genji* by Muraki Shikibu, written around 1000, was and still is one of the most popular tales to come from this period.

The Japanese also developed artistically during this period. Most artistic development was influenced by Zen Buddhism, in which balance and harmony with nature were the focus of life and art. The people of Japan turned to nature as an expression of art, creating simple yet beautiful landscaped gardens. Architecture also reflected this emphasis on balance and harmony; the Golden Pavilion in Kyoto was one of the most frequently cited examples.

NOTABLE QUOTABLE

The gate was extremely small, and one had to bend one's body to enter. Set back deep in the property was a building where everything was made of fine wood. There were ink landscape paintings on all four walls.

—*Hekizan nichiroku,* Anonymous

Little Brother—Korea

Korea has sometimes been referred to as the "little brother" of China, but this little brother developed a distinct cultural outlook. The Korean people emerged independently from the mountainous Korean Peninsula sometime around 500 B.C.E., but by 109 B.C.E., the Chinese controlled Korea. Not until the third century C.E. were the Koreans able to gain their independence from the Chinese.

Independence! And Independence Again!

Three Korean kingdoms—Silla, Koguryo, and Paekche—emerged to rule the peninsula, and for five centuries these kingdoms competed for power and control of the region.

By the eighth century, Silla was able to rise to the top of the pack, but its status did not come without a struggle, nor did it last long. Civil war and weak leadership allowed the kingdom of Koryo to gain control. The kingdom of Koryo, from which Korea gained its name, built a capital at Kaesong and sent emissaries to China, who brought back Chinese models of government and culture.

Eventually Koryo's peaceful rule was abruptly interrupted by the invasion of the Mongols, who were able to seize most of northern Korea. Only by cooperating with the Mongols were the Koryo able to remain in power. Finally, the Korean people drove the Mongols out in 1392. The Koryo, of course, fell out of favor because of their cooperation with the Mongols, and the Yi dynasty was established to rule Korea.

Southeast Asia

Southeast Asia is located between China and India and is generally divided into two geographic portions: the mainland and the archipelagos or island chains in the Pacific Ocean.

Its two geographic portions include mountain ranges, fertile valleys, and rain forests, in which a diverse mixture of races, cultures, and religions emerged. A number of kingdoms or states developed from 500 to 1500 c.e., which looked to the larger neighboring regions of China or India as models but also adapted those models to their own unique needs.

With the variety of states and races found in Southeast Asia, generalizations about society and social structure there are just that. Society in Southeast Asia varied from time to time and place to place.

At the top in most of these states were the hereditary aristocrats who held political and economic power. Most lived in the urban centers of their respective states. Below the aristocrats were the rice farmers, merchants, and artisans, and at the lowest level were subsistence farmers and the poor. Like many other cultures, women did not hold a high rank in the society, but in general women did have more rights than their counterparts in China and India.

Vietnam

The people of Vietnam, much like the people of Korea, were initially conquered by China around 111 b.c.e. For 1,000 years, the Vietnamese people remained under the control of the Chinese government and the influence of Chinese culture.

Eventually, in 939 C.E., they were able to gain independence by driving the Chinese out. Although physically the Vietnamese people were free of China, they were not culturally free. The new government of Vietnam, called Dai Vet or the Great Vet, adopted a Chinese model of central government as well as Confucianism as the state religion. The nation also adopted Chinese court rituals, even going so far as calling the rulers of Dai Vet emperors. The Chinese influence allowed the Vietnamese to stabilize their rule and the region. In due course, Dai Vet was able to expand its kingdom southward (not northward—China was too much of a presence still) to the Gulf of Siam by 1600 and was considered one of the more powerful states to emerge from Southeast Asia.

The Khmer Empire

During the ninth century C.E., a kingdom called Angkor emerged to dominate the region of present-day Cambodia. Jayavarman, the powerful ruler of the kingdom of Angkor, guided this rise to the top, consolidating power, uniting the Khmer people, and setting up a capital at Angkor Thom. Later, Jayavarman named his kingdom the Khmer Empire and, in 802, he was crowned god-king. (From the ruler's perspective, it's always a good move to combine religion and state.)

Of course, the god-king passed away, but his empire remained and continued to rule the region of Cambodia until 1432. In that year, the Khmer Empire's northern neighbors, the Thai, invaded and destroyed the Khmer capital. And although the ruling class had survived the destruction of the capital by fleeing and setting up a new capital near Phnom Penh, the Khmer Empire began a rapid decline.

Thailand

The Thai people emerged from the shadows of the southern border of China during the sixth century C.E. During the eleventh and twelfth centuries, they had migrated southward, coming into conflict with the Khmer Empire. At this junction, the Thai people created the kingdom of Thailand with a capital at Ayutthaya on the Chao Phraya River.

Influenced by both China and India, Thailand adopted Buddhism as its state religion as well as the political practices of neighboring India. In due course it was able to expand its kingdom and become a politically powerful entity in Southeast Asia.

The Burmese and the Kingdom of Pagan

The people of Burma originated from the valleys of the Salween and Irrawaddy rivers, migrating to the highlands of Tibet during the seventh century C.E., mostly in an effort to avoid conflicts with the much more powerful Chinese army.

By the eleventh century, the Burmese created their first state—the kingdom of Pagan. This kingdom, much like Thailand, was influenced by both China and India. It adopted Buddhism as the state religion along with the political practices of India. The kingdom of Pagan initially depended on agriculture as a source of economic vitality, but later it developed into a regional sea-trading power. Its decline was hastened by the arrival of the Mongolian invaders during the thirteenth century.

The Malay Peninsula

In the southern archipelago region of Southeast Asia is the Malay Peninsula, where four unique states emerged. The state of Srivijaya developed on the Malay Peninsula during the eighth century C.E. Influenced by Indian culture and governmental models, Srivijaya dominated the trade routes of the Strait of Malacca.

The state of Sailendra emerged during the same time period on the eastern portion of the island of Java. Like Srivijaya, it was also influenced heavily by Indian culture and government, but unlike Srivijaya, it depended on agriculture rather than trade for its livelihood.

These states existed for five centuries before they were displaced by the kingdom of Majapahit. Majapahit emerged during the thirteenth century, and by the fifteenth century it had replaced Srivijaya and Sailendra as the region's dominant state. Majapahit was able to unite a majority of the archipelago under its empire, benefiting from a combination of trade and agriculture to fuel its economy and to become a political power in Southeast Asia. But the developing empire had one rival, and that was Melaka.

An Islamic state formed around the small city of Melaka during the beginning of the fifteenth century, developing into a major trading port that competed with Majapahit and its trading interests in the region. In due course, Melaka expanded and converted a majority of its people and the areas it controlled to Islam. Islam served as a unifying principle, and Melaka became the *sultanate* of Melaka and a major political force in Southeast Asia.

DEFINITION

A **sultanate** is a term used for a land ruled by the authority and office of a strictly Islamic monarch.

The Least You Need to Know

- Japan's geography isolated it from Asia and set the stage for Japan to develop its own unique culture and government.
- Although originally dominated by China, Korea eventually emerged as a divergent nation politically and culturally.
- Due to the diverse geography of Southeast Asia, countries developed from a series of separate regional kingdoms with their own distinctive cultural traits and languages.

The Mongols Rule!

In This Chapter

- Genghis Khan and the rise of the Mongols
- Pax Mongolia
- The grandsons of Genghis Khan
- Timur the Lane
- The Mongols in world history

Now we'll examine the Mongols, who have been mentioned briefly in previous chapters. The Mongols were a disruptive conquering force in history, but, on the other hand, they opened up a new era of interregional exchange that had not been seen since the classical period of world history.

Introducing the Mongols

The Mongols started out as a group of nomadic tribes in and around the Gobi Desert and the steppes of central Asia. These tribes were hardened by their environmental circumstances as they eked out a life of herding goats and sheep and hunting and gathering. Skills such as riding a horse and bravery in battle and the hunt were essential. Unlike most other societies, men and women were treated equally in Mongolian society.

In due time, the tribes formed related clans, which slowly developed into regional kingdoms that continually competed for power on the steppes of central Asia with the neighboring Turkic peoples. This prevented the Mongolian people from developing any lasting empire, although during the fourth and tenth centuries they controlled portions of northern China.

The Rise of Genghis Khan

The birth of Temujin in 1162 marked an end of the Mongolian age of obscurity. A prince of one of the regional Mongolian kingdoms, Temujin built on his father's success and created a series of tribal alliances that united the eastern and western Mongolian kingdoms. In 1206, Temujin was elected *khan*, or supreme ruler, of the Mongolian kingdoms at the *kuriltai*, a meeting of all Mongol chieftains, and took the name Genghis Khan, meaning "ruler of all."

> **WHAT IN THE WORLD**
>
> Mongol warriors were known to spend days on their horses, even sleeping in the saddle during long marches. It was documented on several occasions that the Mongolian cavalry traveled close to a hundred miles in a day's time.

The Mongol War Machine

Genghis Khan had an army of natural warriors. The harsh environmental conditions in which the Mongolians were raised made them tough and resilient. From years of hunting game, they were expert marksmen with the short bow, able to accurately use the weapon on horseback at a range of 400 yards. Thus Genghis Khan had armies of swift cavalry at his beck and call.

Genghis Khan brought to the Mongolian armies discipline, unity, and a command structure that made the armies not only tough and fast, but efficient. The armies were divided in units of 10. The first unit was the *tumens*, made up of 10,000 warriors, then smaller units of 1,000, 100, and finally 10. Each unit had a commanding officer who received his orders from the commander of the unit above.

The cavalry units (the Mongolians had no foot soldiers) were divided into heavy (with more armor and more weapons) and light cavalry. To help with communication between units, a messenger force was created that could ride for days without stopping and even sleep on their horses—they were actually bandaged to the horses so they did not fall! Finally, they had special units to map the terrain, so the armies were prepared for any environmental eventuality.

Conquest!

With an army waiting, Genghis Khan was ready to expand his empire with an assault on Asia. His first strike was in 1207, when the Mongolian armies humbled the Tangut kingdom of Xi Xia in northwest China. Then Genghis Khan attacked the powerful Qin Empire, established by the Manchu-related Jurchens a century earlier.

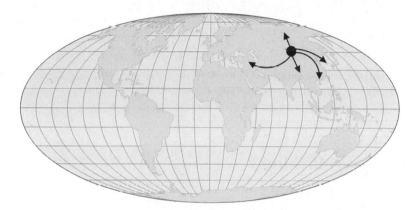

Mongol invasion.

During these campaigns, Genghis Khan used a terrifying policy of retribution in which resistance was met with swift death. Whole towns that resisted the Mongolian armies were killed after defeat, including women and children, usually in a grisly manner. Tales of this policy preceded the Mongolian armies as they moved westward against the Kara Khitai Empire. It was annexed as part of the Mongolian Empire by 1219. The Mongols then overwhelmed the Islamic Khwarazm Empire, and by 1227 the Mongolian Empire stretched from eastern Persia to the North China Sea.

In addition to the policy of retribution, the Mongolian armies used sound military tactics to defeat their adversaries. One tactic was to charge the enemy's main army with a lesser force. After a short engagement, the Mongolians would retreat, apparently defeated. When armies would move to pursue the retreating Mongolians, the other Mongolian units would outflank and surround the disorganized enemy army. As the Mongolian armies conquered more territories with stronger fortresses and cities, their tactics began to include siege weapons, which they acquired from conquered enemies.

After Genghis Khan had established his Mongolian Empire, he created a capital at the city of Karakorum and instituted some policies that few expected from a conquering Mongol. First, he consulted Chinese Confucian scholars, Muslim engineers, and Daoist holy men to build his capital city and develop his governmental policies, which were very progressive.

For example, Genghis Khan's policy of religious tolerance throughout the empire was unique compared to most other civilizations. Thus did the bloodthirsty conqueror bring peace to Asia, which some historians have referred to as a period of Pax Mongolia (Mongolian Peace). Genghis Khan's armies protected the people and trade of the empire. This protection revitalized the commerce of the Silk Road and reestablished interregional connections between Asia, Europe, Africa, and the Middle East.

The Death of Genghis Khan

Of course, all good things must come to an end, and so it was with the rule of Genghis Khan. In 1226, Genghis Khan turned southward to complete his conquest of China, which he had always regretted not finishing earlier. With an army of close to 200,000 warriors, Genghis Khan made short work of the Chinese cities in the north. However, in August 1227, just as China was on the verge of collapse, the great Genghis Khan died. The invasion was discontinued as the Mongolian armies returned to the capital city of Karakorum with the body of Genghis Khan for burial. (Out of respect for their great ruler, they killed every living thing that preceded them on the long march home!)

The Mongolian chiefs then met to elect another grand khan. They elected Ogedei, the third son of Genghis Khan, who was very satisfied with consolidating his rule of the Mongolian Empire from the capital of Karakorum rather than pursuing further conquests. It appeared the rest of Asia could breathe a sigh of relief. The Mongols were done with invading their lands … or were they?

Conquest Again!

Ogedei might have been satisfied staying at home, but his sons, the grandsons of Genghis Khan, were not. Batu, Hulegu, and Kublai all made significant conquests to expand the Mongolian Empire further in Asia and the Middle East and into portions of Europe.

Batu and the Golden Horde

Batu was given charge of Mongolian armies in the western regions of the empire and, in 1236, he invaded Russia. The Russian princes refused to unite under the prince of Kiev, and their kingdoms were individually ravaged and conquered by Batu's 100,000 Mongolian warriors. Eventually Kiev itself was reduced to rubble by the Mongol siege machinery, and the Russian princes were forced to submit and pay tribute to Batu as vassals of the Golden Horde, the name used for Batu's territories and armies.

The impact of this invasion on Russia was great. The Russian princes had to develop better military organization. They also learned from the Mongolians the ins and outs of centralized rulership—something the independent princes had trouble with. Finally, the years of Mongolian rule during the thirteenth, fourteenth, and fifteenth centuries cut Russia off from some of the key cultural movements of Europe, which led to a unique Russian identity that some (especially Peter the Great!) considered "backward."

WHAT IN THE WORLD

The Russians called the Mongolians "tartars." This term was derived from the place of punishment in the underworld of Greek mythology called Tartarus. So calling someone a tartar was referring to him as someone from hell.

For Batu, Russia was just a warm-up exercise for the big show: Europe, which he believed had riches and resources beyond imagination. The Europeans, at first, thought well of Batu and the Golden Horde. The legend of Prester John, a mythical Christian ruler whose kingdom in central Asia was supposedly separated from Europe during the period of Islamic conquest, was still strong in the European consciousness. Europeans believed that one day Prester John's descendants would help to defeat the growing power of Islam in the Middle East. The Mongolians had, of course, come from central Asia conquering Islamic lands. But after the conquest of Christian Russia, the Europeans knew that the Mongolians had not "come in peace."

In the initial military encounter with European forces, the Mongolians defeated an army of Hungarians and German knights led by King Henry of Silesia. It looked like Europe was open for conquest. As fate would have it, however, Batu's father, Ogedei, died, and he had to journey back to the Mongolian empire's capital of Karakorum. After Ogedei's burial, Batu returned to the lands of the Golden Horde and built a new capital at Sarai on the Volga River. By then, Batu had changed his mind about Europe and spent the remainder of his days harassing the Islamic lands of the Middle East and collecting tribute.

Of all of the cities of Russia, Moscow benefited the most from rule of the Golden Horde. The leaders of Moscow collected more from their people than they needed for the tribute and eventually developed the financial resources to resist the Mongols. By the fifteenth century, Moscow united the other princes of Russia, a feat that Kiev could not pull off, and defeated the Golden Horde at the Battle of Kulikova. This established the prince of Moscow as the leader of the Russian princes and ended Mongolian rule in Russia.

> **NOTABLE QUOTABLE**
>
> Swarming like locusts over the face of the earth, they have brought terrible devastation to the eastern parts [of Europe], laying it waste with fire and carnage. After having passed through the land of the Saracens, they have razed cities, cut down forests, overthrown fortresses, pulled up vines, destroyed gardens, killed townspeople and peasants.
>
> —*Chronica Majora,* Matthew Paris

Hulegu and the Islamic Heartlands

Like Batu, Hulegu, another grandson of Genghis Khan, was given command of Mongolian armies in the southwest region of the Mongolian Empire. Hulegu surveyed the surrounding regions and determined that the Islamic territories of the Abbasid dynasty were ripe for conquest. By 1258, Hulegu's Mongolian armies had captured the Abbasid territories and destroyed the city of Baghdad, which was the center of Islamic culture and included the great Islamic libraries that housed the most advanced knowledge of the world at the time. The armies then moved westward across the Middle East, conquering as they went.

They were stopped by a rather strange alliance. The Egyptian slave army of Mamluks, led by Baibars, was given permission to cross over territory in Palestine controlled by Christian crusaders to meet and defeat the Mongolian army. The Islamic Mamluks were the sworn enemies of the Christian crusaders, but both felt that religious differences should be set aside to stop this Mongolian threat. The defeat by the Mamluks convinced Hulegu to settle down and consolidate the rule of his newly conquered territories. His Mongolian kingdom stretched from the borders of the Byzantine Empire to the Oxus River in central Asia.

Kublai Khan and the Yuan Dynasty

Even with all their conquests, the Mongolians had not forgotten the unconquered empire of China. During the powerful Song dynasty, Kublai, yet another grandson of Genghis Khan, started to make advances into China. Unlike his brothers, who conquered vast territories rather quickly, Kublai battled for the Chinese Empire from 1235 to 1271.

During this period (and probably to the chagrin of his brothers), Kublai assumed the title of the Great Khan. Twelve years later, the Great Khan was vindicated when China fell to his armies. But rather than impose Mongolian conventions of rulership on the Chinese, Kublai Khan established the Yuan dynasty, similar to the traditional dynasties of China's past. He then placed the capital at Tatu, which is present-day Beijing.

NOTABLE QUOTABLE

Being the adherent of no religion and the follower of no creed he eschewed bigotry, and the preference of one faith to another, and the placing of some above others; rather he honored and respected the learned and pious of every sect, recognizing such conduct as the way to the Court of God. And as he viewed the Muslims with the eye of respect, so also did he hold the Christians and idolaters in high esteem.

—Ala-ad-Din Juvaini, on Kublai Khan and religious toleration (ca. 1260)

Mongolian culture and ideas also came with Kublai Khan and the Mongolian armies. Muslims from the western region of the empire were brought in for governmental bureaucracy and development. Foreign travelers, once few and far between, came from Europe, the Middle East, and Southeast Asia. Kublai Khan insisted on religious tolerance in all of the territories, making Buddhists and Daoists who had fallen out of favor very supportive of Mongolian rule. Chinese literature and art blossomed, producing one of the most enduring works of Chinese drama, *The Romance of the West Chamber*. With progressive reforms and the protection of the Mongolian armies, the Chinese initially enjoyed the rule of the Great Khan, who had brought prosperity to China. Eventually, though, the honeymoon ended.

The Chinese began to resist the Mongolian cultural influence after contradictions were observed. First, the Mongolians were very resistant to Chinese culture and maintained a wall of separation from the Chinese, which included making it illegal for the Chinese to learn the Mongolian language. Additionally, the Mongolians appeared to play favorites, using foreign rather than Chinese officials. The Mongolians also helped the artisan and merchant classes, who, according to Confucian Chinese standards, were the "mean" people and at the bottom of the Chinese social structure. So Kublai Khan, although progressive, was unintentionally alienating the very important Confucian scholar-gentry class of China.

WHAT IN THE WORLD

Marco Polo (1254–1324) was one of the foreigners whom Kublai Khan employed in the Yuan dynasty government, serving as an advisor to Kublai Khan's court for a short time during his 20-year-plus trek across Asia. Polo later wrote about his travels in the book *Travels of Marco Polo,* which was instantly popular and generated interest in the lands of Asia.

The end of the Yuan dynasty started with the failed invasions of Japan in 1274 and 1280. The Chinese people perceived that the Mongolians were not quite as tough as they appeared to be, and by the 1350s this perception manifested itself in the secret White Lotus Society, which was filled with Yuan dynasty haters and Song dynasty supporters. With their help and many others, a poor peasant family man named Ju Yuanzhang led a revolt that overthrew the Yuan dynasty, marking the rise of the Chinese Ming dynasty. After the takeover, the Mongolians retreated back to Mongolia, marking a decline in their power across Asia.

One Last Mongol

Just as the people of Asia, the Middle East, and even Europe thought that the "all clear" had sounded, another nomadic group stepped forward to strike fear in the hearts of the people with swift cavalry attacks and a policy of retribution.

This nomadic group was the Turks, led by Timur-i-Lang, or Timur the Lane. During the 1360s, after the decline of the Mongolian empire, Timur the Lane very quickly carved a Turkish Empire out of Persia, the Fertile Crescent, India, and southern Russia. After consolidating his conquests, Timur the Lane established a capital city at Samarkund in central Asia from which to rule his newfound empire. But his empire did not have the strength and longevity of the Mongols, and, after his death in 1405, the empire quickly fell into civil war between his army commanders. In the end, Timur the Lane and his Turkic armies were a watered-down version of the conquest and the power of Genghis Khan and the Mongols.

The Upside of Bloodthirsty Mongol Conquerors

Regardless of the bloodshed created by Genghis Khan and the Mongols, the Mongols did much to revitalize interregional exchanges between Asia, Europe, the Middle East, and even Africa. During the Pax Mongolia, trade and commerce was renewed under the watch of Mongol armies.

Additionally, the civilizations conquered by the Mongols learned how to centralize government over diverse peoples and vast territories, so that, when the Mongols declined in power, the kingdoms and states of Europe, Asia, and the Middle East were able to continue centralizing power and developing interregional exchanges. The Mongols started the engine that ushered in the modern period of world history.

The Least You Need to Know

- Genghis Khan established the Mongolian Empire through conquests of Asia.
- Genghis Khan's grandsons expanded the Mongolian Empire farther with the conquest of Russia, Persia, and China.
- Mongol power declined after the loss of China to the Ming dynasty in the mid-fourteenth century.
- Timur the Lane quickly created the Turkish Empire that included portions of central Asia, the Middle East, and Russia, although the empire dissolved after this death.
- The Mongol conquests ushered in a new age of interregional exchange and centralized government in Asia, Europe, and the Middle East.

Those Terrible Middle Ages

In This Chapter

- Europe after the fall of Rome
- Vikings and feudalism
- The power of the Church
- The Crusades
- The Black Death
- The end of the Middle Ages and the Renaissance

The European Middle Ages lasted approximately from the fall of the Roman Empire to the beginning of the European Reformation, or from 500 to 1500 c.e. A thousand years is a huge chunk of time for historians to deal with, so it has been divided into three different periods: the Early Middle Ages (500–1000), the High Middle Ages (1000–1300), and the Late Middle Ages (1300–1500).

However, just to add a little confusion, sometimes historians talk about the Renaissance, which happened during the Late Middle Ages in Italy, as a distinct time period from the Middle Ages. And to make it even more confusing, some historians refer to the Middle Ages as the Medieval Period (actually meaning middle period) or the Dark Ages or the Age of Feudalism or the Age of Faith. But regardless of all the ambiguities, most historians would agree that there were some reoccurring events and themes during the period of 500 to 1500 on the continent of Europe.

After Rome

After the fall of Rome in 476, which was hastened by Germanic invading tribes, Europe had a political vacuum waiting to be filled. Many Germanic tribes tried, including the Lombards, Goths, Visigoths, Vandals, Saxons, Jutes, and Angles, but the Franks were the first tribe to get it all together and fill the void left by the fall of Rome.

The Merovingians

In the early 400s, the Franks migrated from central Europe and settled in the region of France. After some time the Franks emerged as the strongest and dominated the region for years. The early rulers of the Franks came from the Merovingian family. King Clovis (481–511) established a monarchy over the Franks and ruled during the late 400s. He also converted the Frankish kingdom to Christianity, supposedly at the urging of his wife and because he believed he received God's assistance in a particularly important battle. In reality, like the many rulers before him, Clovis saw the cohesive power of religion. Clovis established a strong kingdom during his lifetime, but once he passed away the Merovingian line became weak and the kingdom of the Franks suffered.

As the Merovingian monarchy fell into decline, the office of the mayor of the palace became stronger. Charles Martel was an excellent example of a strong mayor of the palace who defended the kingdom of the Franks while the Merovingian king stayed at home. (Merovingian kings were sometimes called "do-nothing kings.") In 732 Martel led a Frankish army against an invading Muslim army at the Battle of Tours, a critical point in European and world history. Martel's victory ensured that Christianity would be the religion of Europe. His son, Pepin the Short, assumed the hereditary and powerful title of mayor of the palace after his death. Tired of the "do-nothing kings," Pepin, after gaining the blessing of the pope of Rome, deposed the last Merovingian king and became king himself. This was the start of the Carolingian dynasty.

The Carolingians

The Franks were fortunate that the Carolingians gained the throne. Pepin the Short's son became one of the greatest leaders of medieval Europe and helped to build the Frankish kingdom into an empire. Charlemagne, or Charles the Great, became king of the Franks in 771 after the death of his father. Within a few years, he doubled the territory of the Frankish kingdom to include modern-day Germany, France, Italy, and northern Spain. Through the charisma of his rule, the Franks experienced a renaissance, or rebirth in culture.

Although he was never able to read himself, Charlemagne encouraged the construction of schools and hired scholars from across Europe to facilitate learning. (The story goes that he slept with a book under his pillow, hoping he would learn how to read!) Like any good Christian ruler, he protected the churches and monasteries of the empire, and also forcibly converted the Germanic tribe called the Saxons to Christianity. (He continually had trouble with them from then on.)

In 800 Charlemagne took a Frankish army to the gates of Rome to rescue Pope Leo III from an invading Germanic army. The pope was so grateful and eager for continued protection that he crowned Charlemagne the Holy Roman emperor, recalling and associating Charlemagne with the great Roman emperors of the past. But things were not to last.

 NOTABLE QUOTABLE

It was at the time he received the title of emperor and Augustus, to which at first he was so averse that he remarked that had he known the intention of the pope, he would not have entered the church on that day.

—*Life of Charlemagne,* Einhard

Charlemagne did not prepare his successor well. In 814, he died, leaving his throne to his son, Louis the Pious who was, in fact, very pious—he wanted to be at the altar more than on the throne. The Frankish empire weakened with Louis' rule, and even more so when he died in 843.

Louis the Pious left the Frankish empire to his three sons, a division spelled out shortly beforehand in the Treaty of Verdun. Charles the Bald (yes, he was bald) received the western region, which later turned into France. Louis the German (yes, he spoke German) got the eastern portion, which became Germany. Finally, Lothair (no, he didn't have a nickname) acquired the strip of land between the two other brothers called Lorraine.

The saying goes, "United we stand, divided we fall," and with the division of the Frankish empire, its political and military power weakened under the strain of other competing kingdoms and a renewed series of invasions of Europe.

Invasions Again?

Beginning in the ninth century, another series of invasions threatened Europe, much like the fifth-century invasions threatened the Roman Empire. From the north, out of Scandinavia came the Vikings, who traveled across the Baltic Sea in shallow-draft longboats. The Vikings were mainly pirates, interested in quick strikes and easy fights, so they targeted Christian monasteries and small villages and towns.

From across the central steppes of Asia and central Europe came the Magyars. These nomadic tribes terrorized central Europe until they were collectively defeated by the German Holy Roman Emperor Otto I at the Battle of Lechfeld in 955. And finally, the last groups of ninth-century invaders were Islamic forces, which periodically raided the southern coastline of Europe.

These invasions or raids had several effects. They isolated communities by discouraging travel, and trade subsequently declined. The invasions also weakened the authority of the kings, who appeared unable to protect their people and territory. Finally, the most lasting impact was the development of the system of feudalism, which lasted in various forms across Europe for hundreds of years.

Let's Go Serfing

Although the origins of the feudalist system have sometimes been debated, many historians place its beginning during the rule of Charles Martel. After one of Martel's many military campaigns, he was unable to pay his soldiers for the services rendered. Rather than hand the armed men IOUs (which probably would not have gone over well), Martel granted the men fiefs, or estates, populated by peasants.

At the top of the feudal pyramid was the king, followed by the nobles, his lords or vassals. Kings granted or protected the lands of the nobles, who swore an oath and military support to the king, hiring men-at-arms or knights. On the bottom were the peasants, who lived and worked on the land, giving up many freedoms to have the protection of the lords above them. This pyramid was held together by the strength of its alliances, which were hereditary as well as contractual and were secured by a ceremony known as homage. In that ceremony vassals pledged to be loyal and perform their duties for their lord.

The feudal system really caught on during the ninth-century Viking invasions. It was better equipped to handle these types of incursions because people did not have to depend on a distant king and his armies.

Working with the feudal political system was an economic system called the manorial system. Manorialism described the economic ties that existed between the lord of the manor and the peasants. Generally, peasants remained on the manor because they could not afford their own land or they needed protection. Usually these peasants or serfs were bound to the manor and could not leave without permission.

The typical manor included the lord's house, usually a fortified palisade or castle; pastures for livestock; fields for crops; forested areas; and a village or town for the serfs. The stability of manorialism helped to increase crop production during the early Middle Ages. It also helped that a heavier plow was invented that could handle the thick soil of Europe, and the three-field system prevented the erosion of nutrients in the fields. Europe's improved agricultural production benefited the whole population.

WHAT IN THE WORLD

Knights began as weapon-carrying horsemen. As time progressed, early medieval armor called chain mail (small metal rings riveted closely together) became the common garb of a knight. With the development of more deadly weapons such as crossbows, longbows, maces, and strong swords, more protection was needed, leading to the use of plate armor by the 1300s.

The Church

During the Early Middle Ages, the Roman Catholic Church was developing at a rapid and powerful rate. When Rome fell, people looked to the Church not only for spiritual guidance but for political and social support, and it became a major power in Europe. At the head of the Church was the bishop of Rome, the pope, who became one of the strongest political leaders in Europe, sometimes more powerful than emperors and kings. In part, this power came because of the spiritual authority that he held over Christians.

The Church's Religious Role and Organization

In order to take care of the spiritual well-being of the Christian laity of Europe, the Church administered the sacraments, or rituals associated with teachings of Jesus, and conducted church services. The sacraments included baptism, penance, the Eucharist, confirmation, matrimony or marriage, anointing of the sick, and the holy orders. Church services, or Mass, incorporated the sacrament of the Eucharist and were performed in the traditional language of the church, Latin.

All of the spiritual, political, and social work of the church was performed by the clergy, which was divided into two groups. The secular clergy included the pope, cardinals, archbishops, bishops, and priests, who interacted with the secular world. The regular clergy included abbots or monastery heads, abbesses or nunnery heads, monks, and nuns, who worked and lived in monasteries and were generally separated from the world.

> **WHAT IN THE WORLD**
>
> Pretzels originated in the schools of the medieval monasteries. Medieval monks created them for children as rewards for memorizing their prayers. The Latin word *pretiola,* from which pretzel is derived, means "small reward." The knot shape of the edible reward was supposed to represent the folded arms of a child in prayer.

Monks and the Business of Monasteries

The work of the monasteries, even though separated and sheltered from the world, was very important to the culture of Europe. The monastic tradition of Christianity developed in the deserts of Egypt and Syria. At a monastery at Monte Cassino, a former Roman official and monk named Benedict took the desert monastic tradition and transformed it into something quite new, creating the Benedictine Rule.

The rule was much like a constitution for monks and their monasteries to follow. And it wasn't just *a* rule; it was a list of rules for monks to follow, including obligations to perform manual labor, to meditate, and to pray. The rule included vows of poverty, chastity, and obedience to the monastery head. The Benedictine Rule and monastic movement became very popular, and soon monasteries spread across Europe during the early Middle Ages.

The monasteries transmitted learning by creating schools for young people, including schools for peasants to learn trades. They also provided food and shelter for the poor and hospitals and medical treatment for the sick. Culturally the monasteries preserved classical religious and pagan writings. The great writings of antiquity would have been lost if they had not copied the ancient texts, preserving and transmitting them to future generations. Starting with Pope Gregory I in 597, monks spread the message of Christianity throughout Europe, and by the mid-eleventh century, most Europeans were Catholic Christian.

WHAT IN THE WORLD

Today the pope is still elected by a college of cardinals called a "conclave." After the death of the pope, the cardinals meet behind locked doors at the Vatican and are not allowed to leave until a new pope is elected.

Power and Reform in the Church

As the Middle Ages progressed, so did the power of the Church. The Church was a part of the feudal system, so it acquired land through the feudal exchange. Many Church officials were nobles, meaning that they actually fought like all the other vassals in the feudal system. In addition, the Church received many donations of land from Christians concerned about the fate of their soul in the afterlife. By the end of the Middle Ages, the Church was one of the largest landowners in Europe and a very powerful voice in politics. Of course, with great power comes great responsibility, and also corruption. Beginning in the 900s, people within the Church began to call for reform.

The Church reform movement started at one of the major spiritual centers of Europe, the monastery at Cluny, where the clergy called for the Church to be free from the feudal system. That was a long time coming, but other reforms were made. In 1059, cardinals began to choose the pope rather than kings or mobs. Later, in 1073, Pope Gregory VII criticized and fought the German Holy Roman emperor over the practice of *lay investiture.* (More on the clash between the pope and the Holy Roman Empire later in the chapter.) In addition, the Church started in earnest to combat heresy—the denial or misinterpretation of basic church teachings—with the threat of excommunication or expulsion from the Church.

DEFINITION

Lay investiture was the medieval practice in which kings and other secular nobles appointed church officials to positions, such as cardinal or bishop, in their respective kingdoms.

Wandering preachers called friars also inspired reform in the Church. These men moved from town to town preaching the teachings of Jesus found in the Bible and living a simple life. The best known of these holy orders were the Franciscans and the Dominicans, which were started by St. Francis of Assisi and St. Dominic.

Medieval Art and Architecture

Beyond the sacraments, the power, and the reform, the Church inspired people visually with architecture. Two types of Church architecture developed in the Middle Ages. First, from around 900 to 1050, was Romanesque architecture, very similar to Roman architecture. Its prevalent features included thick walls and small windows with rounded arches and barrel vaults.

The Gothic style emerged during the mid-eleventh century. Gothic churches were considered to be a representation of prayer in stone and glass. In addition to the large, beautiful stained-glass windows, Gothic architecture featured flying buttresses that held up thin walls, pointed arches, and ribbed vaults.

The Big Three

As the Germanic tribes organized, filling the void that the disintegration of the Roman Empire created in Europe, three kingdoms arose to dominate the political landscape of the continent. These kingdoms became the modern-day countries of England, France, and Germany, and they had a huge political and cultural impact on the Middle Ages.

Jolly Old England

Prior to the fifth-century Germanic invasions, the island of Britain was inhabited by a mixture of Celtic tribes and Romans, referred to as Britons. As the fifth-century migrations progressed, the Germanic tribes of Angles, Saxons, and Jutes settled on the island and came to dominate it culturally, forming several independent kingdoms across Britain, then called Angleland.

The Anglo-Saxon kingdoms were not immune to the ninth-century Viking invasions and lost power and lands until the mid-ninth century. King Alfred the Great of Wessex finally united the Anglo-Saxon kingdoms to drive out the Viking invaders, but after the death of King Edward the Confessor, William the Bastard of Normandy (a region of France) made a claim for the throne. In 1066, William and his Norman army defeated the other rival for the Anglo-Saxon throne, Harold Godwinson, at the Battle of Hastings. After conquering England he was forever referred to as William the Conqueror.

Starting with William, the Norman kings of England centralized the power of the monarchy. In 1068, King William undertook the first census of England detailed in the *Doomsday Book*. King Henry II (1154–1189) established the traditional use of common law and jury trials, which also helped to centralize power. But this centralization of power brought a backlash from the nobles of England.

In 1215, the Norman nobles forced King John to sign the Magna Carta, or Great Charter, which limited royal power and gave the nobles more of a say in governance. The power of the monarch was limited again in 1295 when King Edward I created the Model Parliament made up of people from the clergy, nobility, and merchant class to advise the king. This Model Parliament gradually developed into the modern English Parliament, with two branches: the House of Lords and the House of Commons. For England, the centralization of the monarchy was tempered by the power of the nobility.

WHAT IN THE WORLD

The Magna Carta, with its limits on the power of the monarchy, is one of the documents that influenced the drafters of the U.S. Constitution in eighteenth-century America.

The French

In France, the centralization of the power of the monarchy took much longer, probably due to the entrenchment of the feudal system. In 987, the noble Hugh Capet seized the French throne from a weak Carolingian king. During the eleventh and twelfth centuries, the Capetian dynasty consolidated power and strengthened France, but it took King Phillip II (1180–1223) and King Louis IX (1226–1270) to overpower the feudal system, weakening the lords and making the royal courts dominant over the feudal courts.

The triumph of the monarchy was soon tempered by the nobles' assertion of power. When King Phillip IV (1285–1314) needed to raise taxes, he required the support of the nobility. As a result, he had to create the Estates-General, an assembly of nobles, clergy, and merchants that checked the power of the monarchy.

Germany

In the region of Germany, or the Holy Roman Empire, King Otto (936–973) began the centralization process in earnest while trying to restore the empire that Charlemagne ruled. Although not completely successful at restoring the glory of the empire, Otto I did end the harassment of the Magyars at the Battle of Lechfeld and was crowned Holy Roman emperor by the pope in 962.

The relationship between the Holy Roman emperor and the pope wasn't always so pleasant. Later Holy Roman emperors came into conflict with papal authority over the policy of lay investiture. Not until 1122 did the pope and the Holy Roman emperor reach a compromise on the issue at the Concordant of Worms. Thus, the centralization of the monarchy in Germany was tempered by the assertion of papal authority.

Let's Go Crusading

There have been many debates over the reasons and the results of the Crusades of the Middle Ages. In general, the centralization of the monarchy and the power of the Church combined to produce a mass migration of people to the Levant. When they finally left the Levant, they connected isolated Europe with the global civilization of Islam, which had a major impact on the history of the world.

The major reason for the European Crusades was that Jerusalem, a holy city not only for Christianity but also for Judaism and Islam, and the region of Palestine fell from Christian hands to Arab invaders in the 600s. The Arabs tolerated Jews and Christians in the city, so there was little problem with this new development; later in the early eleventh century, however, Islamic Seljuk Turks took control of the city and region. In an overzealous act, they closed the city to the religious traditions of Christianity and Judaism. Once news of the closing of Jerusalem reached Christian Europe, the Crusades were underway.

In 1095 the Byzantine emperor wrote Pope Urban II asking for a few armored knights to help open the Holy Land and defend against the Seljuk Turks who had taken the Levant from Byzantium. So Pope Urban II made his official plea to a large crowd at Clermount, France. In his impassioned speech, Urban II called for a crusade, or holy war, against the Islamic forces in the Holy Land, promising penance for the crusaders. As a result, three armies of crusading knights and peasants, numbering close to 100,000, traveled to the Holy Land.

WHAT IN THE WORLD

In 1212 about 50,000 children, led by a boy, decided to go crusading and conquer Jerusalem with love, not war. Sadly, they made it only as far as Marseilles, France, where they were tricked by unsavory merchants and sold as slaves in North Africa and the East.

In 1099, the crusading armies besieged and captured the city of Jerusalem to create a crusader kingdom. Other crusades followed (there were 10 crusades, including the Children's Crusade) after the city of Jerusalem was recaptured by Islamic forces led by Saladin in 1187. Eventually the crusading movement died out as interest waned and it became too expensive, but not before they helped to precipitate the decline of the Byzantine Empire and create a host of bad feelings between Muslims and Christians that in many ways linger to this day.

The Crusades had several other long-term effects on the development of Europe. They helped increase the authority of kings by speeding up the breakdown of feudalism. The Crusades renewed interest in learning and, as knights returned to Europe with goods from the Middle East, spurred demand for more spices, sugar, and silk. Finally, the Crusades helped advance technology, including more accurate maps, magnetic compasses, and improved military techniques.

Economic Improvements

Because of the interest in products from the East generated by the Crusades as well as agricultural advances and a population explosion, Europe's economy began seeing unprecedented growth.

In agriculture, three advances increased production: a heavier plow, the collar harness, and the three-field system. Increased production led to an increased birth rate, as peasants wanted more hands to work the fields. Increased population led to the revival and growth of towns. Some towns gained population and reemerged on the map, but others simply exploded on the scene, such as Venice in Italy and Flanders in France.

All of the trends in the High Middle Ages led to even more economic growth. The development of trade fairs, guilds, banking, and the rise of the merchant or middle class added even more fuel to the economic fire of Europe. This economic abundance had a significant impact on the culture of medieval Europe.

Education and Learning (Not Always Synonymous!)

With the economic boom and the rise of the middle class in towns, education became more in demand and available. The schools moved away from monasteries to universities, which started out as guilds of teachers in a central location. By the thirteenth century, universities had spread throughout Europe. The most notable were the University of Bologna in Italy, known for law; the University of Paris, famous for theology; and the University of Oxford, noted for the liberal arts.

The new universities were infused with old, forgotten sources of knowledge that poured in from the Middle East during the Crusades and Spain during the Reconquista. A majority of the ancient sources were writings of Greek philosophy, especially Aristotle; the Muslims were less shy about preserving ancient pagan writing than the European monks. Many scholars tried to apply and reconcile Aristotle's philosophy to Christian theological questions. Two scholars from the University of Paris led this movement, known as scholasticism: Peter Abelard, who wrote *Sic et Non (Yes and No)*, and Thomas Aquinas, who wrote the massive theological tome *Summa Theologica*, or *Summary of Religious Thought*.

Literature

Literature also flourished during the economic boom of the High Middle Ages. Troubadours, traveling poet musicians, sang about heroic knights and their deeds. These developed into the literary form called *Chansons de geste*, French epic songs that celebrated the courage of the knights and the chivalric code.

Literature started to be written in the vernacular, or everyday language, of the people. The most famous of these early works were *The Divine Comedy* by Dante Alighieri and *The Canterbury Tales* by Geoffrey Chaucer.

With the Highs Come the Lows

The economic and cultural highs of the High Middle Ages were followed by some very low moments during the Late Middle Ages, which shook the foundation of medieval culture and called many of its institutions into question.

The Hundred Years' War

The Hundred Years' War between the developing nations of France and England lasted from 1337 to 1453 and devastated continental Europe. The war began over feudal disputes over lands in northwestern France and English claims on the throne of France. For a majority of the war the English dominated the French, defeating them at the major engagements of the Battle of Crecy (1346) and of the Battle of Agincourt (1415).

Not until a simple 17-year-old peasant girl, Joan of Arc, emerged on the political and military scene did the French begin to turn it around. Joan believed that she received messages from God to help return the French king to the throne. By 1429, she had persuaded Charles, the heir to the French throne, to supply her with an army, and she helped to lift the siege of Orleans and oversaw the crowning of Charles VII as king of France at the traditional site of Reims. Later she was captured and executed as a witch by the English, but her impact on the war could not be stopped. The French rallied around Charles and the memory of Joan and pushed the English forces from France by 1453.

Some positives came out of the Hundred Years' War. The French developed of a sense of unity. Feudalism was adversely affected and continued to decline. But in the long run, it caused devastation and chaos for continental Europe. Trade and agriculture were hampered by the more than 100 years of war, which affected the growth of medieval culture.

Also, England, once defeated, plunged into a civil war called the War of the Roses from 1455 to 1485. This negative symptom of the Hundred Years' War was a dynastic struggle over the throne of England between the noble families of the Yorks and the Lancasters. In the end, neither noble family won and a Tudor ascended the English throne.

The Babylonian Captivity and the Great Schism

Two events related to the politics of the Church during the Late Middle Ages also tore at the fabric of medieval culture. The Babylonian Captivity, which lasted from 1305 to 1377, started when Pope Clement V, under the influence of the French king, moved the papal court from its traditional home of Rome to Avignon, France.

Many feared that the French monarch had too much influence on the pope, and their fears were correct. The popes elected during the Babylonian Captivity were always French, and they represented French interests very well indeed. Finally people became fed up, and when the pope died in 1378 a Roman mob forced the College of Cardinals to elect an Italian pope who would return the papal court to Rome.

This started the Great Schism, which lasted from 1378 to 1414, and deepened when the same College of Cardinals declared their election of the Italian pope invalid and elected a French pope—who then moved the papal court back to Avignon. Both popes then claimed to be the legitimate pope. In 1409, the Council of Pisa tried to eliminate the problem and unite the Church by electing another pope. Now there were three popes, all of them claiming legitimacy.

The crisis didn't end until yet another council convened, forced all three popes to resign, and elected Pope Martin V. He and his court were sent to Rome to rule over the Church, ending the Great Schism. But the damage was done, and the Church's authority over political and spiritual matters was severely tarnished.

NOTABLE QUOTABLE

The ship of Peter is shaken by the waves, the fisherman's net is broken, and the serenity of peace turns to clouds, the disaster of wars devastates the lands of the Roman church and nearby provinces.

—*Sacrorum Conciliorum Nova et Amplissima Collectio*

The Black Death

In this time of political and spiritual turmoil, the Black Death, one of the most virulent episodes of bubonic plague, descended upon Europe. Carried by flea-infested rats, the epidemic came in the caravans that traveled the trade routes of central Asia, where it originated. Tartar armies besieging the Black Sea port of Kaffa contracted the disease, which was brought to Europe when merchant ships that housed infected rats left Kaffa for Italian ports.

The disease spread fast; by 1348, France, England, and Spain were devastated. A year later, Russia, Scandinavia, and Germany were infected. Although the numbers cannot be known exactly, it is estimated that by 1350, when the Black Death disappeared from the continent, over a third of the population—approximately 25 million people— succumbed to its horrific affects.

Those who remained after the Black Death were left looking for reasons and answers. To some degree the economic boom and population increase of the High Middle Ages left Europe open to such a devastating event. Towns grew too large too fast; they were overpopulated and lacked proper sanitation, and the Black Death found good breeding grounds. The increase of trade allowed the disease to spread along all of the land and sea trade routes. Finally, the military conflicts of the Late Middle Ages left the health and constitution of the people in a weakened state. Food and energy had been devoted to war, and when the plague hit, resources were too low to combat the disease.

Reform

Regardless of the debatable causes, there were two very tangible effects. First, the Church's authority came into question. Church authority had already been weakened by the controversies of the fourteenth and fifteenth centuries, and many found the Church unable to respond adequately to those wondering why their religious obedience had failed to prevent the calamity of the Black Death.

A call for reform was heard across Europe. The first reformer of the Late Middle Ages was John Wycliffe, a fourteenth-century scholar at Oxford University who criticized the wealth and corruption of the Church as well as the pope's claim to absolute authority. Wycliffe wanted the monarchs to remove corrupt church officials and believed that the Bible was the sole authority for religious truth, not the Church. He translated the Bible from Latin to English so all English people could read it. After his death his followers, called Lollards, continued to agitate for reform.

The next reformer was Jan Hus, a Czech from the region of modern-day Bohemia, Germany, who started a more violent call for change. As a professor of the University of Prague, he produced copies of the Bible and pamphlets in the Czechoslovakian vernacular. For these actions, in 1415 he was burnt at the stake as a heretic, but his supporters, named Hussites, continued a violent struggle with the crusading knights of Bohemia. Finally in 1436 the German Holy Roman emperor compromised with the Hussite leaders and their reforms.

Rebirth

After the Black Death, survivors were, of course, sad for the death of loved ones but also grateful to be alive, resulting in a renewal of trade and cultural achievements in Europe, later called the Renaissance (1350–1500).

The movements were centered in the independent city-states of Italy, most notably Florence and Venice, which benefited financially from the trade from the Mediterranean Sea basin. With this prosperity and their deep attachment to classical traditions (Roman ruins surrounded them!), scholars delved into Roman and Greek classics gathering dust in monastery libraries. The older traditions of *humanism* and classical culture resurfaced on the European landscape and spread via the universities to those able to hear this message.

> **DEFINITION**
>
> **Humanism** is a system of thought with humanity at the center, the sum of all things.

The Prince, written by Niccolo Machiavelli, had a humanist perspective, focusing on the daily life and true feelings of people and challenging long-accepted traditions, assumptions, and institutions. Some historians point to this period as key to the development of modern literature.

Renaissance art was more individualistic and worldly than the art of the Middle Ages. It also included aspects of pagan classical mythology that were, of course, non-Christian themes that medieval artists never dared depict. New artistic techniques were developed in perspective, anatomical correctness, and human emotions. Famous artists like Donatello, Michelangelo, Leonardo da Vinci, and Raphael (they were Renaissance artists before they were Teenage Mutant Ninja Turtles!) developed new techniques in paintings and sculptures that continue to influence art today. The *Mona Lisa* by Leonardo da Vinci is one of the most recognized paintings in the world.

NOTABLE QUOTABLE

After the darkness has been dispelled, our grandsons will be able to walk back into the pure radiance of the past.

—Petrarch, Italian poet of the Renaissance

The Renaissance could not long be confined to Italy and spread to northern Europe through war, trade, and the invention of the printing press by Johannes Gutenberg. The Northern Renaissance had a more religious tone, represented in the works of Desiderius Erasmus (1466–1536), who wrote the *Praise of Folly*, a work very critical of the Catholic Church, and Thomas More (1478–1535), an English philosopher and writer who wrote *Utopia*. The artwork of the Northern Renaissance retained a distinctive perspective by remaining more medieval than classical in focus, with the oil paintings of Jan and Hubert van Eyek and Pieter Brueghel being the most notable.

The European monarchies and the Church were established powers by the High Middle Ages, but political and natural calamities and the subsequent Renaissance emphasis on humanism brought their authority into serious question. The trend proved unstoppable, and Medieval Europe changed into modern Europe as a result.

The Least You Need to Know

- The European powers of England, France, and Germany trace their origins and forms of government to medieval times.
- The medieval Catholic Church became entrenched in Western culture and laid the basis for modern education and learning.
- The Crusades increased trade and scholarship and changed the European perspective from inward to outward.
- The Black Death decimated Europe during the mid-fourteenth century, bringing the institutions of the Middle Ages, especially the Church, into question.
- The Renaissance renewed interest in the classical traditions of Greece and Rome and a humanistic perspective of the world.

America on the Eve of Invasion

In This Chapter

- Early civilizations of North America
- The Early Mesoamerican civilizations
- The Mayans and the Aztecs
- The early civilizations of South America
- The Incan Empire

The history of the early Americas is not often told in detail, but recent archaeology and scholarship has shed new light on the Americas before exploration.

Early humans crossed the Bering Strait when it was a land bridge into the Americas during the Ice Age. From that time, the first Americans populated the Western Hemisphere with a variety of cultures suited to their environmental settings in North, Central, and South America.

North America

Prehistoric North American civilization can be divided into the Eastern Woodlands and the Southwest. The other regions of North America only had nomadic tribal cultures, which did not leave enough of a historical or anthropological record to make an impact on the world historical stage.

The Eastern Woodlands

Three unique primitive cultures developed in the eastern region, in the fertile river valleys and forests of the Ohio and Mississippi rivers. The Adena thrived in the region from 500 B.C.E. to 100 C.E., to be eclipsed by the Hopewell culture that developed and peaked from around 100 to 400 C.E. Little is known about these cultures; the archaeological record is limited to only a variety of earthen mounds, and these peoples did not develop a written language.

The culture that subsequently emerged in the river valleys of eastern North America from 700 to 1500 C.E. left the clearest historical record to examine. The Mississippian civilization did not develop as a nation or a kingdom but as a loose confederation of tribes, which provided enough cultural stability to allow for the development of a few urban centers, most notably the city of Cahokia in modern-day Illinois. Like its predecessors, the Mississippian culture created a large variety of earthen mounds that most likely served as ceremonial and religious centers.

The Southwest

In the dry desert region of Southwest North America, a civilization called the Anasazi, meaning "ancient ones," emerged and adapted to the harsh environment. They began as small settlements around 450 C.E. Although very little is known about their culture because of a lack of written language, the Anasazi did leave behind elaborate cliff dwellings. These fascinating dwellings made of clay and rocks were carved into canyons high above the desert. The civilization reached its peak around 700 C.E. and thereafter suddenly declined. The reason is unknown, but some historians link its fall to the rise of the Mesoamerican civilizations.

Central America

Central America, or Mesoamerica, witnessed the rise and fall of several unique and advanced civilizations, including the Olmec, Teotihuacán, Mayans, Toltecs, and Aztecs. Their advanced culture provided archaeologists and historians with more information to reconstruct their histories compared to the North American civilizations.

The Olmec

The Olmec emerged in east-central Mexico around 1200 B.C.E. and remained active in Mesoamerica until 400 B.C.E. It is considered by most to be the "mother civilization" of Central America, meaning that most of its descendents drew from its culture in the area of art, architecture, religion, and language.

> **WHAT IN THE WORLD**
>
> The Olmec constructed a series of enormous stone head monuments—incredibly, without the use of any metal tools; they used stone tools. The faces of the monuments are unique because they contain detail unlike any found in early America before arrival of the Europeans. Archaeologists and historians have not been able to explain the reason for or origins of the Olmec monuments.

Teotihuacán

Influenced culturally by the Olmec, the Oaxaca Zapotecan people founded the city of Teotihuacán around 150 to 100 B.C.E. near modern-day Mexico City. It developed into one of the world's largest cities, with a population of over 200,000. Teotihuacán was carefully planned to accommodate its growing population, with streets laid out in a grid pattern with two pyramids in the center of the city, one dedicated to the sun and the other to the moon.

Teotihuacán thrived on intensive agriculture developed around the area of the city and an extensive regional trade network. The city's social structure consisted of two major groups. At the top were the priests and nobles, who lived in lavish homes. The other group was composed of farm peasants and workers who inhabited apartment compounds. The city began to fall into decline between 800 and 1000 C.E., during which it was ruled by a form of militarism, until finally Teotihuacán was conquered by the expanding Mayan people.

The Maya

The Mayan civilization that developed in the early centuries of the Common Era in Mesoamerica has sometimes been called the "Greeks of the New World." They emerged in Central America and eventually occupied an area that included present-day Guatemala, Honduras, Belize, and southern Mexico. The Mayans flourished politically and culturally from 250 to 950 C.E., creating a calendar, a sophisticated written language, superior textiles, and elegant art.

WHAT IN THE WORLD

Around 850, the Mayans built an observatory for astronomy called the Caracol in the city of Chichén Itzá. Its architecture was based on the alignments of different celestial events. The observations of the planet Venus at this observatory proved to be very important to the Mayans, serving as the basis of the Mayan calendar.

Religion was the foundation of the Mayan culture, a complex set of beliefs involving the worship of serpent gods and jaguar deities. The Mayan people built large pyramid complexes in which to perform large-scale human sacrifices to the gods. They also created a ritualistic ball game, much like basketball, which involved shooting a ball through a hoop—but the losers of the competition were then ritually sacrificed to the gods.

The Mayans took religion very seriously, which produced some very positive results. The Mayans developed hieroglyphs to record their history, astronomy, dynastic lineage, and religious practices. This hieroglyphic system was based on a number system of 20. It consisted of an ideographic series of bars and dots that made over 850 characters, which the Mayans carved on stone and wrote on a primitive form of paper. Furthermore, the Mayans made many advances in mathematics and astronomy, including the creation of a calendar system accurate to within a second.

NOTABLE QUOTABLE

This is the account of how all was in suspense, all calm, in silence; all motionless, still, and the expanse of sky was empty. This is the first account, the first narrative. There were neither man, nor animal, birds, fishes, crabs, trees, stones, caves, ravines, grasses, nor forests, there was only the sky.

—*Popul Vih* (Sacred book of Maya), Anonymous

The Mayans were ruled by a *theocracy* that combined civic and religious authority over the people. Generally, these theocrats came from the same family and directed the activities of the elite scribes and priests who administered the affairs of the state. Mayan cities reached populations of 80,000 people, and the Mayans centralized agriculture to drain swamps to raise maize or corn. Eventually, the populations of the cities became a drain on environmental resources. The Mayan civilization fell into decline until the Toltecs invaded their territories and ended the Mayan rule for good.

DEFINITION

A **theocracy** is a government ruled by a person who claims to have the sanction of a god or gods. Generally, these claims have a powerful effect on the people if the religion is culturally very important.

Toltecs

The Toltecs emerged from northern Mesoamerica to invade and conquer most of the Mayan territories and establish a capital at Tula by 968. A very aggressive civilization, the Toltecs were dedicated to a militaristic ethic that included continuous warfare and the cult of sacrifice.

Later successors, most notably the Aztecs, confused and combined the legacy of the Toltecs with that of the city of Teotihuacán. In reality, the Toltec influence on Mesoamerica was very limited, as was their ability to maintain an empire for any length of time. By 1150, the Toltecs fell into decline and no longer dominated the region of Mesoamerica.

The Aztecs

The Aztecs emerged from the struggle for supremacy in Mesoamerica after the fall of the short-lived Toltecs. Although their origins are not altogether clear, most agree that the Aztecs were part of a nomadic group referred to as the *Mexica*. This tribe, which spoke Nahautl, the language of the Toltecs, migrated to the shores of Lake Texcoco in the central valley of Mexico around 1325. At that time the Aztecs founded their major city, Tenochtitlan, on a marshy island in the middle of the lake. From there, the Aztecs began a rapid and spectacular rise to power. With a reputation as fierce warriors and zealous followers of their religion, they became a major power in Mesoamerica by the early fifteenth century until the arrival of the Spanish in the mid-sixteenth century.

As the Aztecs conquered Central America, they developed a tribute system that ensured their short-term dominance. Conquered people were forced to pay tribute, surrender lands, and perform military service. Local rulers were allowed to stay in their positions to act as tribute collectors, allowing for Aztec political dominance without direct administrative control. In exchange, the conquered people were extended Aztec protection, which was dominated by the Great Speaker, the ruler of Tenochtitlan. The Great Speaker was first among equals and a civil power as well as a representative of the gods on earth. For these privileges, the conquered had to give up a few of their own to help feed the fast-developing Aztec cult of human sacrifice.

Aztec Religion

The religion of the Aztecs was vast as well as complex. The Aztec religion made little distinction between the world of the gods and the natural world, and had at least 128 major deities. Each deity served as patron of cities and occupations. The forces of nature had a duality that allowed for a male or female counterpart, which multiplied the complexity and number of the Aztec pantheon.

Religious observances took on many forms, including a variety of festivals and ceremonies with feasting, dancing, penance, and human sacrifices. Not all of Aztec religion had such a polytheistic perspective. The writings of Nezhualcoyotl, king of Texcoco, hinted at a deeper unity of spiritual belief and monotheistic concerns. Nezhualcoyotl questioned the existence of the Aztec pantheon and advanced the notion of an invisible creative force underlying all things, which gave true meaning to existence.

Human sacrifice held a special place in the Aztec religion. The sun god Huitzilopochtli was, in addition to being the Aztec tribal patron, the central figure in the cult of human sacrifice. According to the Aztecs, sacrifice was based on the belief that Huitzilopochtli needed strength to fight the forces of darkness and cold with warmth and light. This warmth and light was derived from human life in the form of the heart and blood. So the Aztecs had to continually perform human sacrifices to help fight the forces of darkness. These performances developed into elaborate rituals and a cult that dominated Aztec society. Central to the cult was the city and temple complex at Tenochtitlan, which was viewed as the foundation of heaven.

Agriculture

To support its growing population, the Aztecs invented a unique system of agriculture to supplement traditional methods. Using Lake Texcoco as a resource, the Aztecs invented *chinampas*, which were beds of aquatic weeds, mud, and earth in frames made of cane that were rooted to the lake floor. These floating fields augmented the production of maize and other staple crops of the region, all of which was controlled and distributed by the Aztec state.

Social Structure

The social structure of the Aztecs mirrored that of other previous civilizations. Of course, at the top were the king and his family, who were representatives of the gods on earth. The nobility, which made up a majority of the military, were next in line. As part of the military, their importance came from taking prisoners in war for sacrifice, which ensured immortality. To have a "flowery death" meant dying while gathering prisoners for the cult, which was one of the noblest ways for someone to die.

Below the nobles were the scribes, artisans, and healers who inhabited the cities of the Aztec Empire. There was also the *pochteca*, or special merchant class, that traded in luxury items that the Aztec command economy did not control. The lower class was the peasantry, which worked in the fields to feed the empire.

The Decline of the Aztec

The most obvious reason for the Aztecs' decline was the invasion of the Spanish, led by Cortez, but there were seeds of a fall years earlier. The lack of technology, and more specifically the lack of the wheel, made basic food preparation laborious and lengthy. The Aztecs had to grind maize for 30 to 40 hours per week by hand. This work was taxing on manpower as the Aztec Empire grew in population.

In addition, the Aztec tribute system caused problems as conquered people grew resentful of Aztec political and cultural domination. Finally, the religious need for more sacrificial victims pushed the empire to expand beyond its ability to effectively control and provide.

The Spanish also contributed to the decline of civilizations to the regions south of the Aztecs, but their development was very different in comparison to the people of the central region.

South America

Humans began to develop settlements in the peaks and valleys of the Andes Mountains in the second millennium B.C.E. The first known human settlement in South America emerged along the Supe River in central Peru in 2600 B.C.E. Eventually the settlements spread northward, developing weaving, pottery, and metallurgy as they grew into urban societies.

The Chavin

The Chavin civilization was the first true civilization to develop in South America and Peru. It flourished from 1000 to 200 B.C.E. and spread for hundreds of miles along the Peruvian coast. The center of the Chavin civilization was at Chavin de Huantar, high in the Andes Mountains north of present-day Lima.

The people of the Chavin civilization were united religiously rather than politically. As their religious authority declined, the people broke up into regional groups that dominated the political landscape of Peru for centuries. Their cultural legacy included improved techniques of cultivating maize, the back-strap loom, and advances in metallurgy.

The Moche

The Moche civilization emerged in the Moche and Chicam valleys of Peru from 200 to 700 C.E. It expanded to adjacent valleys of the northern coast of Peru through conquest. Its expansion and subsequent stability allowed for the development of two large urban cities: Tihuanaco, on the shores of Lake Titicaca in Bolivia, and Huari, in southern Peru, which became dominant in the end.

The Moche rulers oversaw the building of two huge pyramids of adobe blocks known as the Temple of the Sun and the Temple of the Moon, which were painted with polychrome murals. In addition, the Moche people constructed extensive irrigation ditches and fortifications around their cities. To some degree, these measures provided protection and stability, which resulted in the development of an artisan class to create painted water jars and gilded metal objects.

The Moche civilization used the practices of ayllus, reciprocity, and verticality to help to bond their society together. Ayllus were kinship units based on shared mythical ancestors to which everyone belonged. Reciprocity developed cooperative relationships based on Moche religious beliefs. And finally, verticality was the creation of social and political objectives of families and communities based on different economics and altitudes. Over time, these techniques of societal cohesion came to naught and the Moche civilization was conquered by the state of Chimu.

Chimu emerged around 800 c.e. to dominate over 600 miles of the Peruvian and Chilean coast. Its capital city was Chan Chan near present-day Trujillo. This powerful state was quite abruptly conquered at its height by the Incas in 1465.

The Incas

The Incan people emerged from the region of Cuzco in the Andean highlands around 1350 and, before their sudden end at the hands of the Spanish, they became the most powerful empire of South America.

By 1438, the Incas had defeated and conquered all of their surrounding neighbors to create a large and powerful state. But it was the three rulers—Pachacuti (1438–1471), Topac Yupanqui (1471–1493), and Huayna Capac (1493–1527)—who created the Incan Empire. Pachacuti conquered more territory to create not just a powerful state but a large empire. Topac Yupanqui, the son of Pachacuti, added to that empire by conquering the Chimu state by cleverly seizing its irrigation system. Finally, Huayna Capac consolidated the newly conquered lands under Incan rule and suppressed subsequent rebellions against that consolidation.

WHAT IN THE WORLD

Over half of the population of Peru are descendants of the Incan civilization, and its culture is still alive. The Andean pipes, an Incan instrument, are still played in the music of the country. Many Peruvians speak the ancient Incan language of Quecha. The people of Peru also use Incan techniques in farming and clothing.

The Incan Empire developed a proven technique of rule and empire. The empire was divided into four provinces, each with its own governor. Underneath that governor was a provincial bureaucracy in which the Incan nobles played a major role. Local rulers who were conquered by the Incas maintained their positions and received privileges for their loyalty. The conquered people did not pay tribute (remember those unhappy groups who were conquered by the Aztecs?), but instead provided labor on lands. To further help with cohesion in the empire, the Inca spread the Incan language, Quechua. Finally, the Inca constructed a system of roads to connect all of the empire culturally and economically.

The Incan Religion

The Incan religion had many different elements. A royal ancestor cult drove the Inca to expand the empire, maybe to its detriment. Deceased Incan rulers were mummified. After their mummification, the dead rulers were treated as intermediaries between the Incan people and the gods. All of the deceased's land and possessions were used to support the cult surrounding its mummified body. This meant that subsequent Incan rulers received no lands or possessions when they took over the empire, so they continually sought to expand the empire.

The Incas also worshipped many gods, with the sun god being the most revered. The ruler of the Incas was the sun god's representative on earth and thus very important, whether he was alive or dead. The Temple of the Sun in Cuzco combined the cult of the royal ancestor and reverence for the sun god. It became the center of the state religion and housed the mummies of the dead Incan rulers.

Finally, animism was another element found in the Incan religion. *Huacas*, or holy shrines, found in such places as mountains, stones, rivers, caves, and tombs, were believed to be inhabited by spirits. Some of these acknowledged spiritual shrines became pilgrimage sites for the Incas.

Incan Achievements

The stability of the Incan Empire allowed developments in mathematics, architecture, and metallurgy. Incan craftsmen created many beautiful religious and domestic objects out of gold and silver. Copper and bronze were used to make various weapons and tools.

In architecture, the Inca built precise, fitted-stone buildings. In math, they developed the *quipu*, a system of knotted strings to record numerical information for trade and engineering. In agriculture, the Inca developed a terrace system for irrigating and growing crops on hills and mountains. Finally, they laid over 2,500 miles of roads throughout their empire, an engineering feat similar to that of the Roman Empire—with the additional amazing exception that the Inca built all of their roads in the Andes Mountains.

The Least You Need to Know

- The early people of the Americas traveled from Asia across the Bering Strait during the Ice Age, when it was a land bridge.
- The early Americans gradually populated both North and South America, adapting to the different environments.
- Many civilizations developed in the Americas, but the most notable were the Mayans, Aztecs, and Incas.
- The Mayans, Aztecs, and Incas developed and administered complex societies that included large urban centers and government bureaucracies.

The World Gets Much Smaller

Part 3

This part begins the period of modern history, or at least early modern history, which began Europe's dominance over the world. How, is a question better left to sociologists and other historians to debate. Once things stabilized after the Mongolian invasions, trade intensified along interregional networks.

This trade continued to snowball when European nations began to explore and to colonize. For once, the ability to use technology effectively became a key factor in expanding empires. The Europeans ascended to the position of control over most of the world.

Back to Islam

In This Chapter

- The rise of the Ottoman Turks
- The fall of Constantinople
- The spread of the Ottoman Empire
- The Safavid Empire
- The Mughal Empire

Three powerful Islamic civilizations were established in West Asia, North Africa, and southeastern Europe that were very influential to the politics and culture of the Middle East. In the thirteenth century, the Ottoman Turks grew in power in the region of the Middle East to threaten the aging Byzantine Empire. In 1453, the threat became fact when the Turks captured Constantinople. Afterward, the Ottoman Turks expanded into southeastern Europe and North Africa, but the expansion brought problems that started its decline.

To the east of the Ottoman Turks at the beginning of the sixteenth century, the Safavid dynasty was founded and conquered the region of present-day Iran. It also suffered internal problems, which brought its end in the early eighteenth century.

Farther west, during the same time period, the Mughal dynasty was established and ruled the Indian subcontinent, mixing Hindu and Islamic cultures successfully until British incursions in the region.

The Rise of the Ottoman Empire

The group of Turkic people known as the Ottomans emerged during the thirteenth century from the region in the northwest Anatolian Peninsula. Ottoman leader Osman created a sizeable empire, taking territory from the declining Seljuk Empire in the fourteenth century and marking the beginning of the Ottoman dynasty. Following Osman's lead, rulers of the Ottomans took the title of sultan.

As Ottoman ambitions became more militaristic, they mastered the use of gunpowder with muskets and cannons. The Byzantine Empire was on its way out by that point, and the Ottomans dominated the territories of the Bosporus and Dardanelles. The Ottoman Empire was solidified and expanded with the defeat of the Serbs at the Battle of Kosovo in 1389, and by 1400 the Ottomans had conquered the region of Bulgaria. Now they were ready for the "big show," which was the siege and conquest of Constantinople.

NOTABLE QUOTABLE

The soldiers fell on the citizens with anger and great wrath …. Now they killed so as to frighten all the city, and to terrorize and enslave all by the slaughter.

—Greek observer of the fall of Constantinople

The Fall of Constantinople

Ottoman ruler Mehmed II (r. 1451–1481) initiated the attack on Constantinople. After several attempts in 1453, the Ottoman Turks conquered Constantinople and killed the Byzantine emperor. The last remains of the Byzantine Empire were gone from the pages of history. Constantinople was renamed Istanbul and became the capital of the expanding Ottoman Empire.

The Ottomans did not stop there. From 1514 to 1517, the Sultan Selim I (r. 1512–1520) led several successful campaigns into the regions of Mesopotamia, Egypt, and Arabia, leading to Turkish control of Jerusalem, Mecca, and Medina. Later, Selim I led Ottoman forces into North Africa, conquering much of the region, and was declared caliph and the new defender of Islam.

With expansion into the Middle East and North Africa complete, Suleiman I (r. 1520–1566) pushed into Europe. The Ottoman armies advanced up the Danube River, seized the city of Belgrade, and in 1526 defeated the Hungarians in the Battle of Mohacs. The Ottoman armies conquered Hungary and pushed to the borders of Austria.

All hope appeared lost for Christians as the Islamic Ottoman Turks conquered eastern Europe and moved to put Vienna under siege. But it was at Vienna in 1529 that Suleiman I and his armies were finally stopped. With a combined military effort of the Holy Roman emperor and several German princes, the siege failed, and Ottoman expansion northward into Europe ceased.

The Ottoman Turks still extended their territorial domination of North Africa, the Middle East, and eastern Europe into the eastern Mediterranean Sea. In due time, the Turkish navy tried to expand into the western Mediterranean but was rebuffed by the Spanish navy in 1571 at the Battle of Lepanto. Other European nations also worked to push back the Ottoman expansion, and by the late seventeenth century the Turks had been driven out of Hungary by Austrian and Hungarian forces.

WHAT IN THE WORLD

The janissary corps was an elite group of soldiers and administrators of the sultan's army. In general, they were young Christian men taken from their families for their good looks and physical abilities and forced to convert to Islam. After initial recruitment, the janissaries had sons who also inherited the right to be in the corps. But by the early 1800s, the force had become an undisciplined group of over 100,000 men, and a potential political powerhouse—so the sultan was forced to put its entire membership to death!

The Gunpowder Empire

The Ottoman Empire qualified as one of the first "gunpowder empires." These empires were created by ambitious rulers who unified regions that were not originally under their control and which did not have many unifying factors other than the empire itself. Of course, the success of the Ottoman Empire and other gunpowder empires was based on the use of gunpowder.

The achievements of the Turkish Empire can also be attributed to its administrative structure. At the top was the sultan, a hereditary ruler with supreme authority in political and military matters, whose status and prestige increased with the expansion of the empire. The imperial council, headed by the grand *vizier*, advised the sultan on the matters of state and controlled the bureaucracy. The bureaucracy of the empire was efficiently divided into provinces and districts governed by pashas, who were given land by the sultan in exchange for collecting taxes, supplying armies, and maintaining law and order.

Another powerful player in the politics of the Ottoman Empire was the queen mother, the mother of the sultan. Generally, she emerged as a major advisor to the throne, and deservedly so, considering she had to make her son stand out from all of the other sons in the *harem*.

DEFINITION

A **harem** was the part of the household in which the wives and female slaves of the sultan lived. Generally, the sultan favored one or two wives and children over others in the harem, which caused much strife and political intrigue in the harem itself.

Religion in the Ottoman Empire

The Turks of the Ottoman Empire were Sunni Muslim, as were the majority of the Muslims they ruled. As rulers of most of the Islamic world, the sultans claimed the title of caliph by the early sixteenth century, guiding and maintaining Islamic law in the empire through the *ulema*. The ulema administered the Islamic moral code for the sultans of the empire. In addition, they maintained the schools that taught the Islamic religious tradition.

DEFINITION

An **ulema** was a group of religious advisors to the Ottoman sultan who administered the legal and educational system based on Muslim law.

All of this emphasis on Islam did not mean that the Turks were intolerant of other religions. In fact, the empire was quite accepting of other religions as long as the religious groups paid a special tax. So Christian Europe's fear that Ottoman Turks would conquer the whole of Europe and force all Christians to become Muslim was unfounded. In general, the regions conquered by the Turks stayed Christian, although there were a few exceptions, such as the region of present-day Bosnia.

Social Structure

The social structure of the Ottoman Empire was somewhat standard. Of course, on top was the ruling class, followed by the merchant class, which held a privileged position exempt from government taxes and regulations. Artisans, peasants, and nomadic herders were on the bottom of the structure. In spite of the strength of traditional Islamic roots in Turkish culture, women in the empire were given more freedoms. Although restricted in many ways, they were allowed to own and inherit property. Additionally, women could not be forced into marriage and a few even served as government officials.

Ottoman Art

The sultans of the Ottoman Empire were also patrons of Islamic art as caliphs. This patronage manifested itself quite often in the architecture of the mosques. In the sixteenth century, Sinan the Architect, with the encouragement of the sultan, designed and oversaw the construction of more than 80 mosques in the empire. The crowning achievement of this building surge was the Suleimaniye Mosque in Istanbul.

The early eighteenth century was also another period of artistic achievement in the empire, with a surge of textiles, rugs, and wall hangings being produced with intricate and beautiful color schemes and Islamic designs.

Problems in the Ottoman Empire

The high-water mark for the Ottoman Empire was the reign of Suleiman I, sometimes referred to as Suleiman the Magnificent (as opposed to merely great). After his reign in the mid-sixteenth century, a decline began.

Grand viziers and other ministers exercised more power, while the sultans retreated to the tents of their harem. Eventually, an elite group formed, a group that did not seek to benefit the empire but only sought wealth and power. To make matters worse, the pashas also became corrupt, with law, order, and tax collection becoming secondary concerns. Finally the Turkish culture started to be heavily influenced by European or Western standards that were highly contrary to Islamic law. Alcohol, coffee, and tobacco were all used by Turks across the empire during the sixteenth and seventeenth centuries. Unrest smoldered, waiting for the right moment to flame up.

As the Ottoman Empire developed, with its set of problems related to the Islamic tradition, so did the new Islamic Empire of the Safavid in Persia. The Safavid problem was not like the Ottoman tug-of-war between secular Western culture and traditional Islamic culture; it was between subcultures within the traditional Islamic culture: the Sunni and the Shiites.

The Safavid Empire in Persia

After the empire of Timur the Lane fell in the early fifteenth century, the region of Persia fell into a state of anarchy—but not for long. A new Islamic regime, the Safavid dynasty, founded by Ismail, a descendent of Safi al-Din (thus the name Safavid), emerged to take control of Persia.

By 1501, through military action and political bargaining, the Safavids were able to seize much of present-day Iraq and Iran. Ismail and his successors called themselves shahs or kings of the Persian Empire and considered themselves to be the spiritual leaders of Islam, undermining the Ottoman caliph's claim as spiritual leader of Islam. In addition, the Safavid rulers were Shiite Muslims, the traditional enemies of the Sunni who ruled the Ottomans. This meant there was a lot of tension between the Safavids and Ottomans along their borders.

WHAT IN THE WORLD

The Safavid Empire was located in modern-day Iran, which still has a predominantly Shiite Muslim population. This population still has many conflicts with the Sunni Muslims of the region.

The Shiite and Sunni Problem

The tension between Shiite Safavids and Sunni Ottoman Turks arose because of several events in the history of the Persian Empire. The Safavids at one time sent missionaries to the Ottoman Empire to convert Sunnis to the Shiite views, which only caused more tension.

In 1508, the Sunni population that inhabited Baghdad after its fall to the Safavids was killed indiscriminately. In retaliation, Selim I moved against the Safavids and defeated the fast-expanding dynasty at the Battle of Tabriz. By the late sixteenth century, the Turks had taken control of Azerbaijan and the Caspian Sea from the Shiite Safavids. The Safavid power was waning as they started to lose territory and prestige.

The Safavid Culture

The cultural impact of the Safavid dynasty on the region was significant. The arts flourished under the rule of Shah Abba. The capital city of Isfahan was built during his reign with a sense of planned order. Silk and carpet weaving spread through the region, with the government providing clear roads and resting spots for the traders directing the camel caravans. Persian paintings highlighting soft colors and flowing patterns also were traded along these routes. All of these goods were purchased and enjoyed by the empire's bureaucratic and landed classes, and, for a time, Persia benefited from the rule of a relatively stable dynasty.

The Quick Decline of the Safavid

The high point for the Safavid dynasty was the rule of Shah Abbas (r. 1588–1629), who negotiated a peace treaty with the Turks in 1612 to maintain the borders of the Persian Empire. But his successors did not have as much luck, talent, or skill to maintain the empire.

Shiite groups, dissatisfied with peace with the Sunnis and wanting stricter observance of Islamic law, rebelled often. Religious orthodoxy increased even when the Shiite rebellions waned. By the time Shah Hussein came into power in the early eighteenth century, the Safavids were ready to fall.

The bordering nations knew of the troubles of the Safavid dynasty and took the opportunity to seize territory. The Afghans invaded from the east and captured the capital of Isfahan, and the Ottoman Turks invaded and took territories on the western borders. Persia again fell into a state of political chaos and anarchy; to this day the region hasn't been able to shake its tendency for instability or sometimes harsh rule.

NOTABLE QUOTABLE

Few cities in the world surpass Isfahan for wealth, and none come near it for those stately buildings, which for that reason are kept entire.

—*A New Account of East India and Persia, Being Nine Years' Travels, 1672–1681,* John Freyer

The Mughal Dynasty

Since about 1500, the subcontinent of India had been divided into a mixture of Hindu and Muslim kingdoms. It was the Mughals (also spelled Moguls) who finally unified these small kingdoms and brought unity to the region.

Babur

The founder of the Mughal dynasty was a man known as Babur (r. 1526–1530). His father descended from Timur-i-Lang and his mother from Genghis Khan, so one might say he came from good stock! Due to his heritage, Babur inherited the rule of what remained of Timur-i-Lang's short-lived empire. Using this as a springboard, Babur besieged and conquered Kabul in 1504 in his first military expedition. In due time, he crossed the Khyber Pass into the subcontinent of India.

Babur slowly conquered the subcontinent and then finally captured the city of Delhi in 1526 at the Battle of Panipat to establish himself as the premier power in the plains of north India. He continued his military conquests till his death in 1530. Although Babur ruled with an iron hand, he loved learning and culture and even wrote his own memoirs.

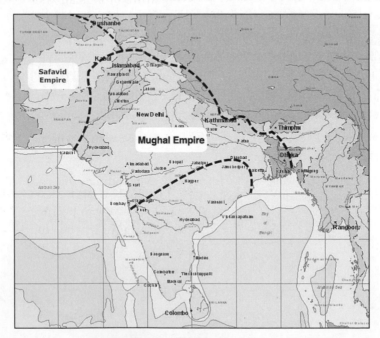

The Safavid and Mughal empires.

Akbar

Akbar, the grandson of Babur, picked up where his grandfather left off. Despite coming to the throne at the age of 14, Akbar was able to unite the entire Indian subcontinent under Mughal rule by 1605. Much like the Ottoman Turks, this rapid expansion was attributed to the use of heavy artillery to conquer the many independent fortresses across India. Akbar created the greatest empire in India since the Mauryan dynasty.

Despite appearances, Akbar was not a ruthless conqueror. His rule was humane in many respects. Although Muslim himself, Akbar was tolerant of other religious traditions in his empire. His administrative policies were also open minded. Akbar recruited non-native Muslims and Hindus to fill his government bureaucracy. Officials known as *zaminders* received plots of land for personal use in return for their service. Additionally, they kept a portion of the taxes they collected for the empire for their salaries. And unlike the taxation policies of other empires, Akbar was fair-minded about his taxes, and as a result foreign trade flourished during this rule.

Mughal Society and Culture

Mughal society and culture were a curious mixture of Persian and Indian elements. The Mughals were Muslims ruling a Hindu nation, but the blend seemed to work in India. At least for the men. Restrictions on women were universal in both cultures, so the practice of the *suttee* continued in Hindu society. Additionally, upper-class Hindus adopted elements of Islamic law that isolated women further.

DEFINITION

Suttee is the Hindu religious custom of cremating a widow on her husband's funeral pyre.

Other exchanges also occurred in the arts. The "Akbar" style of painting used both Muslim and Hindu styles, with the addition of a European perspective and lifelike portraits. These artistic achievements were encouraged by the emperors of the Mughal Empire, who were patrons of the arts.

The Decline of the Mughal Empire

When Akbar died in 1605, he was succeeded by his son Jahangir. At first his rule benefited the empire; Jahangir was able to centralize the government more so than his father. But soon Jahangir fell under the political influence of one of his wives in his harem. She used her position to enrich her offspring and arranged the marriage of Akbar's niece to her son, Shah Jahan, which put him on the throne. This action began the decline of the empire.

Shah Jahan ruled the Mughal Empire from 1628 to 1658. Although he expanded the Mughal Empire and maintained the political system, Shah Jahan spent too much. When his beloved wife died, he began construction of the beautiful (and expensive) Taj Mahal in her honor, completely draining the treasury for the project. Shah Jahan raised land taxes to continue the project, which drove the peasant population in India into poverty. Domestic problems arose, but he failed to deal with them.

As time passed, Shah Jahan became sick and politically weak. His son, Aurangzeb, took that opportunity to try to seize power. Eventually, Aurangzeb won political control over the Mughal Empire and imprisoned his father for the remainder of this life.

The rule of Aurangzeb was not a good period for India. As a devout Muslim, Aurangzeb forbade *suttee* and was not religiously tolerant. Many Hindus in the empire were forced to convert to Islam. Consequently, the populace revolted and the Mughal dynasty was weakened by the unrest.

To add to the problems caused by poor rule, British and French merchant traders arrived to shake up the political landscape, and the Mughal Empire was weakened by the sudden invasion of a Persian army and the sacking of the city of Delhi.

In 1757, Mughal and British trading interests came into conflict, and a small British force led by Sir Robert Clive defeated a numerically superior Mughal army. Afterward, the Mughals were forced to allow the British to collect taxes from the region around Calcutta. By the eighteenth century, the British had moved inland to control more Mughal territory. The British trading interests represented by the British East India Company grew rich from Indian trade and obtaining money from local rulers by selling trading privileges. By 1803, the British East India Company controlled Delhi, and the Mughal emperor only remained so because of British goodwill. Finally in 1857, the last Mughal emperor was exiled and the title was abolished in India.

The Least You Need to Know

- The Ottoman Turks emerged from central Asia to create an empire out of the territories of the Middle East, North Africa, and eastern Europe.
- Suleiman the Magnificent was the most able of all of the Ottoman sultans—his reign also marked the high point in Ottoman power and culture.
- The Safavid dynasty came out of the political chaos and anarchy of Persia to dominate the region and create a short-lived empire.
- The Mughals established an empire that united the Hindu and Muslim kingdoms in India for over 300 years.

As the World Shrinks: South Asia

In This Chapter

- Ming China
- The voyages of Zheng He
- Qing China
- Tokugawa Japan
- The Yi dynasty in Korea

With the Ming dynasty and the reunification of the country, strong central Chinese rule was restored. During this period, Chinese civilization flourished culturally, agriculturally, and commercially, becoming the largest center of civilization at the time. With the eventual decline of the Ming rulers, the Manchu seized control of China, creating the Qing dynasty during the early seventeenth century. Although starting strong, the Qing dynasty did not deal successfully with European expansion in the region. This lapse in policy led to its decline.

Luckily for the Japanese, they were not tested by European expansion so rigorously. This was due in part to the emergence of the Tokugawa Shogunate during the sixteenth century, which had gained enough control to stop contact with the Europeans. They succeeded in this state of isolation until the nineteenth century. In Korea also, the Yi dynasty tried to isolate itself from China, Japan, and the Europeans. But in the seventeenth century it was forced to open its borders through a military invasion by China.

The Ming Dynasty

The Chinese Ming dynasty founded by Ming Hong Wu, or Ming Martial Emperor, filled the political void left by the overthrow of the Mongol Yuan dynasty in 1368. The Ming dynasty provided strength and stability to China for close to 300 years, lasting until 1644.

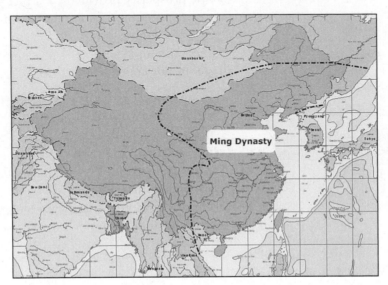

China during the Ming dynasty.

Doing Things Right

The Ming dynasty was able to do many things that helped further advance Chinese power in the region and culture. The dynasty invested time and effort into strengthening the Great Wall to ensure that northern invaders like the Mongols would be kept out. This allowed them to extend their rule into Mongolia and central Asia. (The conquered had become the conquerors!) To rule the expanded nation, the Ming dynasty used the civil service exam to create a highly efficient bureaucracy. To help fill this bureaucracy, the dynasty also created a nationwide school system.

The nationwide school system better-educated the Chinese people, which helped the economy of the country. (The theory is, better-educated people create and buy better products.) But what really helped the Chinese economy was the completion of the

Grand Canal. Shipping of agricultural products from southern to northern China was much faster and cheaper. Commerce and trade received a much-needed boost, and the economy of China continued to grow under the stability of the Ming dynasty.

Zheng He and Chinese Exploration

In some sense the stability and economic prosperity provided by the Ming dynasty allowed for an interesting "almost" turning point in world history. From 1405 to 1433, the Ming dynasty, stable and prosperous, sent ships to explore the Indian Ocean and the east coast of Africa, aided by the Chinese invention of the compass. These explorations were led by the admiral and minor court official Zheng He (d. 1433).

The expeditions returned with wonders heretofore unknown to the Chinese, including giraffes, ostriches, and zebras, as well as information about the world beyond Asia. Still, the Chinese voyages were not well received. Confucian scholars were resistant to it. It put the social order into question. Additionally, the Chinese were not impressed with what they saw of the outside world. When Zheng He died, so ended the explorations, leaving this episode in Chinese history with a big "what if?" What if the Chinese had continued their explorations and discovered America before Columbus? How would world history have been different?

Contact with the West

As the Chinese began to close off from the outside world, the outside world began to find them. In 1514, the Portuguese traders arrived in China, the first direct contact the Chinese had with Europeans since the time of Marco Polo during the Yuan dynasty. This initial contact had a very limited effect on China, but Christian missionaries soon followed. The European influence started to trickle into China.

The Fall of the Ming

During the late sixteenth century, the Ming dynasty was plagued with weak rulers and corruption. In addition, the Ming rulers levied high taxes on the people, which led to peasant unrest. In the 1630s, this unrest increased after several epidemics and bad harvests. Finally, a peasant revolt led by Li Zicheng gained momentum, and in 1644 a peasant army took the capital city of Beijing. The last Ming emperor hung himself from a tree in the palace gardens rather than face capture.

The Rise of the Qing

The Manchu from Manchuria saw the overthrow of the Ming dynasty as their opportunity to seize power. They moved into China and easily defeated the inexperienced Li Zicheng and his peasant army, conquering the capital city. The Manchu then declared the new Qing dynasty, which would rule China for almost 300 years, from 1644 to 1911.

The Manchu Problem

The Manchu had a unique position as rulers. Much like the Mongols, they were ethnically and culturally different than the Chinese. To remedy this, the Manchu forced all the Chinese men to adopt the Manchu style of dress and culture. This included shaved foreheads and braided pigtails called queues. Chinese men who refused this new look were executed. But the Qing dynasty did not always replace Chinese elements with Manchu ones. The dynasty adopted the Chinese political system and brought the Chinese into the imperial administration to share power. And eventually, the Qing dynasty was accepted as legitimate rulers of China.

The Great Kangxi

The Emperor Kangxi was one of the greatest emperors of the Qing dynasty and in Chinese history. During his rule from 1661 to 1722, he stabilized the frontiers of China. Kangxi was also a patron of the arts and scholars, which created a high-water mark in Chinese culture. He was tolerant of the new Christian missionaries; in fact, over 300,000 Chinese converted to Catholicism under his rule. After his death, that policy changed into suppression, pushing the Chinese Christian population underground.

NOTABLE QUOTABLE

On this account men of all ranks and dignities whatsoever, even nearest to him in blood, stand in his presence with the deepest awe, and recognize him as sole ruler.

—Ferdinand Verbiest, European missionary, on Emperor Kangxi

Those Sneaky Europeans

During the rule of Emperor Qianlong from 1736 to 1795, European powers were able to finally make a significant impact on Chinese policy. Also during this time, older Chinese ways fell into decline. The government was filled with corrupt officials, and the taxes levied on the Chinese people had become too burdensome. Additionally, China had a population surge that caused economic hardship on the whole society.

A group of unhappy peasants tried to overthrow the dynasty in the White Lotus Rebellion. It was suppressed, but it weakened the dynasty considerably, and the European powers saw an opportunity to push for more trade privileges with China. The Qing dynasty needed funds and sold limited trading privileges to the European powers, but confined them to an island outside of Guangzhou. The British weren't satisfied and asked for more in 1793. Emperor Qianlong responded by writing George III stating that the Chinese had no need for British manufactured goods (probably being quite truthful). Of course, the British backed off; but the European powers had opened the door to China and there would be little that could shut it again.

WHAT IN THE WORLD

The most famous Jesuit missionary to China was Matteo Ricci. He and his fellow Jesuits were respected by the Chinese because of their ability to use the Chinese language and respect for Confucianism.

Economic Changes

From the sixteenth to the nineteenth centuries, China experienced several economic changes. China remained an agricultural society—more than 80 percent of the population were small farmers—but new agricultural techniques increased food production, and the population increased to more than 300 million, which created a land shortage. The Qing government responded by placing limitations on the amount of land wealthy landowners could hold. This policy did not remedy the situation but did help to control it.

The Chinese also experienced a growth in the trade of silk, porcelain, and cotton goods, in part because of new markets in Europe. The Qing saw this growth as an opportunity and took control of those industries to gain its revenue, and placed high taxes on traded goods.

Chinese Society and Culture

Based on Confucian principles, Chinese society remained much the same as it had for centuries. The society was organized around the family, with the individual desires given up for the good of the family. With an emphasis on respect for the elderly, several generations of one family lived under the same roof. These extended families also connected with dozens of other families to form clans. The clan worked to benefit all of the member families, with wealthier families helping poorer families.

WHAT IN THE WORLD

To this day in China the family is more important than the individual. An example of this comes from the way food is ordered. In America, everyone orders individually, but in China, one order is placed for the whole family.

Women in China

Sadly, the status of women in Chinese society did not change much over time. They were still regarded as inferior to men. Only men could obtain a formal education and have a career. Additionally, Chinese women could not divorce their husbands or inherit property. Plus, the tradition of binding women's feet—seen as a status symbol—continued through the Qing period.

The Arts and Literature

Under the Qing dynasty, Chinese arts and literature flourished. This period witnessed the evolution of the modern novel with *The Golden Lotus*, the first realistic social novel, and also *The Dream of the Red Chamber* by Cao Xuegin published in 1791. Advances in art and architecture matched those in Chinese literature, with the beauty of the Imperial City in Beijing being created at this time.

So despite some economic and political issues, Chinese culture continued to be vibrant and creative. As Chinese civilization experienced growing pains in reaction to outsiders, Japan tried to avoid outsiders entirely and focused inward.

Japan and the Great Unifiers

After the collapse of shogunate power during the early fifteenth century, the island of Japan experienced a century of chaos as daimyo fought constantly for political power and control of lands. But by the mid-sixteenth century, new movement toward unification was led by three men.

The Game Changers

A daimyo named Oda Nobunaga (1534–1582) and his army of samurai, using muskets supplied by the Portuguese, seized control of Kyoto and placed the shogun under his control. He then consolidated his rule in the central plains of Japan, forcing other daimyo to submit to his rule. To help control violence, Oda and his forces used "sword hunts" to gather arms from surrounding areas so they could not be used against the shogun. Apparently one of his own followers took exception to his policies and assassinated Oda.

Oda was succeeded by Toyotomi Hideyoshi, who began life as a farmer's son but became a renowned military leader. By the late sixteenth century, Toyotomi's military prowess had convinced most of the daimyo to accept his rule. He was succeeded by Tokugawa Ieyasu, the daimyo of Edo. In 1603, Tokugawa became the premier political power in Japan and took the title shogun. His successors remained in power until 1868 and, because of the stability the Tokugawa brought to Japan, it was called the period of "Great Peace."

The Rule of the Tokugawa

The followers of Tokugawa wanted to transform the Japanese feudal system, so they separated Japan into 250 territories called hans, or domains. Each han was ruled by the traditional aristocratic daimyo. Knowing that the daimyo were needed but also a threat politically, the Tokugawa created a hostage system to control them. In this system, the daimyo were required to have two residences, one in their own lands and one in the capital of Edo. When the daimyo were away from the capital, their family had to stay at the residence in Edo under the watchful eye of the Tokugawa shogunate. In all, this new system transformed the daimyo into a manager of lands, which heralded the decline of the samurai warrior class as conflict ceased.

Social Changes

The Tokugawa period not only witnessed political changes but also social changes. Trade and industry flourished during the period of stability. The development of banking and paper money also helped. With economic prosperity, the Japanese class system solidified. The emperor and the imperial court were still on top. The warrior class made up of shogun, daimyo, samurai, and *ronin* came next. Peasants and farmers were the next class, followed by the artisan class. A new class of merchants emerged just below the artisans as the economy continued to evolve toward trade and industry. Finally at the very bottom were the *eta*, social outcasts who were strictly regulated by the Tokugawa government.

> **DEFINITION**
>
> A **ronin** was a samurai who lost his lord and was forced to roam the countryside, often becoming a bandit.

Tokugawa Culture

The peace and prosperity of the Tokugawa shogunate allowed Japanese culture to thrive. New urban fictional novels, lighthearted in nature, were being written at a rapid pace. Of course, it was not all fun and games. Ihara Saikaku wrote one of the most famous novels of this period, *Five Women Who Loved Love*, which was a tragic novel. Poetry was also being written at almost the same pace as the fictional novels; Matsuo Basho, who lived during the seventeenth century, was one of the most renowned of the Japanese poets.

Kabuki theater also grew in popularity with its action, music, and dramatic gestures about life in teahouses and dancehalls. Finally, art and architecture prospered as daimyo competed to create the most beautiful and elaborate residences in Edo.

> **NOTABLE QUOTABLE**
>
> The ancient pond
> A frog leaps in
> The sound of water.
> On the withered branch
> A crow has alighted—
> The end of autumn.
>
> —Matsuo Basho, Japanese poet (1644–1694)

Contact with Europeans

In 1543, during the early Tokugawa period, Portuguese traders landed in Japan. At first, the Japanese welcomed the Europeans; the daimyo were especially interested in buying European muskets. In 1549, Jesuit missionaries arrived, led by Francis Xavier, and by the end of the sixteenth century, thousands of Japanese had converted to Catholicism. The new converts were not tolerant of other religious traditions and subsequently destroyed some Buddhist shrines.

By 1587, Hideyoshi had enough of this destructive activity and issued an edict prohibiting Christian activities. Later, Tokugawa Ieyasu expelled all Jesuit missionaries from the island and persecuted Japanese Christians. Finally, all European merchants were expelled from Japan with the exception of a small Dutch community that remained in Nagasaki. The Japanese had enough of the problems associated with those hairy and smelly Europeans; but it was not the end of the European problem.

WHAT IN THE WORLD

The Portuguese introduced playing cards to Japan during the late 1500s. Playing cards spread like wildfire with the populace of Japan. Eventually, to protect the honor of the samurai, the daimyo created an amendment to the warrior code that forbade gambling with cards.

The Hermit Kingdom

As in the past, Korea continued to remain isolated from even China and Japan, so it has been referred to as the "Hermit Kingdom." The Yi dynasty, founded at the end of the fourteenth century, ruled over Korea and patterned their society after the Chinese. During the late sixteenth century, a Japanese army led by Toyotomi Hideyoshi tried to invade and conquer Korea. Korean forces were able to defeat the Japanese but were substantially weakened as a result. The Chinese saw this as an opportunity and in the 1630s invaded Korea from the north, making the Yi dynasty subject to China.

The Least You Need to Know

- After the overthrow of the Yuan dynasty, the Ming dynasty emerged to take political control of China from the late fourteenth century until 1644.
- The voyages of Zheng He during the early fifteenth century were an unsuccessful attempt by China to look beyond its borders.
- The Manchu from Manchuria seized control of the failing Ming dynasty to create the Qing dynasty, which ruled China until 1911.
- Oda Nobunaga, Toyotomi Hideyoshi, and Tokugawa Ieyasu worked to unite a politically chaotic and divided Japan under the Tokugawa shogunate.
- The Yi dynasty of Korea continued to isolate itself until it was forced into submission by China during the early seventeenth century.

Exploration or Exploitation?

In This Chapter

- The motives for European exploration
- Christopher Columbus and the New World
- The Spanish Empire
- The impact of European exploration

If the Mongols revitalized the interregional exchange among Europe, Asia, Africa, and the Middle East, it was the Europeans who developed the most interest in maintaining and developing these contacts. Thus, the world was on the verge of a new era of history.

Means and Motives

The European states had several motives for wanting to explore other regions. While fighting in the Middle East, European crusaders discovered that they liked a lot of what the Muslims had, including spices and fine linens from the Far East. Of course, after many years of fighting with the Christians, the Muslims did not care to do business with the Europeans (except the Venetians!), so to acquire exotic goods from the Far East, European monarchs and merchants started to look for ways around the Middle East. The European states and the various churches also saw it as their duty to spread Christianity, and it was time to find some new prospects. And many explorers were out for the purely selfish goals of fortune and glory. Finally, Europe's developing nation-states could not sit idle while a neighbor was exploring and gathering increased wealth, influence, territory, and revenue streams. Competition was intense and meant life or death.

This combination of motives and economic means developed rapidly after the last of feudalism was wiped out by the Black Death. Europe now had the right mix to begin the Age of Exploration.

First, Portugal

Portugal was the first European nation to make attempts at exploration by probing the western coast of Africa with several expeditions beginning in 1420. Why Portugal and not some other nation of Europe? The debate will continue about the specific cultural, social, and geographic reasons, but one individual factor was Prince Henry the Navigator, who took a strong interest in exploration and sponsored the expeditions.

The expeditions discovered new sources of gold in a region in Africa and justifiably called it the Gold Coast. In 1488, Bartholomeu Dias rounded the Cape of Good Hope. Vasco da Gama went even farther, rounding the cape and sailing to India, returning to Portugal with a cargo hold filled with spices. For his labors, Vasco da Gama made over 1,000 percent in profits, making him a rich man and generating a lot of interest with Portuguese spice traders.

As the Portuguese spice trade grew, it conflicted with the already existent Muslim spice trade with India. In 1509, things came to a head, and a better-prepared Portuguese fleet defeated a fleet of Turkish and Indian ships. From that point forward, Portugal was an active participant in the Indian spice trade, with the Port of Goa on the western coast created for just that purpose.

The merchants of Portugal also saw money in the Southeast Asia nation of Melaka, so Admiral Albuquerque and his fleet forced it to submit to Portuguese rule. This gave Portugal a jumping-off point for trade with China and the Spice Islands, connecting it back to Portugal after stopping at India and the Cape of Good Hope. The first European trading empire had been created. It was not the last.

Next Comes Spain

Rather than compete with Portuguese interests in the East, Spain decided to explore westward, beginning with the voyages of Christopher Columbus. In 1492, Columbus, an Italian sailing for Spanish monarchs Isabella and Ferdinand, sailed the Atlantic Ocean in hopes of finding a direct route to Asia.

By October 1492, Columbus reached land and, thinking he had reached Asia, proceeded to call the inhabitants he and his men met "Indians." In reality, Columbus had reached the Caribbean Islands off of North America. In three more voyages he discovered all of the major islands of the Caribbean and Honduras, still believing he had reached Asia.

The Treaty of Tordesillas

The Catholic Church saw a possible conflict on the horizon between two Catholic nations, Portugal and Spain, who from all appearances had conflicting claims on territory in Asia. So in 1494 with the help of the Church, the Treaty of Tordesillas was signed by the two nations in hopes of averting a war. This treaty created an imaginary line north and south through the Atlantic Ocean and South America. The unexplored territories east of the line belonged to Portugal while the unexplored territories west of the line belonged to Spain. Of course, the parties of the treaty did not know until later that Columbus had discovered a "new world." Thus, the treaty proved to be much more advantageous to Spain, because they acquired the majority of the rights to America while Portugal only acquired rights to the trade route around Africa. Spain was set up to be the next leading European trading empire.

WHAT IN THE WORLD

The citrus industry in Florida has its origins in Columbus's second voyage to America. Columbus carried with him citrus seeds that were planted in the West Indies and eventually spread to Mexico and finally Florida.

Racing Across the Americas

Christopher Columbus's legacy has been questioned, but in his time Columbus was an inspiration. Many explorers from several different nations followed in his wake. John Cabot, who represented England, explored the area of New England during the early sixteenth century. Portuguese captain Pedro Cabral led an expedition to explore parts of South America around the same time. And finally, Amerigo Vespucci, who coined the name "America" in his letters to describe the lands he was discovering on his voyages, explored even more of South America for Spain. These and other expeditions led to one general conclusion: that the land they were exploring was not Asia but a "new world" that had never been seen by Europeans.

NOTABLE QUOTABLE

They are credulous and aware that there is a god in heaven and convinced that we come from there. And they repeat very quickly any prayer we tell them and make the sign of the cross. So your Highness should resolve to make them Christians.

—Christopher Columbus, letter to Queen Isabella and King Ferdinand (1492)

The Spanish Empire

According to the Treaty of Tordesillas, the New World that explorers were discovering belonged to Spain, so Spain had an instant empire. As far as Europeans were concerned, an empire was something to control and exploit for the benefit of the mother country. So Spain sent men called conquistadors to subdue or conquer the natives of their empire, bringing with them weapons that the native Americans had not seen: muskets, horses, and, most devastatingly, infectious diseases.

Cortés and Pizarro

Hernán Cortés was the first man to make it to the New World with conquest, not exploration, as his main objective. Cortés and his small army of Spanish conquistadors landed in Central America in 1518, coming from the nearby Caribbean Islands. To motivate his men, he burned all of his ships, so there could be no turning back.

After some quick reconnaissance, Cortés found out that he was in the middle of the large empire of the Aztecs. Using the discontentment of neighboring native tribes to recruit allies, Cortés and his men were able to subdue the whole powerful Aztec Empire led by Montezuma, who at first thought Cortés was a god returning to the Aztecs. They conquered the Aztec capital city of Tenochtitlan by 1521. By 1550, the Spanish controlled a majority of Central America. Much of the success a few hundred Spanish soldiers had in subjugating an entire nation was due to the muskets and horses that the Aztecs did not have.

Another reason for the Spanish success was the diseases they unintentionally brought to the New World. Native Americans had no immunities to smallpox, measles, typhus, and influenza. These diseases came with the Spanish and spread quickly through the Native American population, decimating the entire continent.

Francisco Pizarro followed in Cortés's footsteps. Setting out from Panama in 1531, he and his small army of conquistadors crossed the mountains into the empire of the Incas. By 1533, Pizarro had defeated the Incas and killed the Incan emperor, Athahualpa. Afterward he built a capital at the city of Lima and set up a puppet monarchy to rule the territory.

To Administer an Empire

After the conquests of Cortés and Pizarro, the Spanish created a complex colonial administration system to control their empire. One of the first actions was to declare all Native Americans subjects of Spain.

Although they were subjects, they did not receive many rights. The system of *encomienda* allowed Spanish settlers to use Native Americans as forced labor. Eventually this policy of forced labor, combined with disease and starvation, took a heavy toll on the native population. Close to half of the natives died from smallpox, measles, typhus, and influenza. There was a concerted effort by Catholic missionaries to convert the Native Americans in hopes of protecting them. Hundreds of thousands were converted to Christianity, which only hastened the destruction of Native American social and political structures, to be abruptly replaced with alien European structures.

WHAT IN THE WORLD

The creation of a castelike system is a very important development in Latin American history. In the system, the "pure-blood" Spaniards had a higher status than those of mixed ancestry, which included Native/Spanish, African/Indian, and African/Spanish; indigenous populations; and imported African slaves. Remnants of this unjust system can still be found in the culture and politics of the region.

The Impact of Exploration

Spain, Portugal, and the other European nations saw several benefits of their explorations. Gold and silver found in the New World flowed to Spain, making it one of the richest and most powerful nations of Europe. Portugal became the chief entry point of spices into Europe, displacing the Venetians from that rich and important role. All of Europe acquired new agricultural products—potatoes, corn, tobacco, and coffee—which became staple and luxury crops for Europeans in the modern period. This trading exchange is sometimes referred to as the *Columbian Exchange*. Finally a new competition developed among sixteenth-century European nation-states.

> **DEFINITION**
>
> The **Columbian Exchange** was an exchange of goods, plants, animals, and also diseases that followed Columbus's initial connection of Europe and the Americas. Agricultural staples such as potatoes and corn were introduced to Europe, while wheat production was brought to the Americas. Animals such as horses, sheep, goats, and cattle were brought to the Americas, while Europe received the turkey and squirrel. Diseases were also exchanged, with the Europeans spreading small-pox, typhus, influenza, and measles among the Native Americans.

Finally, the English, Dutch, and French

The English, Dutch, and French did not sit idly by as the competition started to heat up. These nations did not recognize the validity of the Treaty of Tordesillas for a variety of religious and political reasons, so they also funded explorations with varying degrees of success.

The English were able to establish themselves in both Asia and the Americas in the seventeenth century. In Asia, England explored the region of northwest India, staying clear of Portuguese claims as much as possible. In North America, the colony at Jamestown, Virginia, was founded in 1607; by 1700, English colonies dotted the eastern seaboard of North America.

The Dutch were also able to set up colonies in both Asia and the Americas. In 1595, they set up their first trading colony in India, administered by a company created to oversee trade in Asia called the East India Company. A similar company was founded to conduct trade in America called the West India Company. It financed the colonization of the Dutch colony of New Netherlands in the Hudson Valley.

The French tailed the English and the Dutch and were unable to colonize the Americas until the eighteenth century. It was then, spurred by the French exploration of the Mississippi River valley, that the French created a colonial territory in present-day Canada.

Mercantilism, or What Can You Do for Me?

As the colonization of the New World and Asia continued, the European nations developed a new economic policy regarding the colonies. Called *mercantilism*, the policy was very simple: to make sure that the colony served the mother country's interests, a favorable balance of trade was established in which the mother country imported raw materials from the colony and exported finished goods back.

DEFINITION

Mercantilism is an economic policy that many European governments pursued during the eighteenth and nineteenth centuries in which a nation was to import raw goods and export valuable finished goods. Theoretically, the pursuit of this policy made a nation rich and powerful by keeping the economic resources in the country.

To maintain that favorable balance, the mother country used high tariffs on foreign goods so the colonists could only afford goods from the mother country. Does this seem fair? The colonists didn't think much of it, either, and eventually it came back to haunt the European nations.

The Impact of Exploration on Africa

We examined the impact of exploration on the Americas and Europe, but another continent was profoundly affected by the exploration of the European nations: Africa.

WHAT IN THE WORLD

The composer of the famous Christian hymn "Amazing Grace," John Newton, was a former slave trader. In the hymn, John described his spiritual journey from an abusive slave trader to a Christian. Later, Newton became involved with William Wilberforce in the slavery abolition movement.

The Beginnings of Slavery in the New World

During the sixteenth century, sugar cane plantations flourished in the Caribbean Islands and South America as people in Europe acquired a taste for sweets. These plantations needed a large number of workers to operate, but the Native American population had been severely depleted. They needed a new workforce, so in 1518 the first load of African slaves was brought to the Americas.

Slavery had existed for centuries in Africa prior to the European contact. Traditionally, Africans traded slaves, mostly acquired as prisoners of war, with each other and Arab traders in small numbers. The Portuguese and Spanish were the first to purchase these slaves in small numbers at coastal trading ports. As demand for them increased from the plantations, the Europeans went farther inland to acquire more and more slaves.

It is estimated that over 10 million slaves were brought to America from the sixteenth to the nineteenth centuries. This forced migration to America was known as the Diaspora. Slaves often did not make it across what was known as the Middle Passage because of the poor conditions of the cargo holds of the European ships. Disease, starvation, and despair accompanied this group to the New World.

The Triangular Trade Network

The slave trade from Africa to the Americas was the starting point of a trading system called the triangular trade network. Manufactured goods like guns and cloth were traded in Africa for slaves; slaves were shipped to the Americas where they were exchanged for sugar, tobacco, and raw cotton; and those products were shipped to Europe to be made into finished goods that either went back to the colonies or to Africa to begin the trading network again.

NOTABLE QUOTABLE

Some gentleman may, indeed, object to the slave trade as inhuman and impious; let us consider that if our colonies are to be maintained and cultivated … [it] can only be done by African Negroes.

—Temple Luttrell, speech to British House of Commons (1777)

The End Result in Africa

The expansion of the slave trade in Africa had effects that still resonate in the continent into the modern age. Socially, the trade tore the fabric of African society, creating conflict and war among the African people as they competed for the slave market. Coupled with the exportation of Africans as slaves, these conflicts depopulated the African continent. The conflicts also brought into question African cultural values, causing their rapid deterioration. As trade routes shifted to the coast, the old Songhai Empire weakened considerably, which helped to strengthen the Moroccan dynasty that emerged in the later sixteenth century to destroy the empire of Songhai.

With all of these changes, some things in Africa continued regardless. The traditional monarchial form of government remained highly centralized in most African kingdoms. Christianity remained constant in South Africa and Ethiopia, while Islam continued to spread throughout the remaining portions of Africa.

The Global Impact of Exploration

In the end, what was the global impact of European exploration? First and foremost, earlier interregional connections were solidified to create a truly global economy. Regional trade networks were disrupted and declined in importance, which allowed for a shift in trade dominance, with Europe now the center of the global market. Naturally the shift in trade brought a shift in political power, and European nations became *the* global leaders for next 400 years.

The Least You Need to Know

- European exploration was facilitated by the revitalization of interregional connections between Europe, Asia, and the Middle East.
- Portugal was the first European nation to make substantial efforts at exploration and creating a trading empire.
- Christopher Columbus, sailing for the Spanish, discovered the New World, establishing Spain as a world power.
- Other European nations followed the example of Spain in exploring North America.
- European exploration established those nations as the dominant world powers for the next 400 years.

Religion and Reformation

In This Chapter

- Martin Luther
- The Protestant Reformation
- Zwingli and Calvin
- The Catholic Counter-Reformation
- The wars of religion

The Protestant Reformation was one of the most divisive events in European history, and its impact on world history can't be overstated. Many of the ideas and institutions of the West—and, as a result, the world—are influenced by the ideas and results of the Reformation.

The Monk Who Changed Europe

Every story has a starting point, and the Reformation's starting point was a German monk named Martin Luther (1483–1546). Luther was born to middle-class parents who wanted him to be a lawyer, but legal training was not his style and he decided to become a monk. (There's a story that Luther, coming home late one night, got caught in a storm and, after lightning nearly struck him, decided to enter a monastery.)

After joining the ranks of the Augustinian order and becoming a teacher of religion at the University of Wittenberg, he appeared to struggle with his soul's salvation. Some claimed to have heard him wrestling with the devil late at night in his cell at the monastery. In fact, what Luther was wrestling with turned Europe inside out and struck at one of the sources of the European structure and tradition.

NOTABLE QUOTABLE

As a monk I led an irreproachable life. Nevertheless, I felt that I was a sinner before God. My conscience was restless …. I actually hated the righteous God who punishes sinners …. Then finally God had mercy on me, and I began to understand that the righteousness of God is that gift of God by which a righteous man lives—namely faith—and that … the merciful God justifies us by faith.

—Martin Luther

Salvation by Faith

While reading the letters of Paul in the New Testament, Luther was struck by the apostle's idea of faith. At this time, the Church taught that people entered heaven through their good works. What bothered Luther was that, no matter how many good works he performed, he did not feel worthy to enter heaven. Paul, in his letters, approached it from an angle the Church seemed to ignore. Paul believed that we enter heaven by faith alone. Simply and truly believing in God was all that we need to enter heaven.

Luther took Paul's idea and advanced it further by teaching that works of the Church—rituals of the sacraments and other actions—were meaningless and useless for one's salvation. Thus Luther dropped a bombshell at the University of Wittenberg, where he began to teach this new perspective of salvation, putting the Church's teachings into question. And he wasn't done yet.

The Ninety-Five Theses

Luther also began to protest what he saw as abuses by the Church. The abuse that most bothered him was the selling of indulgences, certificates awarded by the Church that reduced the punishment for people's sins. During Luther's time the Church pushed this practice to raise money to rebuild St. Peter's Basilica in Rome.

By 1517 Luther had had enough of the Church, its teachings, and indulgences. So on October 31, he submitted the Ninety-Five Theses, or statements, to the church in Wittenberg, detailing what he saw as all of the wrongs of the Roman Catholic Church, hoping to generate debate and reform in the Church. The response Luther got was quite unexpected.

WHAT IN THE WORLD

The official story is that on October 31, 1517, Martin Luther nailed his Ninety-Five Theses to the door of the church in Wittenberg, starting the Protestant Reformation. But the image of Luther performing this act, popularized by numerous paintings, is probably false. Historians have no eyewitness accounts of the event, and Luther never mentioned it during his lifetime. It is just a legend that was created after this death.

To say that the Catholic Church was not entirely open to Luther's criticism would be an understatement. Once the news of Luther's Ninety-Five Theses reached Pope Leo X in Rome, Luther was excommunicated, and his writings on the subject of justification by faith and the abuses of the Church were banned. It would appear that all had gone wrong for Luther and that his issues with the Church were not going to be heard. But several German princes were listening.

The German princes were motivated to do the morally responsible thing for the people of their respective small German kingdoms. In addition, the Church had traditionally appeared to represent Italian, not German, interests. The fact that most of the popes were Italian seemed to prove the point. Finally, the Church was one of the largest landowners in Europe. A break from the Church might mean that Church lands were up for grabs and available for the German princes.

The Teachings of Luther

So with the support of the German princes, particularly Prince Frederick of Saxony, Luther continued teaching and writing despite the disapproval of the Church. He went on to translate the Latin Bible into German, so all people would have the opportunity to read it. Eventually giving up on reform within the Church, Luther broke completely from the Roman Catholic Church to form the first Protestant (from the word "protest") faith: Lutheranism. He also developed his ideas and teachings through the years as his new version of the Christian faith grew. The following points represent the belief system that Luther advanced:

- Salvation is obtained by faith alone, not works.

- Religious truth and authority can only be found in the Bible.

- The Church should not be a hierarchy of clergy but a community of believers.

- All jobs are important, not just the occupations of priests, monks, or nuns.

- The worship service should be in the language of the people for them to understand.

- There are only two sacraments—baptism and marriage.

Once Luther challenged the Church, others followed in his path. While the teachings of the Church began to be questioned, a variety of theological teachings sprang up, as religious-minded reformers began to develop new ideas that did not agree with the teachings of Luther, much less the Church.

Zwingli in Switzerland

In Switzerland, a priest named Ulrich Zwingli (1484–1531) started the call for reform. Eventually the churches in Switzerland broke away from the Roman Catholic Church. Much like Luther, Zwingli stressed that salvation was obtained by faith alone. But unlike Luther, Zwingli was very interested in setting up a theocracy, or church-run state. He thought that the state could best keep the people in line with the backing of church doctrine.

For a time, Zwingli was able to set up his version of a theocracy in the city of Zurich. Then in 1531, Catholic forces defeated Zwingli and his army in the field of battle. With this Catholic victory and Zwingli's death in battle, the Protestant reform movement seemed to be over in Switzerland. But another reformer emerged.

NOTABLE QUOTABLE

Three times Zwingli was thrown to the ground by the advancing forces, but in each case he stood up again. On the fourth occasion a spear reached his chin and he fell to his knees saying, "They can destroy the body but not the soul." And after these words he fell asleep in the Lord.

—*Ulrich Zwingli*, Oswald Myconius

Calvinism

John Calvin (1509–1564) was a reform-minded Protestant theologian from France. His teachings drew from Martin Luther and put him in hot water in his homeland, and he was forced to leave the country. By the mid-sixteenth century, Calvin established a reformed church in Geneva, Switzerland.

In Geneva, Calvin was able to teach the Christian doctrines he professed in his book *The Institutes of the Christian Religion*. Influenced by the writings of the fourth-century Doctor of the Church Augustine of Hippo, Calvin taught that everyone was already *predestined* for heaven or hell since God is the Alpha and Omega—the beginning and the end. If a man loves God, he will try to have faith and perform good works, but salvation is in God's hands alone, for He is the master of man's destiny.

DEFINITION

Predestination is the belief that God determines beforehand whether souls have either salvation or damnation.

Through the strength of his teachings, Calvin took over the government in Geneva and created a strict theocracy to help maintain his reformed church, now known as the Calvinists. Other reformers observed Calvin's success and used his ideas in their own Protestant reform movements.

Anabaptists and Radicals

As the door for protest against the Church and its teachings opened up, so did the chance for things to go horribly wrong. After all, the very order of society was rooted in Church doctrine. People started to question the authority of established Protestant teachers such as Luther and Calvin.

The Anabaptist movement began in response to the teaching on the sacrament of baptism. *Anabaptists* believed that baptism should only occur when someone was an adult and fully able to understand the meaning of the sacrament. All well and good, but within the Anabaptist movement, radicals began to deny the very authority of local government to rule their lives, since local officials had no spiritual authority to do so.

DEFINITION

Anabaptists were a sixteenth-century sect of the Reformation that opposed the taking of oaths, the holding of public office, military service, and—most famously—infant baptisms.

Eventually the radical Anabaptists were a force to be reckoned with. They seized the city of Munster in Germany in a violent uprising. Once sealed off in the city, the radical Anabaptists practiced polygamy, burnt books, and killed members of other religious groups, Protestant and Catholic. Finally the surrounding cities had had enough and an army of Lutherans and Catholics besieged the city and destroyed the radical movement. From that point most Anabaptists, radical or otherwise, knew they were not welcome in Europe, and many left for America. With them went two ideas that resonated in the colonies of North America. These were the ideas of religious liberty and the separation of church and state.

In Need of a Divorce

Unlike the Protestant movements prior, the one in England did not have theological doctrine as its focus. Its focus was divorce. King Henry VIII needed a male heir to his throne, as all kings do. The problem was that he just couldn't produce one, and he went through several wives trying.

Such was the state of affairs in 1527, when Henry VIII asked the pope to grant a divorce from his current wife, Catherine of Aragon, so he could marry his mistress, Anne Boleyn. The pope, who had granted several divorces at this point, refused Henry VIII's request—politically, he didn't want to cross the King of Spain. In response, Henry VIII broke from the Roman Catholic Church to form the Church of England, with the monarch—him—as the head of the church. As head of the Church of England, Henry VIII then granted himself a divorce. Case closed, problem solved! But Henry's move ushered in a period of religious strife in England that plagued the country and the monarchy for two centuries before it was finally resolved.

WHAT IN THE WORLD

To gain a male heir to the throne, Henry VIII was married a total of six times. What he produced was a daughter and the first female monarch to assert political power over England. She was Queen Elizabeth I, one of the greatest monarchs of English history, whose rule marked a cultural peak called the Elizabethan Age.

You Know ... You Might Be Right

With the Protestant Reform movement in Europe, the Church conceded that the Protestants might be right. In 1536, Pope Paul III officially called for reform in the Catholic Church. The Counter-Reformation, as it is sometimes referred, can be divided into two phases.

The Society of Jesus

The first phase started with the establishment of the Jesuits, or Society of Jesus, led by Ignatius Loyola. This society was organized militarily, requiring members to obey blindly and with absolute faith. The Jesuits served as the militant arm of the Counter-Reformation and tried to hinder Protestantism in a number of ways:

- They engaged in missionary activities around the world.

- They established schools in Catholic nations to help perpetuate the Catholic faith.

- They rooted out heresy through the Inquisition, a general tribunal that employed a variety of methods, from house arrest to execution by being burned at the stake.

- They served as advisors in the courts of Catholic kings.

- They helped to create and maintain the *Index of Forbidden Books.*

WHAT IN THE WORLD

The *Index of Forbidden Books* got its start in the early fifth century, but it wasn't until the sixteenth century under Pope Paul IV that it took the form in which it remained for over 400 years. During those years, the texts of many great thinkers and philosophers were put on the list, including Erasmus, Thomas Hobbes, and Voltaire. The list also had some very strange and interesting uses. The Bodleian library, founded in the 1600s at the University of Oxford, purchased its first books from the list found in the *Index*. They figured if the Catholic Church didn't like it, it must be worth having!

The Jesuits performed all of these actions very zealously, and in all likelihood they did prevent the spread of Protestantism in the majority of Europe. But another Church action might have done even more to prevent that spread, and that was the Council of Trent.

The Council of Trent

The Council of Trent was a meeting of the top bishops and theologians of Catholic Europe held in Trent, Italy, from 1545 to 1563 (they must have needed a lot of espresso!). The purpose of this meeting was to define a new Catholic doctrine in response to the complaints of the Protestants. In the end the Church decided upon the following things:

- First and foremost, the sale of indulgences was forbidden.

- Salvation is achieved by a combination of good works and faith.

- The *seven sacraments* are true and valid in the life of the Church.

- Religious authority is found in the Bible, the traditions of the Church, and the writings of the Church leaders.

- The Latin Vulgate Bible is to be used.

- People cannot interpret the message of the Bible without the guidance of the Church.

DEFINITION

The **seven sacraments** of the medieval Church were ceremonies that only a priest possessed the right to perform through the authority of the Church: baptism, confirmation into the Church, the consecration of the Eucharist, the administration of penance, the ordination of the clergy, and the marriage ceremony.

The Results of the Catholic Counter-Reformation

The actions of the Jesuits and the mandates of the Council of Trent had several results. First, the Counter-Reformation helped to correct some of the abuses of the Roman Catholic Church. It also increased religious devotion, which led to a new art and musical style called baroque that emerged in Catholic Europe. And finally, the Protestant movement was prevented from spreading across the entirety of Europe, making it essentially a northern European movement.

Of course, all of the efforts of the Council of Trent to address the complaints of the Protestants beg the question: Why did the Protestant reformers and churches remain separated from the Catholic Church after the Counter-Reformation? The Catholic Church was reformed and better, wasn't it? In reality, regardless of the changes, things had gone too far.

The Protestants were very sincere in their religious beliefs and convictions. In addition, there were political reasons to remain separate from the Church. Monarchs and rulers wanted church lands and the ability to use religion to benefit their own state. Northern European nations were only too happy to defy the Italian-controlled Roman Catholic Church. They wanted autonomous, local control over their lands and people, so separation seemed to be the better political course. Merchants and townspeople also liked the new Protestant Christianity. Protestant doctrine on the value of all vocations or work seemed to support business practices and the accumulation of wealth.

So what were the long-term results of the Protestant Reformation on Europe? In the end, the Protestant churches became well established in northern Europe, while the Roman Catholic Church remained entrenched in the southern regions of Europe. The Reformation also helped the monarchs of Europe to centralize power and completely end the feudal system. But the Reformation also had violent long-term consequences, which culminated in the seventeenth century's Wars of Religion.

The Wars of Religion

Three separate wars were caused in part by the religious differences created by the Protestant Reformation and Counter-Reformation. These were the French Wars of Religion (1562–1598), the Thirty Years' War (1618–1648), and, to some degree, the English Civil War (1642–1649).

The French First

The French Wars of Religion, although they ended in the sixteenth century, gave Europeans an idea of the strife that was to emerge from behind the Protestant Reformation. The series of wars between 1562 and 1598 focused on the fight between French Protestants, or Huguenots, and French Catholics for the throne of the Valois dynasty after the death of King Henry II.

Tracing the wars and their various conflicts is a complex task better left to European histories; what matters is that, in the end, Henry of Navarre rose to the top of the political heap by adopting Catholicism and became king of France in 1593 as Henry IV. Later he established official tolerance of Protestantism in France with the Edict on Nantes in 1598. Henry IV spent the rest of his rule trying to repair the damage to the power and prestige of the French monarchy, which had been upturned by the religious dissention in France.

The Thirty Years' War

The next series of wars over religion in Europe was even more chaotic and disruptive than the French wars. The reasons for war were not only religious but also political. The princes of the independent German kingdoms wanted autonomy from the Holy Roman Empire. France wanted to limit the power of the Hapsburg family, which ruled the Holy Roman Empire. The Spanish, also ruled by the Hapsburgs, wanted to help extend the Hapsburg power in Germany over the German princes. And finally, the nations of both Sweden and Denmark wanted to strengthen their sphere of influence in the Baltic Sea region.

WHAT IN THE WORLD

By the early seventeenth century, firearms dominated the battlefield. The flint-lock musket was a front-loaded gun. A flint striking metal at the closed end of the musket ignited the gunpowder. This flintlock mechanism made it easier and more reliable than previous muskets. Trained armies of musketeers were able to fire up to two shots per minute. This technological development changed the face of war. The nations of Europe started to fund standing armies, and from then on wars were fought by professional soldiers.

Regardless of the political reasons for the war, the overarching conflict was between Catholics and Protestants over religious doctrine. For this doctrine, the people of Europe descended into the first continent-wide war involving all the major nations in their history.

Again, the track of the war is the subject of a European history, not a world history. But the result was that the Peace of Westphalia in 1648 reinstated the earlier Peace of Augsburg of 1555, which allowed the German princes to choose their subjects' form of Christian religion—limited, of course, to Catholicism, Lutheranism, and now Calvinism. The idea of *Cuius region, eius religio* or "whose the region, his the religion," was the maxim for the German states. In addition, the German princes were made sovereign, independent rulers of their kingdoms. This curtailed the political power of the Holy Roman Emperor and the Hapsburgs, beginning their slow decline.

The Results of the Wars of Religion

There were also several long-term results of the war. Germany had been ravaged and devastated. One third of its population had been wiped out, and it took the region two centuries to regain its composure culturally and politically. Later, the English

Civil War acquainted England with the problems that religious differences cause. This war, from 1642 to 1649, beheaded a king, King Charles, and gave them a tyrant, Oliver Cromwell, before things returned to a state of normalcy.

By the seventeenth century, the European nations had learned their lesson about wars of religion. From now on, they'd only go to war for political reasons! The people of Europe associated religious absolutism and zealotry with death and destruction, and began to look elsewhere for the answers religion used to provide. The stage was set for the age of science and reason.

The Least You Need to Know

- Martin Luther's Ninety-Five Theses led to the emergence of the Protestant Reformation.
- During the Catholic Counter-Reformation, the Catholic Church enacted a series of reforms that helped to strengthen the Church.
- The French Wars of Religion fought between French Huguenots and French Catholics started a period of religious warfare in seventeenth-century Europe.
- The Thirty Years' War devastated the region of Germany economically, socially, and culturally.
- After the Reformation and the Wars of Religion, people started to examine other worldviews rather than from a religious point of view.

Science and Philosophy Brighten Things Up

In This Chapter

- The beginnings of the Scientific Revolution
- Bacon and Descartes
- Sir Isaac Newton
- The Enlightenment
- The enlightened monarchs

The Scientific Revolution, sometimes referred to as the Newtonian Revolution, ushered in the modern period of European and world history. It marked a distinct break from the old framework of Europe and the adoption of something quite new. Its influence throughout the world is felt to this day and can be seen in many scientific and technological advances of world civilization. More important, it affected how people saw and interacted with the world around them.

In the Beginning

Advances in the field of stargazing (astronomy, if you want to get scientific) got the Scientific Revolution going during the fifteenth and sixteenth centuries. The Polish astronomer Nicolas Copernicus (1473–1543) started the ball rolling when he theorized that Earth, in fact, revolved around the sun, referred to now as heliocentric theory. Danish astronomer Tycho Brahe (1546–1601) kept the scientific inquiry moving with his voluminous set of observations of the night sky, which became the foundation for the theories of the solar system.

The Italian astronomer Galileo Galilei (1564–1642) kicked the ball into orbit. Galileo pioneered the use of the telescope to observe the night sky. More important, he was a vocal advocate of the Copernican system rather than the Church-accepted *Ptolemaic model* of the solar system. Galileo's criticism of Ptolemy's model landed him in hot water with the Roman Catholic Church, which did not appreciate the questioning of tradition. He was put on trial for heresy. After being found guilty of heresy at the trial, Galileo had to recant his findings and was put under house arrest until his death.

Finally, German astronomer Johannes Kepler (1571–1630), who assisted Tycho Brahe in his final years, determined that, although the planets moved around the sun, they did so in an elliptical orbit, not a circular orbit as had been suggested. So these four astronomers developed the basics of scientific observation, which were used throughout the Scientific Revolution.

DEFINITION

The **Ptolemaic model** was the belief advanced by the second-century Greek mathematician Ptolemy that Earth was a fixed point and the celestial bodies orbited around it.

Philosophers of Science

Following the developments in fifteenth- and sixteenth-century astronomy, two philosophers of science applied the practices of scientific observation to their respective fields to mark the beginning of the Scientific Revolution.

Englishman Francis Bacon (1561–1626) was a philosopher who developed and argued for the use of the inductive or experimental method. According to Bacon, the steps of the inductive method that a "man of science" should follow were as follows:

- One observes a natural occurrence or phenomena.
- One accumulates data from observations.
- One experiments with the observation to gather better data.
- One draws conclusions and creates principles.
- One tests principles again with more experiments and observations.
- One becomes a famous "man of science."

Of course, I added the last step—but it has some truth to it. Bacon did become a very famous man of science (regrettably, women were generally excluded) and his inductive method became even more famous and influential on the next generation of scientists.

The next philosopher of science who helped begin the Scientific Revolution was the Frenchman René Descartes (1596–1650). In his famous 1637 work *Discourse on Method*, he argued that all things should be confirmed by observation. If it can't be observed, it should be doubted. To Descartes, the only thing that was truly known was his own existence, proven by the proposition, *"Cogito ergo sum"* or "I think, therefore I am." He also divided all existence into the material and the spiritual, creating what is termed a Cartesian Dualism. According to Descartes, the material world was subject to the inductive method developed by Bacon and the spiritual world was subject to the deductive method. Although it wasn't his goal (he was attempting to reconcile religion and science), Descartes's dualistic approach to the world created a separation and tension between the humanities and the sciences that has lasted well into modern times.

NOTABLE QUOTABLE

But I immediately became aware that while I was thus disposed to think that all was false, it was absolutely necessary that I who thus thought should be something; and noting this truth I think, therefore I am … I concluded … it as being the first principle of the philosophy I was seeking.

—*Discourse on Method,* René Descartes

Newton and the Laws of Gravity

During the Scientific Revolution, one man, Sir Isaac Newton (1642–1727), stood far above the rest—although if you asked him, he would have responded that he was "standing on the shoulders of giants." Newton ascertained the preeminence of science in modern Europe and the world. Using natural law as his guide, his account of the movements of the planets and the stars as well as objects here on Earth is found in his *Mathematical Principles of Natural Philosophy.*

Newton's theory set aside the medieval assumption that God's active participation explained forces of nature. Natural laws like the law of gravity are predictable and unchanging and demonstrate that there is little need for theological explanations of worldly operations. Newton's discoveries advanced the theological notion called Deism. In Deism, God is akin to a watchmaker who creates a watch with all its inner workings and parts in place. He then winds the watch and watches it run without intervention of any kind. With Deism, God is not a personal God but a Creator who may only be a disinterested observer of the world. Of course, that kind of talk rocked the foundations of Christianity, Protestant and Catholic alike. Newton also advocated rationalism, the belief that the laws of nature can be understood with human reason and that mankind can be perfected. From Newton onward, man was the center of the universe—not God.

The revolution that Sir Isaac Newton started with an apple and the law of gravity was the beginning of the modern age. It also led to the next important break from the medieval past, the Age of Enlightenment.

NOTABLE QUOTABLE

The notion of the world's being a great machine, going on without the interposition of God, as a clock continues to go without the assistance of a clockmaker, is a notion of materialism and fate.

—Samuel Clarke, follower of Sir Isaac Newton

Anybody Need a Light?

The Enlightenment, also known as the Age of Reason, was the name given to the eighteenth-century intellectual movement that focused on humanism, science, rationalism, and philosophy. Originally known as the Aufklarung, in German, the Enlightenment was the application of the new methods of science to the humanities and philosophy. It was also a response to the irrational and chaotic Wars of Religion in sixteenth-century Europe. Human science and reason, not religion, it was thought, would provide order to Europe.

John Locke

Who was the first to begin applying the new methods of science and reason to the humanities and philosophy? Arguably, the first was the Englishman John Locke (1632–1704), a contemporary and friend of Newton considered by most to be the founder of Enlightenment *empiricism* and political liberalism.

> **DEFINITION**
>
> **Empiricism** is the belief that sensory experience through observations and experiments is the only source of human knowledge.

Locke wrote two works published in 1690. In *Two Treatises on Government*, he argued against the theory of the divine right of kings and suggested that the authority of rulers had a human origin and as such was limited—meaning if government did not protect the natural rights of the people (life, liberty, and property), the people could toss it. Locke stressed the importance of religious liberty in government and society, laying the foundation for the principle of separation of church and state. In *An Essay Concerning Human Understanding*, Locke argued for the empirical perspective but did not rule out the fact that knowledge was limited and must be reinforced by faith. Locke's argument for empiricism served as the basis for the Enlightenment doctrine that emerged with Locke's writings:

- Reason is the most significant and positive capacity of a human.

- Reason allows humans to free themselves from primitive, superstitious, and dogmatic beliefs that keep humans ignorant and irrational.

- Reason allows humans to learn and to think correctly.

- Reason can lead humans to perfection and to a heavenly existence on earth.

- Human belief should not base itself on human traditions or authority.

- Reason, endowed to humans by a creator, makes all equal and deserving of liberty and justice.

- Humans should seek to impart and/or gain knowledge, not feelings or emotions.

The French Philosophes

If Newton was the inspirational origin of the Enlightenment and Locke the foundation, five French philosophes, or philosophers, shaped it. They were Voltaire, Jean Jacques Rousseau, Baron de Montesquieu, François Quesnay, and Denis Diderot.

Voltaire (1694–1778) was definitely a poster boy for the Enlightenment. Although he was more of a social critic than philosopher, his criticisms brought up questions that later Enlightenment thinkers tried to answer. He wrote against injustice and inequality and for the dignity of all humans and the importance of science. His motto was *"Ecrasez l'infame,"* or "Crush the infamous," which was a warning to dogmatic religion, abusive governments, and old traditions to beware.

Of course, being born in Europe during the seventeenth century, Voltaire was raised a Christian, but Voltaire believed that God or the Creator made the laws that put the universe in order, and the evil of the world resulted from man straying from his understanding of natural law. It was mankind's job to rediscover those laws using reason and bring order back into the world. Voltaire believed that prayer and miracles violated the natural order of things, and therefore did not work.

None of this made Voltaire a hit with churchmen, but it did interest other philosophers and monarchs. Frederick the Great, King of Prussia, invited Voltaire to stay at his court and Voltaire gladly accepted. (Who wouldn't? A king paying for you to just sit and think!) There Voltaire gained an international reputation and influenced succeeding French philosophes.

Jean-Jacques Rousseau (1712–1778) was a contemporary of Voltaire who also helped to spread Enlightenment thinking. Rousseau's concept of the noble savage advanced the notion that civilization corrupts man, and that to return to a more pure and free state of nature would make man more virtuous. But mankind is restrained by the institutions of society, or, in his words from his work *The Social Contract*, "Man is born free, but everywhere he is in chains."

Rousseau's solution was to create a society through a social contract that would allow mankind to be free as possible. This society should be guided by the general will of the people. This, of course, was a cry for a democratic form of government. But his idea of the general will doesn't recognize minorities in society and the tyranny of the majority.

All of these ideas that took shape in Rousseau's writing were and still are very influential in the area of political philosophy, but he had even more to say in other fields such as education. Building on John Locke's idea of *tabula rasa*, Rousseau wrote that children develop according to the environment around them. Additionally, he argued that kids should be understood as individuals and they need caring, not strictness and rigidity, from their parents and teachers.

DEFINITION

Tabula rasa means "blank slate" and is the state, John Locke argued in his *Essay Concerning Human Understanding,* in which humans are born.

The Other Three

The other three French philosophes who shaped the Enlightenment did so in a less broad fashion. Baron de Montesquieu (1689–1755), in his volume *Spirit of the Laws*, argued that the powers of the government should be separated in order to prevent any one person or institution from gaining too much power. Montesquieu believed that there should be three branches of government—the legislative, executive, and judicial. Each branch should have some power over the others, which he termed checks and balances. His ideas generated a lot of interest and served as the foundation of the governmental structure of the United States.

As a leading *physiocrat*, François Quesnay (1694–1774) believed in laissez-faire economics, in which government removed all restraints to free trade, including taxes and tariffs. With the restraints removed, the natural laws of economics would be free to operate and society would obtain its highest good.

DEFINITION

A **physiocrat** believes that land is the only source of wealth and revenue. Because of this, the freedom of opportunity to trade and secure property Is essential to prosperity.

Denis Diderot (1713–1784) was not so much a thinker as a compiler, collecting the writings and ideas of the philosophes of the Enlightenment. He then published these writings in his *Encyclopedia*, which was more of a collection of political and social criticisms. The *Encyclopedia* was a bestseller for the times and helped to popularize and spread the ideas of the Enlightenment.

WHAT IN THE WORLD

Very few women were able to break into the man's world of the Scientific Revolution and the Enlightenment. Mary Wollstonecraft (1759–1797) was an exception. Her well-known writing, *A Vindication of the Rights of Woman*, argued that women should have the same political and educational rights of men. Interestingly enough, she was also the mother of the famous author, Mary Shelley, who wrote *Frankenstein*.

The Later Enlightenment

The ideas of the Enlightenment were shaped in France and built upon by later English and German enlightened thinkers. Adam Smith (1727–1790), in *The Wealth of Nations*, expanded the philosophies of the French physiocrats and the idea of laissez-faire economics. The book was published in 1776 and is considered by most to provide the essential justification for capitalism, governed by these tenets:

- The economy of a nation is governed by natural laws.

- The essential natural law of economy is the law of supply and demand.

- In a free-market economy, competition will bring producers to produce goods more efficiently so they can sell quality, lower-cost goods.

- Government laws and regulations interfere with the natural laws of a self-governing economy.

Immanuel Kant (1724–1804) was a German enlightened philosopher who possibly ranks among the most influential thinkers in history. Kant led a quiet life. While teaching logic and metaphysics at a small university in Germany, he produced several volumes that detail the development of a complicated philosophical system. Needless to say, a complete summary of his works would be impossible in this volume; other philosophers such as Friedrich Hegel have spent years puzzling over and trying to organize his philosophies. But there are some general ideas that he argued decisively which have proven to be very influential on later thinkers.

Focusing on morality, Kant argued for the categorical imperative, that everyone should treat all actions as an end, not a means to an end. He also taught that the basis of moral order should be the freedom of will guided by absolute duty. Theologically, Kant believed that knowledge such as the existence of God or a Creator cannot be attained by human reason. Human reason has limits. Of course, so did Kant. His philosophy, sometimes called Kantianism, although thought-provoking and influential, was sometimes vague and contradictory. But others did build successfully on his system.

NOTABLE QUOTABLE

Enlightenment is man's emergence from his self-incurred immaturity. Immaturity is the inability to use one's own understanding without the guidance of another. This immaturity is self-incurred if its cause is not lack of understanding, but lack of resolution and courage to use it without the guidance of another.

—"An Answer to the Question: What is Enlightenment?," Immanuel Kant

A Recipe for Revolution

All of this Enlightenment not only had an effect on the intellectual life of Europe, but also the political life. Enlightened despotism became the rage among the monarchs of Europe. An enlightened monarch tried to advance the society of his state by fostering education, economic freedom, and social justice. In general the ruler used his power to promote the good of the people because he or she knew best.

Several European rulers qualified for the distinction of enlightened despot. Frederick the Great (r. 1740–1786) was one of the more famous. Using his military genius, he made Prussia into a major European power. Once established, Frederick became a patron of Voltaire, who influenced him to undertake domestic reforms, improve education, and codify laws in Prussia. Frederick also encouraged industry and immigration, and started a policy of religious tolerance.

WHAT IN THE WORLD

Frederick the Great built a summer palace named Sans Souci, French for "without cares." It was Frederick's favorite retreat from the politics of the court. The palace was also famous for midnight suppers that were attended by philosophers and artists who discussed the exciting new ideas of the Enlightenment.

Catherine the Great (r. 1762–1796), ruler of Russia, was a German who succeeded to the throne after the death of her husband, Czar Peter III. Catherine was heavily influenced by European continental culture and the ideas of the Enlightenment. She became a patron of French philosophes and instituted enlightened policies in Russia. But her enlightened side came to an end shortly after Pugachev's Rebellion, a social revolution that aimed to depose the monarch. From then on, Catherine kept a tight grip on the throne and the freedoms of the Russian people.

The final two enlightened monarchs were Maria Theresa (r. 1740–1780) and her son Joseph II (r. 1780–1790), who ruled the empire of Austria. Theresa was able, after some trouble claiming the throne, to centralize the government, promote free trade, and limit the power of the nobility. Her son took Enlightenment reform even further by guaranteeing the freedom of the press and religion and dismantling the remnants of serfdom.

The problem with enlightened despotism is that it was, in general, all wrong. An absolute ruler who controlled people's freedom wasn't what many thinkers envisioned the Enlightenment to be about. The Enlightenment was more bottom up, not top down. The people wanted more control over their freedoms and they were not going to take no for an answer, no matter how enlightened the ruler claimed to be. The stage was set for revolutions: the American and the French revolutions, to be exact, and these changed the course of European and world history.

The Least You Need to Know

- The astronomical discoveries of the sixteenth century created the ingredients necessary for the Scientific Revolution.
- Sir Isaac Newton's discovery of the law of gravity influenced scientists of the Scientific Revolution and philosophers of the Enlightenment.
- The Scientific Revolution and the Enlightenment created the foundations for the modern worldview based on science and reason.
- Enlightenment philosophies led some monarchs to work for the equality of their subjects.
- Enlightenment ideas also led to the events of the American and French revolutions.

Western Domination

Things only continued to improve for the European nations as they industrialized before everyone else. This industrialization helped to transform the interregional networks into a truly global trade network. The European nations started a renewed program of colonization called imperialism. As a result, most of the events from this time are other people's reaction to the West's assertion of power throughout the world. But just when Europe was on top, western nationalism became too potent of a force and, beginning with World War I, the European domination of the world ceased to be.

Revolutions

In This Chapter

- The British Empire
- The American Revolution
- The French Revolution
- The rise and fall of Napoleon
- The Latin American revolutions

The ideas of the Enlightenment created a series of revolutions against monarchs and empires of Europe during the same period that the European powers were expanding their explorations and creating global empires.

The United Kingdom of Great Britain

England succeeded in colonizing North America and many other portions of the world, creating a united empire upon which "the sun never set."

In 1707, England consolidated its rule over Scotland to create the United Kingdom of Great Britain. Soon afterward, in 1714, a new dynasty, the Hanoverians, sat on the throne after the death of the last Stuart, Queen Anne.

The Hanoverian Kings

The Hanoverian monarchs, being German in origin, did not understand the nature of British government and law. So George I (r. 1714–1727) and George II (r. 1727–1760) handed the reins of government to their chief ministers and Parliament. Two ministers, George Walpole and William Pitt, the Elder, used their positions to strengthen Great Britain. Walpole was chief minister from 1721 to 1742 and pursued a peaceful foreign policy, favoring the expansion of trade throughout the British Empire. Pitt expanded the empire by acquiring territories in Canada and India during the Seven Years' War.

All together, the British Empire consisted of territories in North America including the 13 American colonies, India, and Africa. The expansion of the empire increased the United Kingdom's political and economic power in Europe and globally.

The British Colonies in North America

The colonies on the eastern seaboard of North America were populated with a diverse group of English settlers who came to America for a variety of reasons. Some sought religious freedom, some self-government, and others the acquisition of land and wealth. In general, the British left the colonies to themselves, governed loosely by the British Board of Trade, the Royal Council, and Parliament. Everything appeared to be in order, but the roots of revolt were there.

The American Revolution

There were several long- and short-term reasons the North American colonies revolted. In the long term, the colonies had a history of self-government that could not be ignored. The Pilgrims who came to America seeking religious freedom in 1620 created the Mayflower Compact, a charter of self-government. In Virginia, the colony of Jamestown created a representative government based on the English parliamentary model with the Virginia House of Burgesses. Other colonies followed their examples.

Also in the long term, the territory of America, with its open spaces and vast lands to the West, seemed to engender independent spirits. Couple this with the Enlightenment ideas that spread throughout the libraries of Europe and America, and freedom became an important ideal for the colonists.

In the short term, several events and policies pushed the colonists to seek independence. The Seven Years' War in North America (known in America as the French and Indian War) lasted from 1756 to 1763. This war pitted the British against the French and various Native American tribes on the western borders of the colonies. The British were able to win out, and as a result were able to acquire more territory west of the colonies. The colonists saw the new territories as new areas to settle, but the British did not see the same vision. They saw the territories as a buffer zone between the colonists and the Native American population, who came into conflict often. If the colonists settled these territories, the British would have to spend economic resources that they did not have to protect them—on top of their expenditures on the war itself.

NOTABLE QUOTABLE

Is life so dear, or peace so sweet, as to be purchased at the price of chains and slavery? Forbid it, Almighty God! I know not what course others may take, but as for me, give me liberty or give me death!

—Patrick Henry to Virginia House of Burgesses

Read Our Lips: No New Taxes!

To make tensions between the British government and the colonists worse, the British government began to pursue an economic policy of mercantilism. Then George III (r. 1760–1820) and Parliament levied new taxes on the colonists to pay for the debts of the French and Indian War. The colonists in America, used to self-government, were outraged by the heavy-handedness of the government in England.

The first tax that outraged the colonists was the Stamp Act of 1765, which placed a tax on all printed materials, such as legal documents and newspapers. (The "stamp" on the document would show proof that the tax had been paid.) The colonists' opposition, centered in the Boston area, was violent and spread through the colonies. Tax collectors were tarred and feathered. Shocked and aghast at the reaction, Parliament repealed the tax in 1766, but tried several more methods of collecting taxes from the colonists, including the addition of more British soldiers to keep the peace.

The colonists united in protest in 1774 at the First Continental Congress in Philadelphia and wrote a strongly worded letter of protest to King George III. In April 1775, a colonist militia engaged British occupation forces at Lexington and Concord, Massachusetts, with mixed results. Finally the colonists had had enough of the British, and on July 4, 1776, the Second Continental Congress declared independence and established an army to be led by former British officer and colonist George Washington. The American Revolution was underway.

Yankee Doodle Dandies

Washington and his ragtag army spent most of its time in constant retreat. The British controlled most of the northern colonies during the revolution. The French, rivals of the British in Europe, saw the revolution as an opportunity to spite the British in America. They supplied the colonists with money and arms. The French also supplied officers to help Washington with his command, one of whom was the famous Marquis de Lafayette. The Spanish and Dutch eventually entered on the side of the French to provide naval support to the colonists, all to spite the British and their growing empire.

These combined efforts paid off and, in 1781, American forces led by Washington and helped by a French navy forced General Cornwallis and British forces to surrender at Yorktown. At that point, the British had enough of the war and a treaty was drawn up in 1783. The Treaty of Paris recognized American independence and gave the former colonists all of the territories west to the Mississippi River.

Forming a New Nation

The Americans had a formidable job ahead in forming a new nation. Using a huge helping of Enlightenment political philosophy, the former colonists drafted the Articles of Confederation in 1781 to serve as a framework for their government. This decentralized government did not work well when confronted with domestic problems, so 55 delegates from the 13 states met in the summer of 1787 to draft a new constitution.

The United States Constitution created a federal system of government that balanced power between the state and national governments. It also provided for a separation of powers between three branches of government: judicial, legislative, and executive. Finally, the U.S. Constitution based its powers on the sovereignty of the people.

Not all of the delegates were happy with the Constitution. Many complained that it lacked the explicit guarantee of certain rights. As a result, in 1789, 10 amendments were added to the Constitution and called the Bill of Rights. These amendments guaranteed the freedom of religion, press, speech, petition, and assembly. The amendments also gave Americans the right to bear arms; protection from unreasonable searches, seizures, and arrests; the right to trial by jury and due process of law; and property rights. All of the Bill of Rights derived from the ideas of natural rights found in Enlightenment philosophy. Sadly, initially these rights did not apply to women and blacks, but eventually they were extended to all Americans.

The French Revolution—Off With His Head!

Not to be outdone and also influenced by Enlightenment philosophy, the French followed the Americans in revolution. But their revolution had some other distinct causes and more bloody twists and turns.

The Old Regime

One of the older and deeper causes involved the French social structure. During the eighteenth century this social structure was still dominated by the Old Regime, a rigid structure of the feudal past. The Old Regime had divided French society into three estates. The first estate was the Catholic clergy, which numbered roughly over 1,000 and controlled 10 percent of the land in France. The second estate consisted of the nobility, which numbered over 300,000 and owned 30 percent of the land. Both of these estates were exempt from the government *taille*, or tax.

The third estate, which made up 95 percent of the population, included peasants and the growing middle class, or bourgeoisie. They shouldered the tax burden for France. Of course, this social inequality did not hold much water with the spreading ideas of the Enlightenment, and as the bourgeois classes grew in numbers and economic power, many resented the tradition of the Old Regime.

Economic Problems

There were also other, more immediate causes of the French Revolution. For the last century the French government had spent more money than it had on palaces and wars, including helping colonists during the American Revolution. The government was close to bankruptcy and the French economy was in bad shape. Additionally, French farmers experienced two very bad harvests in 1787 and 1789, which caused food prices to rise considerably. In contrast to this economic hardship, the French royal court continued its extravagant ways at the Palace of Versailles, and Queen Marie Antoinette was not shy about publicizing her excess.

So in 1789, with the economy suffering and the government in need of money, King Louis XVI (r. 1774–1792) called a meeting of the Estates General, France's legislative body, which had not met since 1614. He wanted the Estates General to rubber-stamp his proposal to raise taxes. What Louis XVI got was something he did not want: revolution!

The Estates General, made up of representatives of each of the estates of the Old Regime, met at the Palace at Versailles on May 5, 1789. Almost immediately, the third estate wanted to abolish the tax exemptions of the other two estates, since they paid the lion's share of the taxes (up to 50 percent of their income). In addition, the third estate wanted to create a constitutional government. This type of measure could never be passed because each estate had one vote and the first two estates would always protect their interests. The third estate, sensing the inequity of the situation, called for each member to have a vote rather than the old system of one estate and one vote. At this point, Louis XVI ordered the old system of voting in the Estates General to remain. If the third estate was going to abolish the inequality of the system, they were going to have to do it themselves.

Gauls Gone Wild

On June 17, 1789, the third estate declared itself a National Assembly. Outraged, the other two estates locked the third estate out, so they assembled at a nearby indoor tennis court and wrote the French constitution. By this time Louis XVI had had enough of the third estate's little rebellion and threatened to use force to put them back in their place. It was then that Parisians, led by members of the third estate, responded by marching on the prison fortress of the Bastille on July 14 (which remains a national holiday to this day and a symbol of the revolution). The fall of the Bastille put weapons in the hands of the Parisians, who were fearful that the king would send an army to take the city. Everyone was on a high state of alert.

The third estate was not idle during this time. On August 4, they abolished the special rights of the first and second estates. More important, on August 26, the third estate drafted the Declaration of the Rights of Man and the Citizen, inspired by the United States' Declaration of Independence and Constitution and the English Bill of Rights.

In the document, the basic liberties of French citizens were spelled out. Freedoms and equal rights for all men were assured. No longer would there be tax exemptions for the first and second estates. All male citizens had a right to take part in the lawmaking process and all public offices were open to men of talent. Oddly, with all of these rights, nothing was guaranteed for French women. It was Olympe de Gouges who wrote the Declaration of the Rights of Woman and the Female Citizen, which was promptly ignored by the male population.

During this time King Louis XVI remained at the Palace of Versailles and refused to accept any of the pronouncements of the National Assembly. Finally, a group of women had had enough of his sandbagging. On October 5, the mob, tired of the lack of bread in Paris, marched on Versailles. They forced the king to accept the decrees of the National Assembly and also made the king and his family return to Paris as prisoners of the French people.

WHAT IN THE WORLD

Bread was the major component of the diet of an average Parisian in 1789. Typically, each person ate four pounds of bread a day. So supplying the city of Paris with a population of 600,000 was a huge production.

The National Assembly was not finished. They wanted to reform the Church in France, which was seen as a pillar of the old order. As a result, the National Assembly seized and sold all of the lands of the Church. They also enacted the Civil Constitution of the Clergy, which made provisions for bishops and priests to be elected by the people and paid by the state. Additionally, any Catholic who did not accept this new state of affairs was considered an enemy of the revolution.

The final act of the National Assembly was to write the Constitution of 1791. With this document the National Assembly dissolved itself and created a constitutional monarchy with a legislative assembly of 745 members having the majority of the political power. Males continued to have the same rights, and additionally only men over 25 who paid taxes could vote. Many opposed this new constitutional monarchy, including Catholics, priests, nobles, the lower classes, and radicals. To make matters worse, war loomed on the horizon.

War

Austria and Prussia were not happy with the goings-on in France; they wanted the French monarchy restored to its proper place. Most of the monarchies of Europe were interrelated through various marriages and desired to have a conservative and stable Europe. Not wanting Austria and Prussia to strike first, the Legislative Assembly declared war on Austria in the spring of 1792. But the war did not go well for the French, and the revolution seemed to lose its shine as economic hardship gripped the entire country.

To some degree the economic hardship made the revolution go radical. The hardship led to the rise of the radical communes in Paris. These radical groups, dissatisfied with the direction of the Legislative Assembly and the revolution, attacked the royal palace and the Legislative Assembly in Paris. They took the king captive and called for a National Convention to be chosen based on universal male suffrage.

The National Convention Meets

In September 1792, the National Convention, acting as a ruling body, abolished the monarchy completely and established the French Republic. Some refused to accept its decisions. The Paris Commune favored radical change, while some provinces did not acknowledge its existence. The National Convention also decided the fate of King Louis XVI. A group called the Girondins feared mob retaliation and wanted to keep the king alive. A group of Paris radicals called the Mountain wanted the king dead. In the end, the Mountain won and in 1793 the National Convention ordered the king put to death by a new method called the guillotine.

> **NOTABLE QUOTABLE**
>
> The tree of liberty does not flourish unless moistened with the blood of kings. I vote for death.
>
> —Bertrand Barère in the National Convention on the fate of Louis XVI

Reign of Terror, Republic of Virtue

The death of King Louis XVI and Marie Antoinette by the guillotine sent shockwaves throughout Europe. The monarchs of Europe were nervous about the implications and probably collectively rubbed their necks. As a result, an informal coalition was assembled to put an end to the Revolution. Spain, Portugal, Britain, the Dutch Republic, and Russia armed for war against France and were ready to invade by 1793.

The informal coalition of nations scared the French people and the National Convention. As a result, the convention gave special powers to a committee of 12 men known as the Committee of Public Safety. This committee was dominated by George Danton and Maximilien Robespierre. From 1793 to 1794, a period known as the Reign of Terror, they ordered the execution (most by guillotine) of over 40,000 people, supposedly in defense of the Revolution and France. Most were people who openly questioned the convention. Paranoia was rampant. The Revolution had been radicalized.

It was also during this time that the convention instituted the Republic of Virtue. The main thrust of this movement was the de-Christianization of public life. All references to saints were removed from the public. Churches were closed. A new calendar was adopted that incorporated terms of the Revolution with the first year of the

Republic as the first year. Church holidays and Sundays were eliminated and people were told to worship at the altar of reason at the Cathedral of Notre Dame. Most of these efforts failed to work on the French people, but it did demonstrate the zealotry of the radicals of the Revolution.

The National Convention mobilized the entire French nation for war on August 23, 1793. The mobilization produced an army of over a million men. By its sheer size, this army was able to push the invading informal alliance out of France and even conquer the Austrian Netherlands. The People's Army had prevailed, the Revolution was saved, and there was no longer a need for the Committee of Public Safety. Robespierre had made many enemies, and on July 28, 1794, the National Convention ordered his execution by guillotine. (Poetic justice!)

Revolution in Moderation

At this point in the revolution, moderates took over the National Convention. They allowed churches to reopen and created a new constitution in August 1795. The new constitution created a National Legislative Assembly made of two houses. The lower house, called the Council of 500, initiated legislation. The upper house, called the Council of Elders, accepted or rejected the laws and also elected five directors who served as an executive committee. Universal male suffrage proved too radical for the moderates, so this new legislative body was elected by only owners of property.

The executive committee known as the Directory ruled from 1795 to 1799. During this time, corruption spread throughout the National Legislative Assembly. France's economic problems again started to escalate, while an end to the Directory was plotted by a tide of royalists who supported the return of the monarchy and radicals who wanted a return to the radical Revolution. The Directory needed strong leadership, and it got more than it needed.

The Rise of Napoleon

Napoleon Bonaparte was an unlikely candidate to end up ruler of France and—for a time—master of Europe. He was born on the island of Corsica to an Italian family in 1769. Napoleon was ambitious enough to receive a scholarship to study at military school in France. In 1785, he was commissioned as a lieutenant of artillery in the French army. Napoleon rose quickly in the ranks to brigadier general by the age of 25.

In 1796, as commander of the French armies in Italy, he defeated the Italian states and forced them into signing a peace treaty with France. These victories made him a hero and resulted in a cult following. As a result, Napoleon was given command of an army to invade Britain. Rather than invade the island nation, he struck at Britain's territorial possessions in Egypt. This strategy failed miserably, due in part to the fact that the British Admiral Nelson controlled the Mediterranean Sea. So Napoleon abandoned his army to die in the sands of Egypt and returned to France. Strangely, he was welcomed as a returning hero.

The Takeover

With his hero status intact, Napoleon took part in a *coup d'état* that overthrew the Directory. The new government, called the Consulate, was led by three men, including Napoleon. Eventually Napoleon, as first consul, took control of the entire French government, appointing members of the bureaucracy, controlling the army, conducting foreign affairs, and influencing the legislature. In 1802, he was made consul for life, and in 1804, with all pretenses of democratic rule set aside, Napoleon crowned himself Emperor Napoleon Bonaparte I. The French Revolution had come full circle.

DEFINITION

A **coup d'état** is a French term used to designate a sudden, violent, and forcible overthrow of a government by a small group of people with military or political authority.

As political leader of France, Napoleon recognized that several changes were needed to gain stability. In 1801, he established peace with the pope and the Roman Catholic Church by recognizing Catholicism as the religion of France. In return, the pope agreed not to seek the restoration of Church lands in France. Napoleon also consolidated France's hundreds of legal systems into seven simplified legal systems. The most progressive of those legal systems was the Napoleonic Code. It codified the laws of equality, religious toleration, abolition of serfdom and feudalism, and property rights. Sadly, the Napoleonic Code took the right of property from women and treated them as minors in the legal system. Napoleon also established a new French bureaucracy in which promotion was based on merit and ability. As a result, the French bureaucracy started to be populated by a middle-class majority that supported Napoleon's policies.

WHAT IN THE WORLD

Napoleon exported the Napoleonic Code to Europe and even France's colonies in North America. Today, Louisiana, once part of the French Empire in North America, still has laws based on the Napoleonic Code.

Questions nagged the people of France when Napoleon became emperor. Was the revolution over? Was the revolution going to continue? Napoleon's civil code and his new bureaucracy suggested that the revolution was still alive. But the liberties given to the French were provided by a despot, not the people. Government police routinely opened private mail and stopped publications that printed materials against Napoleon.

The Grand Empire

Regardless of the question at home, Napoleon saw himself as an extension of the revolution, and he wanted to take it on the road. But in order to spread the revolution, he needed peace and time to regroup. So in 1802, Napoleon negotiated a peace treaty with Russia, Great Britain, and Austria, with whom France had been at war off and on since 1799. He prepared his armies and by 1803 was back at war with Great Britain, Austria, Russia, and Prussia. This time Napoleon and the French armies were ready. They were able to defeat and force all of the nations of Europe except for Great Britain into submission by 1807. Napoleon had created the Grand Empire.

The Grand Empire lasted from 1807 to 1812. It consisted of several different groupings of nations and territories. The first was the French Empire, which included the territory of France to the Rhine River and the northern half of Italy. The Dependent states included Spain, Holland, Italy, the Swiss Republic, the Grand Duchy of Warsaw, and all of the German states except Prussia and Austria. A majority of these states were ruled by relatives of Napoleon. Finally, the last part of the Grand Empire was the Allied states of Prussia, Austria, Russia, and Sweden, all of which promised support to Napoleon.

To some degree, Napoleon's Grand Empire did spread the Revolution. He force-fed the conquered states the Napoleonic Code, which provided for legal equality, religious toleration, and economic freedom. Napoleon also abolished the privileges of the nobility and clergy in the European states. For a while, these measures made Napoleon a popular ruler with the people of Europe.

The Thorn in the Lion's Paw

The lion that was the Grand Empire did have a thorn in its paw. Napoleon could not get Great Britain to submit. Although Napoleon controlled the European continent, the British controlled the seas around it, a point punctuated when the British soundly destroyed the combined French and Spanish naval fleets at the Battle of Trafalgar in 1805.

Napoleon retaliated by creating a policy called the Continental System. The policy banned all import of British goods to Europe. Napoleon hoped to weaken the British economy, but the Allied states cheated and imported British goods anyway. In the end British exports were at an all-time high, and so was the British economy.

Napoleon's Big Mistake

As the British thumbed their collective noses at Napoleon, a new movement called nationalism spread throughout Europe, indirectly influenced by the ideas of the Enlightenment and the Revolution. Nationalism was the belief that each nation should be based on the cultural identity of its people, including their language, religion, ethnicity, and national symbols. The different nationalist movements looked to France as a model of nationalism, but it was a love/hate relationship. Nationalist movements hated foreign oppressors, and the French were oppressing most of Europe.

Nations began to resist the directives of Napoleon and the Grand Empire. In 1812, the Russians refused to be part of the Continental System. In retaliation, Napoleon invaded Russia in June 1812 with the Grand Army, which numbered over 600,000 men. He was hoping for a quick and decisive battle, but the Russians, knowing that Napoleon would need supplies for his army, refused to fight and retreated eastward, burning the countryside as they did. By the time Napoleon reached Moscow on September 15, 1812, it was empty and on fire, providing the French armies no supplies or haven from the harsh Russian winter. Napoleon was forced to retreat; much like in Egypt, he deserted his army to return to Paris. Only 40,000 men of the Grand Army made it back to France.

With Napoleon's Grand Army in shambles, the nations of Europe rose up against France. Their combined armies captured Paris in March of 1814. Napoleon was sent into exile to the island of Elba in the Mediterranean Sea. The Bourbon monarchy was restored and Louis XVIII (r. 1814–1825), the brother of Louis XVI, was placed on the throne. The nations of Europe breathed a collective sigh of relief. The revolution was over.

Waterloo

Just as everyone let their guard down, Napoleon slipped back into France. The king of France, who had little support amongst the French people, sent troops to capture Napoleon. They promptly welcomed the emperor and joined him in his march to Paris. Napoleon entered Paris on March 20, 1815, and raised an army to attack the nearest allied forces in Belgium.

On June 18, 1815, the French engaged a combined force of British and Prussians under the command of the Duke of Wellington at Waterloo. The Battle of Waterloo remained close most of the day, but in the end Napoleon and his forces were defeated. This time the European nations sent Napoleon into exile even farther away, to a small island in the south Atlantic Ocean called St. Helena, where he died in 1821. Again the European nations hoped it was the end of revolutions, but it was just the beginning.

The Revolutions Never Seem to End

The Spanish territories in Central and South America also followed the Americans and the French with revolutions.

The first took place in the French colony of Saint Domingue on the island of Hispaniola, east of Cuba. Over 100,000 slaves led by Toussaint L'Ouverture took control of the western portion of the island. On January 1, 1804, they declared their freedom and became Haiti, the first independent state of Latin America.

Mexico followed in 1821 by declaring its independence from Spain. By the end of 1824, Peru, Uruguay, Paraguay, Colombia, Venezuela, Argentina, Bolivia, and Chile had all gained independence from Spain, with the inspired leadership of the Latin American generals Simón Bolívar and José de San Martín. These men have been compared to the founders of the United States, such as George Washington and Alexander Hamilton. In 1822, Brazil had gained independence from Portugal. The Central American states gained freedom in 1823 and by 1839 had emerged as Guatemala, El Salvador, Honduras, Costa Rica, and Nicaragua.

Most of these countries wrote constitutions similar to those of the United States and European democracies. However, large landowners, becoming very prosperous growing export crops such as coffee, limited voting rights to keep political and economic power. Not until the twentieth century did freedoms and liberties truly give power to the entire populations of these countries.

The Least You Need to Know

- The British Empire became the most powerful economic entity during the eighteenth century.
- The American Revolution against British rule and taxes was inspired by the ideas of the Enlightenment.
- The French Revolution was the result of poor economic conditions in France and poor judgment by the French monarchy.
- Napoleon rose to rule France and brought the ideals of the French Revolution to the rest of Europe.
- The American and French revolutions inspired the revolutions of the Latin American nations as they cast off European rule.

The Industrial Revolution

In This Chapter

- The origins of the Industrial Revolution
- The early industrialization
- Reaction to the Industrial Revolution
- The Industrial Revolution expands
- The transformation of culture and industrialization

The Industrial Revolution that started in Great Britain during the late 1700s was the practical application of the knowledge gained from the Scientific Revolution and the Enlightenment. This revolution created and spread modernization to the world.

The Industrial Revolution Begins

Why did the Industrial Revolution start in Great Britain during the 1780s rather than elsewhere? The agricultural practices of Great Britain during the eighteenth century had changed, resulting in more food at lower prices. Ordinary families had more money with which to buy manufactured goods. More food also meant families had more children, resulting in a population surge that became a large labor force.

The import/export policies of the British Empire based on Enlightenment ideas about free trade also helped. Many entrepreneurs had become wealthy off of commerce and wanted to invest that newfound wealth. The British Empire itself was a large, untapped market for manufactured goods, which encouraged industrial development. Finally, natural resources such as coal and iron ore—used to fuel the Industrial Revolution—were abundant and easy to acquire in Great Britain.

Oh, So Soft

The cotton industry in Britain was originally a cottage industry, in which industrial production was actually done by individual families who produced cloth in their homes. The process of producing cotton was broken down into two parts: spinning and weaving. Spinning, or making thread, became faster with the invention of the spinning jenny by James Hargreaves in 1768. Weaving also became much faster with the flying shuttle and then the water-powered loom invented by Edmund Cartwright in 1787.

WHAT IN THE WORLD

James Hargreaves, who named his invention the spinning jenny after his wife, tried to keep the invention a secret, but to no avail. Others became suspicious of the large amounts of yarn his family produced. In anger they broke into his house, and when they found his spinning jenny, the mob of workers destroyed it.

Soon cotton mills emerged near streams and rivers across Britain. With the invention of the steam engine by James Watt, looms and machinery did not need to be located near rivers and streams. The cotton industry had become quite profitable. Raw cotton was imported from the southern United States and India, made into cotton cloth, and exported throughout the world. By 1840, it was Britain's most valuable export.

Black Coal and Iron Rails

With the invention of the coal-fired steam engine, coal had to be mined in Britain in large quantities. Additionally, iron was used to build the tools and machines of the mills. This industrial production also depended on coal mining. Thus the new industry of coal mining spread across Britain.

Iron production also improved to keep pace with the demands of the cotton mills. The process of puddling was invented by Henry Cort. In this process, *coke* derived from coal was used to burn away the impurities found in crude iron. This allowed for the production of better-quality iron. With better-quality iron, the demand for iron increased and the iron industry grew exponentially in Britain.

DEFINITION

Coke is the coal created after most of the gases have been removed from it by heating it. This form of coal burns with intense heat and little smoke.

With the expanding production and demand for cotton, coal, and iron, transportation became a priority. As a result, in 1804 the first steam-powered locomotive operated on an industrial rail line. By the mid-nineteenth century, there were over 5,000 miles of railroad in Britain.

The emergence of the railroad meant that it was less expensive to ship goods to the market, which helped lower prices across the board. Additionally, there were more and larger markets for goods, which meant more sales ... which meant that the economy of Britain was booming.

NOTABLE QUOTABLE

By machines mankind are able to do that which their own bodily powers would never effect to the same extent. Machines are the produce of the mind of man; and their existence distinguishes the civilized man from the savage.

—William Cobbett, "A Letter to the Luddites," 1816

The Spread of the Industrial Revolution

By industrializing first, Britain was producing one half of the world's coal and manufactured goods. As a result, it became one of the richest and most powerful nations of the nineteenth century. The British wanted to keep the technology of industrialization to themselves, but they could not. During the early nineteenth century, Belgium, France, and the German states actively encouraged industrialization with strong government support for industry.

In due time, the Industrial Revolution spread to North America. Six out of seven workers were involved in agriculture at the start of the nineteenth century. By the mid-nineteenth century, only 50 percent of the workers in America were farmers. The geographic center of this industrialization was the Northeast; eventually, roads and canals linked this region to the rest of the United States and the goods of industrialization became readily available to the whole population. Transportation of goods and people also improved with the invention of the wheel steamboat in 1807. Additionally, by the mid-nineteenth century there were over 30,000 miles of railroad in the United States. All of these factors allowed industrialization in the United States to catch up with Europe.

The social impact of the Industrial Revolution was significant. The population of Europe and America exploded—world population doubled from 1800 to 1850. There was a decline in death, wars, and diseases. People were well fed and more resistant to diseases. Famine in Europe and America virtually disappeared.

With Britain's economic boom, factories for different industries emerged across the country. These factories created new jobs and a new labor system. Workers now were scheduled in shifts based on set hours and duties. Families, including women and children, went to work in the factories, which were not entirely safe. British society began to change as a result of this population shift.

An industrial middle class emerged—the people who built and managed the factories, bought the machines, and predicted the markets for goods. Another class also emerged, the working class. Men, women, and children typically worked in the factories, sometimes 12 to 16 hours a day. Most were unskilled and replaceable. In time, children and women were prevented from working excessive hours, but working-class men continued the long hours well into the early twentieth century.

Both classes of people flocked to the cities, most of which were unprepared for the population surge and became large, crowded, unclean, and unsafe.

The Industrial Revolution Reloaded

The Industrial Revolution advanced even further during the second half of the nineteenth century. From 1870 to 1914, steel replaced iron in industry. It was lighter and could be used in the production of faster machines, engines, railways, ships, and weapons.

Electricity was converted into heat, light, and motion. Factories became filled with conveyor belts and cranes, which sped up production. Electric lightbulbs, invented by Thomas Edison, allowed factories to operate effectively night and day. The invention of the telephone in 1876 by Alexander Graham Bell and the harnessing of radio waves courtesy of Guglielmo Marconi in 1901 improved communication and commerce.

Finally, the internal combustion engine powered not by steam but by oil and gasoline revolutionized transportation. Goods traveled to market faster and cheaper than ever before. The world suddenly grew smaller as more people traveled greater distances with the emergence of ocean liners, airplanes, and automobiles.

New Trends and Global Patterns

These new developments created new trends in Europe and America. There was a sharp increase in the use of manufactured products. People became more dependent on the work of others to provide food, clothing, and shelter. Wages for workers increased as production became more advanced and specialized. The price of production goods fell as transportation and production became cheaper. And finally, the first department stores emerged during the late nineteenth century as the population spent more money on more produced goods.

As a result of the Industrial Revolution in Europe and America, a new global economic pattern emerged. Western Europe advanced industrially, while eastern Europe and the Iberian Peninsula remained primarily agricultural. Additionally, Europeans received beef and wool from Argentina and Australia, coffee from Brazil, iron ore from Algeria, and sugar from Java. In exchange for these raw materials, the Europeans supplied those countries manufactured goods. In this exchange the Europeans received the most control and profit, making those countries dependent on Europe. By the beginning of the twentieth century, Europe dominated the world market, and as a result dominated the world politically.

Competing Philosophies

During the late nineteenth century, in reaction to industrialization and its inequities, social parties, trade unions, and other more radical philosophies emerged in Europe and America. The negative results of the Industrial Revolution brought some creative and progressive responses.

Utopians Seek Perfection

Some people sought to create alternative utopian societies based on the belief that humans would show their natural goodness if they lived in a cooperative environment. Robert Owen, a successful cotton manufacturer, was a prominent utopian socialist who sponsored two *utopian communities*. The community in New Lanark, Scotland, was a success, but his community in New Harmony, Indiana, was a failure.

DEFINITION

A **utopian community** is founded upon ideas envisioning perfection in social and political organization. These communities are generally considered to be very idealistic.

Workers Wake Up

Marxism was a radical movement that formed as the result of the inequalities of industrialization. It was based on the case for a new social system Karl Marx and Friedrich Engels made in their joint work, *The Communist Manifesto.*

According to Marx and Engels, world history was a history of "class struggles" between the bourgeoisie, or middle class, and the proletariat, or working class. They believed that, eventually, the proletariat would revolt and take control of the means of production and see to it that resources and rewards were distributed evenly. The end result would be a classless society.

The theory was that this was a natural process ... but it might need a little push, in the form of a violent revolution. Not surprisingly, Marx and Engels were popular with the working class and not so popular with the middle class. Marxists tried to spread their ideas among the working class through newspapers and meetings and gained enough support to create political parties in the late nineteenth century.

Adherents to socialism were less radical than the Marxists and took a reformist approach to the inequalities of worldwide industrialization and capitalism. They believed in the equality of all people and wanted competition to be replaced with cooperation, but they wanted government to control the means of production to create equity. Socialist parties organized in the late nineteenth century in Europe. For example, the German Social Democratic Party (SPD) worked to improve the conditions of the working class, and by 1912, they held a majority of the seats in Germany's parliament. The Second International was a group of independent socialist parties from different countries who met frequently from 1889 to 1916.

Partly as an outgrowth of Marxist and socialist thought, the workers' union movement gained strength during the second half of the nineteenth century. Helped by the ability to strike, unions improved the working conditions for workers by shortening work hours and increasing wages.

WHAT IN THE WORLD

Peasants in the Netherlands wore traditional wooden shoes, called sabots, to work. When they started to be employed in the factories, they were intimidated by the speed and efficiency of the machines, and the workers threw their sabots into the machines to destroy the machines. Later the act of deliberately but secretively destroying an employer's property became known as sabotage.

This Is the Modern World

The push and pull of forces of progress and reform unleashed by the Industrial Revolution continued to significantly change the urban landscape and social structure.

Cities and Societies

A new urban landscape emerged from the crowded industrialized cities. Society's poor and working classes became a political concern like never before because, in dense urban populations, they were the key to political power. Elected officials in city governments started to regulate housing and initiate the development of new city systems of aqueducts, tunnels, and pipes to improve sanitation. As a result, although cities grew at a fast rate, living conditions actually began to improve.

Social structures in industrialized countries also continued to change during the second half of the nineteenth century. A new elite class emerged at the top of the social structure. Five percent of the population controlled 40 percent of the wealth and included landed aristocrats, industrialists, bankers, merchants, and government leaders. Below the elite class were the middle class, who were hard working and usually followed a strict Christian morality. The upper middle class included the managers of industry, while the lower middle class were generally shopkeepers who provided goods and services. Finally, the working class, mostly skilled and unskilled factory workers and domestic servants, continued to grow. They made up close to 80 percent of the population of Europe, and thanks to the spread of democracy and Enlightenment reforms, they had better political and economic prospects than lower classes of society had ever enjoyed.

Improvements for Women

The Industrial Revolution also brought a change in the status of women in Europe and America. Traditional farms had needed lots of farmhands—kids—but, since most of the population migrated from the farm, the number of births per woman declined. This gave women a degree of freedom. Middle-class women used this freedom to stay at home and raise the family. Working-class women used this freedom to enter the workforce as unskilled laborers, clerks, or domestic servants.

During the early nineteenth century, the feminist movement emerged from Europe, possibly in response to new positions in society that women obtained. By 1870 in Great Britain, women received the right to own property and gained access to universities. Women also fought for political rights beginning in the mid-nineteenth century. By the early twentieth century, women had acquired the right to vote. And although careers were still socially limited to women, they made initial steps in the career fields of education and nursing.

Yes, You Have to Go to School!

During the time of the Industrial Revolution, universal education for all citizens became a priority, for several reasons. First, if children were in school, they weren't running in the streets or working in unsafe factories. There also was a new need for skilled laborers in the factories of the late nineteenth century, and education created better skilled laborers.

Finally, education made informed citizens who could be trusted to vote and defend the interests of the nation. With these benefits in mind, governments financed primary schools and forced children to attend from the ages of 6 to 12 at least. As a result, literacy rates in Europe and America rose dramatically. This also gave rise to the importance of newspapers in the late nineteenth century, which tended to be sensationalistic and easy to read. (Not much has changed!)

Too Much Time on Their Hands

The last development that resulted from the Industrial Revolution was the increase of leisure time among the population. People had more time available to them than ever before. Unions and technological developments gave the public evening hours, weekends, and sometimes even two weeks in the summer to enjoy. Electric lights allowed events and activities to go on all night. Tacky, colorful, and fun amusement parks sprouted up across Europe and America. Governments created nature parks for families to get away from urban crowding and stress.

Athletic events such as baseball, football, soccer, rugby, cricket, and basketball became popular to play. People also watched professionals play these games in the new stadiums being built in the cities. If those activities were not interesting, the public went to the theater in the evenings to see plays and musicals.

Mixed Reviews

In the end, the Industrial Revolution began the modernization of the world, at first in Europe and the United States. This was a good thing. The quality of life increased with each passing year throughout the world. But this development allowed the West to continue its domination of global economics and politics. Most of the other countries of the world were forced to play catch-up. Resentment toward the West started to build while competition in the West also started to heat up, all of which led to a tumultuous twentieth century.

The Least You Need to Know

- The Industrial Revolution was the result of the practical application of the ideas of the Scientific Revolution and the Enlightenment.
- The Industrial Revolution spread from Great Britain to Europe and America during the first half of the nineteenth century.
- The industrialization of nations changed the nature of culture and society significantly by the second half of the nineteenth century.
- Marxism, socialism, and unions represent some of the response to the inequalities of a new industrialized society.

Revolutions and Reactions

In This Chapter

- The Congress of Vienna
- The Concerts of Europe
- Nationalism and liberalism
- The revolutions of 1830 and 1848
- The other movements of the nineteenth century

During the nineteenth century, two important ideologies, nationalism and liberalism, emerged to have a significant effect on Europe and the world. The Congress of Vienna and the Concerts of Europe were a conservative response to these ideas, which appeared to undermine European stability and the old conservative order. The conservative order ended in political infighting, and by the late nineteenth century, democracy influenced by nationalism and liberalism gained ground among a majority of the nations of Europe. In addition, other ideologies like Romanticism, realism, modernism, Marxism, and socialism reflected a shift in Western thought.

The Congress of Vienna

After the fall of Napoleon, most of the European nations wanted to restore things back to the old order. Great Britain, Austria, Prussia, and Russia met at the Congress of Vienna in September 1814, led by the Austrian foreign minister Prince Klemons von Metternich.

With Metternich's guidance and direction, the Congress made several decisions. Monarchs were to be restored based on dynastic legitimacy. Additionally, nations, states, and territories were to be rearranged to create a balance of power among the European nations. Little attention was given to the different nationalities and ethnic groups within these territories. In other words, the emerging nationalist movement wasn't considered at the Congress of Vienna.

The Congress of Vienna was a victory for *conservatives* against the ideas and forces of the French Revolution. To maintain this conservative balance in Europe, the nations of Europe held periodic meetings called the Concerts of Europe to discuss issues and problems. The Concerts also advocated military intervention to maintain the conservative order and put out the flames of revolution in any European nation. Of the nations of the Concert, Great Britain refused to accept this principle, believing that internal affairs of nations were best left alone. Regardless, the Concerts of Europe used military force to crush revolutions in Spain and Italy.

> **DEFINITION**
>
> The term **conservative** designates policies that support tradition and stability. During the early nineteenth century, conservatives believed in obedience to political authority and organized religion. Generally, conservatives were unfriendly toward revolution, mostly because the demands of people who wanted individual rights and representative governments were a threat to conservatives' property and influence.

Liberalism and Nationalism

Despite the Concerts of Europe's efforts, the ideas of Enlightenment and revolution spread throughout the continent. Two intellectual movements that swept Europe especially caused the Concerts problems.

Liberalism was a philosophical movement based on the ideas of the Enlightenment that asserted several loosely assembled tenets. First, people were to be as free as possible from government restraint. Government was to be used only to protect the civil liberties of the people, especially with religious tolerance and the separation of church and state. Liberalism also put an emphasis on the use of representative assemblies in which voting and office should be limited to men of property and the rule of constitutions.

Nationalism was also based on the ideas of the Enlightenment and spread indirectly with the conquests of Napoleon. Most nationalists believed that a nation should be made of people who had a common language, traditions, religions, and customs, and each nationality should have its own government. As a result of this thinking, for example, Germans wanted the rule of a single government, and so did the Hungarians. Of course, conservatives of the Concerts of Europe wanted to suppress this type of thinking, while followers of the tenets of liberalism supported it.

Revolution Reloaded

So the Concerts of Europe had their collective hands full. The movements of liberalism and nationalism fueled the European revolutions of 1830 and 1848.

The Revolutions of 1830 started with French liberals. They forcibly overthrew the French king, Charles X, who ruled like the kings of old, not realizing that times had changed. The liberals replaced the king with Louis-Philippe, the cousin of Charles X, and created a constitutional monarchy. During the same year, the Belgians instituted a nationalist rebellion against Dutch rule and became an independent nation. But rebellion and revolution did not work out well for everyone. Revolutions in Poland and Italy were crushed by the Russians and the Austrians, who remained loyal to the conservative perspective.

Just when it appeared that the fires of revolution had been put out, revolutionary movements broke out in France, Germany, and Austria in 1848. In France the seeds of revolution started with the economic problems of 1846. The lower middle class and working class were suffering. The landless middle class also wanted a right to vote, which the king refused. So in 1848 the monarchy was overthrown and a group of republicans created a provisional government, calling for an election based on universal male suffrage to create a Constituent Assembly to draft a new constitution for France. By November 4, 1848, a new constitution was written that built the Second Republic. This new government was the most democratic form of government that France had seen. It consisted of a single legislature and a president who was elected every four years. The first elections were held in December 1848, and Louis-Napoleon, the nephew of Napoleon, won by a huge margin.

In Germany, the cries for political change were just as loud as in France. The many different German princes and rulers responded with the promise of constitutions, free press, and jury trials. The German people also wanted the unification of Germany as a nation. As a result, a German parliament called the Frankfurt Assembly met in 1848 to prepare a constitution for a united Germany. But the political infighting was too much for the drafting process and unification was not achieved, to the disappointment of the German people.

Austria—a truly multinational nation made of Germans, Czechs, Hungarians, Slovaks, Romanians, Poles, Croats, Serbians, and Italians—also had a very hard time confining nationalistic tendencies and the problems associated with it. In March 1848, nationalist demonstrations took place in all of the major cities across Austria. Each nationality demanded self-rule. Quickly, the demonstrations got out of hand and revolutionary forces took control of Vienna, the capital, and demanded a liberal constitution. In response, the Austrian government gave Hungary its own legislature. Now with renewed Hungarian support, the Austrian government was able to crush the Czech and Viennese rebels. In 1849, Austria gained control of more territory, including the Italian states of Lombardy and Venetia. So nationalism in Austria had suffered a setback.

> **NOTABLE QUOTABLE**
>
> There will be no wars on questions of partition, domination, nationality and influence. No more weak and strong, oppressed and oppressors. Every country, free to enjoy its liberties and to live its own life, will hasten to enjoy the life and liberty of all.
>
> —*Histoire de la Révolution de 1848,* Etienne Garnier-Pagès

The End of the Concert

After the Revolutions of 1848, the Concerts of Europe began to unravel, creating the right environment for the unification movements of Italy and Germany.

The Crimean War

The beginning of the end of the Concerts started with the Crimean War. This war began as a conflict between Russia and the Ottoman Empire over political control in the Balkan Peninsula. In 1853, Russia invaded the kingdoms of Moldavia and Walachia. In response, the Ottoman Empire, Great Britain, and France declared war on Russia for threatening the balance of power of Europe.

The war was poorly planned and fought by all of the nations. The technology of weapons had improved with the Industrial Revolution, but the strategies had not. At the end of the conflict, Russia lost; with the Treaty of Paris of 1856, Moldavia and Walachia were placed under the protective custody of the great European powers. (Russia was excluded from the club!)

It spelled the end of the Concerts of Europe. The European nations who had tried to maintain a balance of power now reverted back to political games. Austria and Russia, which had previously worked together, became enemies because of their conflicts of interest in the Balkans (and because Austria refused to support Russia during the war). Russia, sulking after the loss of the war, withdrew from European political affairs. France and Great Britain also pulled back from European politics. With Austria politically weak and having no allies, the process of Italian and German reunification began.

Italian Unification

At first the Italian unification movement started with the Italian people. Eventually understanding the enormous task before them, the people looked to the north Italian state of Piedmont and King Victor Emmanuel II to provide leadership. Emmanuel II named Camillo di Cavour, a very able politician, prime minister and gave him the task of Italian unification. Cavour, being politically savvy, made a political alliance with France and then provoked the weak Austrians to invade Piedmont in 1859. Of course, Cavour's new French allies jumped at a chance to humble Austria. They invaded northern Italy and convinced other northern Italian states to overthrow their governments and unite with Piedmont before the Austrians were finally defeated.

WHAT IN THE WORLD

During the years of Italian unification, many Italians, unsure of political instability, immigrated to America. During a 50-year period, more than five million Italians came to America.

In southern Italy, a similar unification movement occurred. The Italian patriot Giuseppe Garibaldi raised an army of volunteers called Red Shirts to fight for unification. The Red Shirts took over Sicily and Naples in 1860. Afterward, Garibaldi turned over the territories to the state of Piedmont. On March 17, 1861, the new kingdom of Italy was proclaimed by King Victor Emmanuel II. Later, Italian unification advanced with the acquisition of Venetia in 1866 during the Austro-Prussian War, and in 1870 when the French withdrew from the Papal States during the Franco-Prussian War. On September 20, 1870, the unification of Italy was complete, with Rome as its capital.

German Unification

As in Italy, the German unification movement really began in earnest in the mid-nineteenth century. The German people looked to the militaristic state of Prussia for leadership. The Prussian King William I appointed Otto von Bismarck as prime minister. Bismarck, far from being idealistic, used realpolitik, or the politics of reality, to guide his actions. (For example, from 1862 to 1866 he governed Prussia without the approval of Parliament but with the approval of the people!) Bismarck did well collecting taxes and creating a better-trained and equipped army. He also pursued an active and militaristic foreign policy, which helped to unite Germany.

WHAT IN THE WORLD

Bismarck used German-caused wars to unify Germany, but, ironically, another German-caused war, World War II, divided the German nation. Germany wasn't united again until 1990.

In 1866, Austria and Prussia came to blows in the Austro-Prussian War. The well-equipped Prussian army won the war easily, with the payoff that the German states north of the Main River were organized into the North German Confederation, one step closer to unification. Seeing war as a great gateway to unification, Bismarck pushed France into declaring war on Prussia on July 15, 1870, over the succession of the Spanish throne. In support, the southern German states joined Prussia to fight France. On September 2, 1870, after a few quick strikes, the Prussian and German armies captured Napoleon III and the entire French army at Paris.

The dividends of the Franco-Prussian War were even better than those of the Austro-Prussian War. Now the German states were unified under one government—the Second German Empire. Additionally, France had to pay reparations to the tune of 5 billion francs and give up the territory of Alsace and Lorraine to the newly unified Germany. And on January 18, 1871, William I of Prussia was proclaimed kaiser. Germany was now the most powerful industrial and military power on continental Europe.

Liberalism and Nationalism in Other Nations

The revolutions and unification movements inspired by the ideas of liberalism and nationalism affected the other nations of the West as well.

The Victorian Age in Great Britain

In Great Britain, the rise of the industrial middle class increased the participation of male voters. In order to keep up, politicians pursued social and political reforms to keep this group happy and maintain stability, aided by the economic growth from the Industrial Revolution.

So nationalism manifested itself with the British in a safer form—national pride. The focal point of that national pride was Queen Victoria, who sat on the throne from 1837 to 1901, the longest-ruling British monarch. With the help of the queen, the British developed a sense of duty and moral responsibility toward their nation. This period in British history was known as the Victorian Age.

The Return of a Napoleon in France

In France, nationalism resulted in an authoritarian government. In the mid-nineteenth century, Louis-Napoleon entreated the French people to help him restore the glories of the empire. In response, an election was held in which 97 percent of the population voted to restore the empire and have Louis-Napoleon as emperor. On December 2, 1852, Napoleon III was crowned emperor of France.

Although nationalistic in origin, the Second Empire of France did not follow the ideals of liberalism. It was extremely authoritarian, with Napoleon having complete control over military, civil, and police forces. In addition, despite the appearances presented by the representative assembly called the Legislative Corps, Napoleon was the only one who introduced legislation and declared war. He also curtailed civil liberties and placed heavy-handed controls on the French government.

Despite Napoleon III's despotic rule, his first five years went well. Government-sponsored public works projects rebuilt Paris and put the unemployed French back to work. But the surge was only temporary; economic hardships eventually returned, and so did unrest among the people and the legislative assembly. Just when things appeared to be on the verge of revolution, the Franco-Prussian War ended Napoleon III's rule and the Second Empire in 1870.

Austria

Nationalism also forced changes in the Austrian Empire. After the Austro-Prussian War of 1866, Austria began to make concessions to different ethnic groups within the empire, the largest being the Compromise of 1867, which created a dual monarchy of Austria and Hungary. Each state had its own constitution, legislature, government bureaucracy, and capital. They did, however, share a common army, foreign policy, finances, and a single monarch, Francis Joseph, who also served as emperor of Austria and king of Hungary.

Russia and the End of Serfdom

Russia was less influenced by nationalism and more influenced by liberalism. Generally considered a backward nation because of its continued reliance on the institution of serfdom, Russia emancipated the serfs in 1861 at the bequest of Czar Alexander II. Peasants were allowed to own property and marry as they chose. The Russian government also provided land to the peasants by buying it from their former landlords.

These liberalized policies were not initially successful. Peasants usually received the poorest lands from the landlords, and starvation and disease increased dramatically. As a consequence, a radical group assassinated Alexander II in 1881. The heir to the throne, Alexander III, subsequently turned against the liberal policies of reform and returned to old repressive ways.

NOTABLE QUOTABLE

I claim not to have controlled events, but confess plainly that events have controlled me.

—Abraham Lincoln

The American Civil War

The United States was experiencing nationalist turmoil during this period as well. During the American Civil War from 1861 to 1865, the Northern and Southern states fought over the issues of slavery and state rule versus federal rule. Seven Southern states seceded from the Union in 1861 in response to the election of Abraham Lincoln as president, believing he represented a threat to states' rights, the institution of slavery, and their way of life in general. Eventually 11 states created the Confederate States of America.

Lincoln sent federal armies into the Confederates states, ostensibly to reclaim federal facilities seized by the Confederates, but also to force the issue of the union of the United States. The Confederates, although outgunned and outmanned, successfully resisted through superior generalship, led by General Robert E. Lee, and the war stretched into a long and bloody four-year struggle. As the war progressed, Lincoln issued the Emancipation Proclamation, which freed all slaves in the South. Eventually, Confederate forces were forced to surrender on April 9, 1865. The federal government in the United States reestablished its authority, and the enslaved African American population gained its freedom.

Oh, Canada!

Like many of the other Western nations, the nation of Canada had its origins associated with nationalism and liberalism. The British received the territory of Canada from the French in the Treaty of Paris at the end of the French and Indian War in 1763. By 1840, it had become known as the United Provinces of Canada, made up of Upper Canada, or Ontario, and Lower Canada, or Quebec.

Led by John MacDonald, the Conservative Party in Canada pushed Great Britain for independence. They received that independence in 1867 with the British North American Act, which established a Canadian nation, the Dominion of Canada. The nation drafted its own constitution based on the parliamentary system. John MacDonald was elected the dominion's first prime minister. Although the Canadians had self-rule on the domestic front, foreign affairs still remained in British hands. This did not bother the Canadians much, and to this day they extend that courtesy to Britain.

Other "Isms" of the Nineteenth Century

A whole host of other "isms" were very influential during the nineteenth century and into the twentieth century. They include Romanticism, secularism, realism, anti-Semitism, Zionism, and modernism.

Romantics and Realists

The movement called Romanticism emerged in Europe during the end of the eighteenth century as a reaction against what some thought was the overuse of reason in the Enlightenment. It emphasized feelings, emotion, and imagination, valuing individualism or the uniqueness of the person. Within the movement, there was also a strong interest in the medieval past, which led to the revival of Gothic styles called neo-Gothic.

In literature, these sentiments were reflected in the stories and poems of Walter Scott, Edgar Allen Poe, Mary Shelley, and William Wordsworth. Most of their works were viewed as direct expressions of the soul and exhibited a love of nature, criticism of science, and an exploration of the alienation of humans due to industrialization. In romantic art, there was an abandonment of classical reason for warmth and emotion with the use of exotic and passionate colors. Romantic art was also a reflection of the artist's innermost feelings. Romanticism circulated through music, too. Ludwig van Beethoven served as the bridge between the classical and romantic periods of music; most of his early works reflected the classical, while later works like the Ninth Symphony showed his romantic inner feelings.

The realism movement that developed during the second half of the nineteenth century was a reaction against Romanticism. Writers and artists of this movement wanted to portray ordinary life as it was (keep it real!). They tried to avoid romantic settings and language and, in literature, preferred novels to poems. Charles Dickens represented realist literature with books like *Oliver Twist* that focused on the harsh realities of working and middle-class life in Great Britain's Industrial Revolution.

Darwin and Natural Selection

In contrast to Romanticism was the movement called secularism, which reflected a general growing faith in the sciences. Sometimes this faith undermined the religious traditions of the people. Secularism advocated the belief that truth was to be found in the sciences, not religion or the humanities.

Charles Darwin represented the secular movement at its peak. In 1859, he published the volume *On the Origin of Species*. In the text, Darwin posited the theory of the evolution of species from earlier, simpler species. According to Darwin, the evolved species were naturally selected, meaning that those species that adapted more readily to the environment survived.

If this idea caused a stir, Darwin's next work, *The Descent of Man*, published in 1871, caused an explosion. Darwin stated that man was not exempt from natural selection, suggesting that man was related to other primates. All of this caused a controversy of ideas about the meaning and origin of life and religion.

Others, like Herbert Spenser, took Darwin's concepts of survival of the fittest and applied them to human society. Spenser saw social progress coming from the struggle for survival. This application became the rationale for many movements and injustices of the nineteenth and twentieth centuries, including imperialism, nationalism, capitalism, and racism.

Modernism

Modernism as a literary and artistic movement emerged as a reaction against realism during the late nineteenth and early twentieth centuries. This movement saw art and literature as symbols that reflected the true reality of the human mind. Within this movement were impressionism, postimpressionism, cubism, abstract expressionism, and functionalism.

Impressionism developed during the 1870s in France. Artists rejected the studio and painted outdoors, finding inspiration in the interplay of light and subject. Claude Monet best represented this school. Postimpressionism naturally followed impressionism during the 1880s, with artists like Vincent van Gogh, who saw art as spiritual and painted as he felt. Cubism followed postimpressionism with Pablo Picasso and his use of geometric designs to recreate reality. Next came abstract expressionism, with Wassily Kandinsky, who used line and color to avoid visual reality and believed that art should speak directly to the soul. Later, in architecture, Frank Lloyd Wright developed the idea of functionalism, designing useful buildings with no unnecessary ornamentation.

While modernism and its different creations progressed through the late nineteenth century, realism declined. In part this occurred because of the advent of photography. Artists came to the belief that they should not mirror reality, but create one as an individual expression. This was the beginning of what most have considered modern art.

Anti-Semitism

Sadly, during the second half of the nineteenth century, *anti-Semitism* reemerged in Europe. The Jewish people received the legal equalities of liberal reforms but still faced discrimination.

DEFINITION

Anti-Semitism is prejudice, discrimination, and hostility toward the Jewish people.

This was demonstrated in 1895 with the Alfred Dreyfus Affair, when a French Jew was unjustly found guilty of selling military secrets and condemned to life in prison. His guilt was really based on him being Jewish. In 1899, the real criminal, a French aristocrat, was brought to justice and Dreyfus was pardoned, but the case still illuminated the depth of anti-Semitism in Europe.

Houston Stewart Chamberlain also proved the point. This German leader preached the unfounded belief that Germans were pure successors of the Aryan race and Jews were enemies who wanted to destroy the Aryans. Although his beliefs were only nominally accepted, they did influence others at a later time.

Zionism

Almost in response to the anti-Semitism in Europe, the Zionist movement developed. During the nineteenth century, eastern Europe had a large Jewish population, but they faced many persecutions and pogroms, or organized massacres. So over 100,000 of these Eastern European Jews migrated to Palestine, although the Ottoman Turks opposed them stringently. This immigration to Palestine was the beginning of a nationalist movement to make the Jewish nation of Israel a reality in Palestine.

Spread of Democracy

The last movement of the nineteenth century was not an "ism," but it's just as important. Influenced by liberalism, democratic reforms spread across the West, with legislative assemblies and male and female suffrage. It advanced quicker in Great Britain and France, and slower in Germany, Italy, and Austria-Hungary. Democracy did not catch on at all in Russia, where Czar Nicholas II believed in the absolute power of the czar, although the Revolution of 1905 forced him to create the Duma with some legislative powers. It also moved forward in the United States after the American Civil War, when suffrage was granted to African American males. Women in America had to wait until later in the early twentieth century to gain suffrage. So democracy made advances in the West, but other parts of the world would have to wait.

The Least You Need to Know

- After the fall of Napoleon, two important ideologies—nationalism and liberalism—emerged to make a significant impact on Europe and the West during the nineteenth century.

- The Congress of Vienna and the Concerts of Europe were a conservative response to the ideas of nationalism and liberalism aimed at maintaining European stability.

- The conservativism of the Concerts of Europe came to an end with the Crimean War and the return of political infighting between the European powers.

- Other ideologies like Romanticism and realism reflected changes in Western culture.

- By the late nineteenth century, democracy started to gain ground among a majority of the nations of the West.

Imperialism

In This Chapter

- Imperialist motives
- Imperialism in Africa
- Nationalism in India
- The decline of the Qing dynasty
- The rise of Japan

At the beginning of the nineteenth century, a new stage of competition developed between the European nations. No longer was European exploration and colonization used to create trading posts; now the aim was vast territorial holdings. This new imperialism caused intense political rivalries between the nations of Europe.

Who Wants an Empire?

The motives for this imperialism were varied. Most of the nations needed raw materials like rubber, oil, tin, and iron to fuel industrialization, and wanted new markets for their products—and direct control over them.

Nationalism created rivalries that at times forced the nations to compete, whether they wanted to or not. Some justified the new imperialism with social Darwinism and the belief that only strong nations survived. Others were racist in their beliefs and motives, thinking that white men had a right to dominate. Missionaries supported imperialism with the view that it helped to spread Christianity to the "pagans." Finally, many had a humanitarian perspective and saw imperialism as an extension of the "white man's burden" to bring the benefits of democracy and capitalism to other countries. Regardless of the reasons, the ideas of imperialism dominated European interactions with the world during the nineteenth century.

> **NOTABLE QUOTABLE**
>
> It was the mission of the Anglo-Saxon race to penetrate into every part of the world, and to help in the great work of civilization.
>
> —*The Aborigines' Friend*, Thomas Hodgkin (July 1896)

Imperialism in Southeast Asia

By 1900, a majority of Southeast Asia was dominated by imperialist policies of Britain, France, and even the United States. Great Britain started its control of the region in 1819 with the founding of the port of Singapore on the tip of the Malay Peninsula. Later, the British took command of the kingdom of Burma to protect its possessions in India and the route to south Asia.

France first started its imperial policies by promoting Christian missionaries in Vietnam. Eventually, France forced the state of Vietnam to accept French protection. From there, France occupied the city of Saigon and then the rest of the country. In 1884, French armies seized the other major city of Vietnam, Hanoi, and made Vietnam an official French *protectorate*. With Vietnam as a base, the French extended control over the states and regions of Cambodia, Annam, Tonkin, and Laos. These territories were united in 1900 into the Union of French Indochina.

> **DEFINITION**
>
> A **protectorate** is a state or nation that is dominated or controlled by a much stronger state or nation.

The only state that remained free of Britain and France on the mainland of Southeast Asia was the state of Thailand. King Mongkut and his son King Chulalongkorn promoted Western learning and friendly relations with the European powers, occasionally playing one off the other to remain independent. As a result, in 1896 Britain and France agreed not to try to control Thailand and left it as an independent buffer state.

The United States also got into the imperialist act in the archipelagos of Southeast Asia, starting in 1898 with the Spanish-American War. Commodore George Dewey defeated Spanish naval forces at the Battle of Manila Bay in the Philippines, and the Philippine Islands became an American territory to be used as a jumping-off point for trade with China. The Filipino population did not appreciate the imperialist policies of the United States. Emilio Aguinaldo led a group of Filipino freedom fighters against the American occupying forces, but was defeated.

The imperial regimes in Southeast Asia were ruled in two different ways: indirect and direct. Indirect rule depended on local elites to maintain law and order and collect taxes for the imperial country. This method made it easier to access resources and lowered the cost of governance. In addition, it made less of an impact on the local culture, making it somewhat more tolerable to the native inhabitants. The Dutch East Indies was an excellent example of this type of rule.

Imperial direct rule was used when local rulers resisted. In these cases, an imperial government was created to rule directly over the local inhabitants. The problem with this was that it was difficult to administer from afar and created resentment among the inhabitants.

Scramble for Africa

Imperialism also dominated the continent of Africa from the early 1880s to the early twentieth century. Beginning with the Berlin Conference in 1884, this period is characterized with the European nations competing for territory in what has been dubbed the "Scramble for Africa."

West Africa

With the abolishment of slavery, the economy in west Africa was in decline. Eventually the export of timber, peanuts, oil, and hides replaced slavery as an economic resource. Britain saw the advantage of controlling these exports, and in 1874 annexed the west coastal states called the Gold Coast. In addition, it established a protectorate over Nigeria. Not wanting to be left out, France also established itself in the region in 1900 with French West Africa. Germany established territories in Togo, Cameroon, and German Southwest Africa.

North Africa

The British were also the first to gain territories in north Africa. Egypt, which had been part of the Ottoman Empire, was established as an independent state in 1805 by Muhammad Ali. This helped to bring Egypt into the modern world and to the attention of European powers. In 1869, the Egyptian government completed the massive project of digging the Suez Canal. The British saw the canal as a lifeline to their trading interests in India, and so, in 1875, bought the Egyptian share of the canal. With the canal under their control, the British felt justified in putting down an Egyptian revolt against foreign influence in 1881. In 1898, the British seized the Sudan located south of Egypt and, by 1915, Egypt was considered a British protectorate and well under British control.

France, again not wanting to be left out of the race for territory, also made imperialist maneuvers in north Africa. In 1879, they took control of the region of Algeria. In 1881, the French made Tunisia a protectorate, and in 1912 Morocco became a French protectorate. The Italians got into the act, too, and in 1911 took over the Turkish territory of Tripoli, which became the Italian colony of Libya.

Central Africa

Central Africa also came under the influence of imperialist Europe. From 1841 to 1871, David Livingstone explored the region of central Africa. He was followed by Richard Burton, who sought the source of the Nile River. Later in the 1870s, Henry Morton Stanley explored the region by sailing the Congo River to the Atlantic Ocean. After his trip, he tried to convince some to settle the Congo River. Only Belgium responded and, in 1876, King Leopold II hired Stanley to help establish Belgian settlements south of the Congo River. France followed Stanley and the Belgians and established settlements north of the Congo River.

WHAT IN THE WORLD

David Livingstone loved the continent of Africa so much that he gave instructions that his heart was to remain in Africa when he died. Today, his body is buried in Westminster Abby while his heart is buried in Blantyre, Malawi, a city named after his birthplace in Scotland.

East Africa

In east Africa, the competition for imperial control heated up between Great Britain and Germany. Germany had possessions in west Africa, and for political purposes the German Chancellor Bismarck was interested in colonizing east Africa. The British saw east Africa as a bridge between their territories in north and south Africa.

Eventually the conflict was settled in 1884 at the Berlin Conference, where official recognition was given to both British and German territorial claims while Portugal received Mozambique. In typical imperialist fashion, no Africans were present at the conference to give their view of the division of their territory!

South Africa and the Boers

Developments in south Africa were also influenced by the imperial policies of European nations. The Dutch first settled the region permanently and by 1865 there were over 200,000 Dutch settlers in south Africa. After the Napoleonic wars, the British had received control of the region and encouraged British settlers to come to the Cape Colony.

In response, the Dutch settlers, or Boers, fled from the cape into the region north of the colony—a time period referred to as the Great Trek. The Boers believed that God ordained white superiority over the indigenous population. They fought the native tribes in the regions that they settled and confined them to reservations. The Zulus, a tribe with a strong military tradition, fought back but were defeated by the combined efforts of the Boers and British.

WHAT IN THE WORLD

The Zulus divided their regiments of soldiers by age group. Each regiment lived in a different village during times of peace. Also, young men were not the only warriors the Zulus retained. They had regiments in the Zulu War of men in their 60s.

British Rule and Cecil Rhodes

When Cecil Rhodes became prime minister of the Cape Colony, things appeared to be well in hand. With Rhodes's guidance, resources were used to found diamond and gold companies that were very economically viable. Rhodes even expanded British settlement in south Africa and got to name a territory after himself (Rhodesia). But eventually Rhodes's rule went south, and the British government discovered secret plans he had been making to overthrow the Boer government of the South African Republic. These plans angered the Boers and started the Boer War, which lasted from 1899 to 1902.

The British won the war and combined the British and Boer territories in south Africa to create the independent Union of South Africa in 1910. To aid its establishment, the British used a policy of appeasement, and per Boer insistence allowed only whites to vote in the nation. This set up a system of *apartheid*, which lasted until the end of the twentieth century.

At the end of the nineteenth century, Africa was dominated by the imperial rule of the various European nations. Only Liberia and Ethiopia remained free and independent states. Although it appeared that foreign domination was bad, imperialism in Africa and elsewhere was not without paradoxes. Imperialism provided what might be considered the blessings of Western civilization. This included freedom and democracy, capitalism and industry, roads and railroads, and the development of the export market.

DEFINITION

Apartheid refers to a legal and institutional separation of blacks and whites that existed in South Africa during most of the twentieth century.

Imperialism in India

The paradox of imperialism created different reactions in the Indian subcontinent, Asia, and Africa. Resistance movements started with the ruling classes, gradually turned to peasant revolts, and finally became the responsibility of Westernized intellectuals and nationalists. This last group had a better comprehension of Western values and institutions, so they understood the deep contradiction of imperialism and Western ideas of democracy. But resistance in the form of revolution and independence was not the only reaction to imperialism. Other countries had more unique ways of dealing with the European incursions.

British power in India increased with the decline of the Mogul rulers. To make rule more convenient, the British government gave power to the British East India Company. This commercial company ruled India during the eighteenth and nineteenth centuries using *sepoys*, or Indian soldiers, to protect its interests in the region.

This system worked well until the mid-nineteenth century. In 1857, the Indians' distrust of the British erupted into the Great Rebellion. The immediate cause of the Sepoy Mutiny, as the British called it, was a rumor that the British were giving bullets greased with cow and pig fat to the *sepoy* soldiers. Of course, cow was sacred to Hindus and pig was taboo to Muslims, making this rumor, if true, a big problem. As a result, the *sepoys* resisted British orders to use the possibly tainted bullets in their rifles. This resistance turned into a revolt in which 50 Europeans were killed, but the revolt was disorganized. The Muslim and Hindu *sepoys* quarreled over leadership and the British army crushed the revolt by 1858. From that point, the British government took over direct control of India from the British East India Company; in 1876, Queen Victoria was given the title Empress of India.

British direct rule in India was through a viceroy or governor. This proved to be of some benefit to the Indian subcontinent; order and stability were established with an efficient government that created a school system and an infrastructure including railroads, telegraphs, and a postal service. But British rule was not without its costs. The agriculture of the subcontinent became focused on cotton to supply the mills of Great Britain. Local Indian industries were destroyed, and at times food supplies ran short as Indians switched their field production to cotton. As a result, in the nineteenth century over 30 million Indians died of starvation.

Shortly after the beginning of direct British rule, Indian nationalism emerged. In 1885, the Indian National Congress formed with the expressed desire to share in the governance of India. But the organization had problems—namely, religious differences divided the group. During the early twentieth century, Mohandas Gandhi came forward to help the Indian nationalist movement. Gandhi came from the native intellectual crowd. He studied in London and became a lawyer in 1915, practicing in South Africa. Gandhi advocated the use of nonviolent resistance to highlight British exploitation and obtain the Indian nationalist goals, which included independence and improving the lot of the poor.

Imperialism and Its Impact on China

Despite being at the height of its power in 1800, the Qing dynasty in China also succumbed to the imperial ambitions of the European nations. Coupled with the internal problems of corruption, peasant unrest, incompetence, rapid population growth, and food shortages, China experienced a difficult period during the nineteenth century.

The First War on Drugs

The first event that set off the Qing decline was the Opium War. Europeans had maintained a trading post at the Chinese city of Canton for close to 200 years, but the British had grown dissatisfied with the arrangement. Chinese trade restrictions had created a British trade imbalance. To improve this balance of trade, the British used opium rather than silver to trade with the Chinese. Opium was a highly addictive drug that came from the British-controlled region of India.

In an effort to protect their people, the Chinese made opium illegal, but the British refused to stop its trade. The Chinese blockaded the city of Canton, and the British responded with force, triggering a war that lasted from 1839 to 1842. Of course, the British, using superior gun and cannon tactics, won.

The Chinese were forced to open five coastal Chinese ports to the British, where Europeans were not subject to Chinese law—a tradition known as *extraterritoriality*. The Chinese also agreed to limit the taxation of imports and pay war reparations to the British. Finally, the Qing dynasty was forced to give the port city and island of Hong Kong to the British. The only question that remained open was the legality of the opium trade.

DEFINITION

Extraterritoriality is the policy of a host nation to create a section of the country for foreigners that is not subject to the host nation's laws.

The Taiping Rebellion

The Taiping Rebellion was the peasant response to the humiliation of the terms of the Opium War, a revolt that lasted from 1850 to 1864. The leader of the revolt was a Christian convert named Hong Xiuquan, who believed fervently that God had given him the mission to put an end to the Qing dynasty, considered outsiders to most Chinese. Xiuquan also had other goals for this peasant revolt, including providing land to the peasant population, treating women as equals, and sharing possessions equally.

By March 1853, the peasant rebellion was in full swing and had captured the town of Nanjing. After the death toll in the town reached 25,000, the European nations decided to come to the aid of the Qing dynasty. With their intermittent assistance, the Chinese crushed the rebellion, but not without a cost. Over 20 million Chinese died during the conflict.

During the time of the Taiping Rebellion, the Second Opium War erupted in 1856, again over the issue of the opium trade in China. This time Great Britain and France joined forces and seized the Qing dynasty capital at Beijing. At the end of the conflict, the Chinese government agreed to legalize opium and open another port to foreign trade.

A Need for Reform

By the 1870s, with the outlook extremely bad for the Qing dynasty, Chinese reformers advocated self-strengthening, meaning that China should adopt Western technology but hang on to Confucian values. This ideology became the basis for Chinese government and culture until the beginning of the twentieth century. The reform movement proved to be of some benefit. New railroads and factories were built and the civil service examination was updated to help the governmental bureaucracy.

But the reforms were not enough to prevent imperial European nations from having their way with China. Russia took Chinese territories north of the Amur River in Siberia. The territory of Tibet broke free of Chinese rule and became a free state. And then European nations, including Great Britain, France, Russia, and Germany, along with Japan, negotiated with regional Chinese warlords rather than the Qing dynasty to create spheres of influence within the country.

So at the end of the nineteenth century, the Qing dynasty suffered growing internal and external obstacles to rule and stability. In 1894, China went to war with Japan over involvement in the Korean Peninsula; remember that Korea was China's "little brother"? At the end of the conflict, China was defeated. In return for peace with Japan, China had to give up control of the island of Taiwan and the Liaodong Peninsula. Later, the European powers, for political reasons, forced Japan to return the territories.

In 1897, the Chinese fought with Germany, resulting in a German win and Germany acquiring the Shandong Peninsula. In 1898, more problems arose. The Qing emperor Guang Xu declared 100 days of reform in China, issuing edicts creating major political, administrative, and educational reforms. Not everyone was happy. The emperor's aunt, Empress Dowager Ci Xi, opposed the reforms and imprisoned Guang Xu.

The Boxer Rebellion

Just when it appeared that China could not suffer any more problems, the United States came on the scene in 1899. The U.S. Secretary of State John Hay issued the Open Door Policy with China. This policy reduced the limits on foreign imports imposed on each sphere of influence. It also lessened the fears of foreign domination of Chinese markets. Of course, it benefited most every nation but China.

> **NOTABLE QUOTABLE**
>
> The existence of the present day China hangs upon the patience of foreign governments, who have too great a stake in the country to sink the ship so long as there is a hope of her floating.
>
> —*The Attaché at Peking,* A.B. Freeman-Mitford (1900)

The people of China started to attribute all of the internal and external problems of the Qing dynasty to the foreign powers. Of course, they were not far from the mark. As a result, a secret society called the Society of Harmonious Fists was created; its members were called "Boxers," and their slogan was "Destroy the Foreigner!"

The Boxers disliked Christian missionaries and Chinese Christian converts, and, in 1900, they rounded up Christians and killed them. The Qing dynasty could not get a handle on the situation, so the cavalry was called. An allied army of 20,000 soldiers from Britain, Germany, Russia, Japan, and the United States descended on China and seized the capital of Beijing in August 1900. Once the allies restored order, they demanded more concessions from the Qing dynasty, and the Chinese government was forced to pay indemnity to the nations that stopped the Boxer Rebellion.

A New Republic

The Qing dynasty seemed to be taking a long time to fall, but in 1905 it was becoming inevitable. Legislative assemblies started to meet at the local levels. They reformed the civil service examination and in 1910 called for an election of a national assembly to give advice to the emperor. Regardless of the democratic reforms, living conditions worsened and taxes increased.

Sun Yat-sen was a Chinese leader who emerged during the late nineteenth century to help rid China of the Qing dynasty. He formed the Revive China Society, which had revolutionary goals such as military takeover, preparation of democratic rule, and the creation of a constitutional democracy. In 1905, to gain support, Sun Yat-sen united the Revive China Society with other more radical groups and formed the Revolutionary Alliance. The stage was set for revolution in China.

In 1908, Empress Dowager Ci Xi died and left the throne in the infant hands of Henry Pu Yi. Sun Yat-sen saw this as the moment for the Revolutionary Alliance to strike. In October 1911, an uprising was started in central China and the Qing dynasty collapsed. Unfortunately, Sun did not have the strength to form a successor government, so he turned to General Yuan Shigai and his army for help. Yuan became the first president of the new Chinese Republic.

Yuan was corrupted by the power that he wielded in China with this army, and he tried to create a new imperial dynasty out of the Chinese Republic. He destroyed the democratic institutions that had been put in place and dissolved parliament, which of course put him in conflict with Sun's Nationalist Party. The Nationalist Party tried to overthrow Yuan and his new imperial dynasty, but Sun was forced to flee to Japan. But the dynasty that Yuan established was unstable and when he died in 1916, the country slipped into civil war with local warlords fighting for control of the country.

Changes in Chinese Culture

During all this time of imperialism and internal and external crisis, Chinese society and culture changed considerably. The Chinese adopted many advances in Western communication and transportation, integrating China into the world economy. New crops were grown, increasing food production. Local industries declined as industrial centers emerged in Chinese cities, financed by foreign investment. This created a new middle and working class in China. Traditional farming still existed, but more of the Chinese people lived in the cities, where radical reformers wanted to completely Westernize the nation and create a new China. Finally, literature and art reflected Western movements rather than traditional Chinese culture.

The end result of imperialism in China was not good. It ended a dynasty and created instability in south Asia, which endured until after World War II.

Japan's Different Take on Imperialism

Japan had a completely different reaction to the imperial movement of the nineteenth century. When the West started to notice Japan, the Tokugawa Shogunate had ruled Japan for close to 250 years, with a policy of isolation from the outside world. Of course, the West saw this as a challenge. It wanted Japan to open up to Western economic interests.

Commodore Perry Comes A-Knocking

In the summer of 1853, U.S. Commodore Perry sailed into Tokyo Bay. He brought a letter from President Fillmore demanding better treatment of shipwrecked sailors and the opening of relations between the United States and Japan. The commodore then sailed away, promising to return in a few months for an answer.

The Japanese debated the issue and, when Perry returned, finally agreed to the Treaty of Kanagawa that was favorable to America while unfavorable to Japan. The treaty opened up two Japanese ports to Western traders. In addition, it gave better treatment to shipwrecked sailors and established a U.S. consulate in Japan. Later U.S. Consul Townsend Harris signed a better treaty with the Japanese, providing the United States with more open ports and an exchange of foreign ministers. Other treaties with other European nations soon followed the U.S. initiative.

The problem with this opening to the West was that it was unpopular with the Japanese. Resistance to the new policy was especially strong with samurai warriors in the territories of Satsuma and Choshu, who had strong military traditions and apparently did not know the Americans had lots of big guns.

> **WHAT IN THE WORLD**
>
> To impress the Japanese officials when he arrived, Commodore Perry set up a miniature railroad and gave officials rides at break-neck speeds.

The Meiji Restoration

In 1863, the Sat-Cho military alliance made the Tokugawa Shogunate promise to end its relationship with the West. When that seemed to fail, the Sat-Cho alliance attacked and destroyed the shogunate, proclaiming that the wishes of the Japanese emperor were restored. The Tokugawa Shogunate and the shogunate system were ended, but not contact with the West. The Sat-Cho alliance realized that it needed to use the West and Western ideas to remain in power.

The Meiji Restoration period started at the end of the shogunate. It was a period of reform in Japan, with the goal of creating a modern industrial nation. The symbol of this reform movement was the new young emperor, Mutsuhito, who called his rule the Meiji or the Enlightened Rule. In reality, the Sat-Cho rulers controlled Mutsuhito, but needed reforms were made to keep up with what was seen in the West.

First, the capital was moved from Kyoto to Edo (Tokyo). Then the daimyo were stripped of their titles and lands in 1871 in return for government bonds. The island was divided into territories called prefectures, with a governor to rule over each.

The Japanese government had studied Western political systems, and decided imperial Germany was the best fit. So in 1890, the Meiji Constitution was drafted and enacted. In the government created by the Constitution, the executive branch, made up of the prime minister and his cabinet picked by Meiji leaders, had the most authority. There was also a legislative branch made up of two houses—one appointed and one elected. So the Meiji Constitution gave the Japanese a democratic look, but it had an authoritarian edge.

Beyond the structural and political changes, the Meiji leader worked with the economics of the island. The land reform program gave former daimyo lands to peasants and levied new taxes on the lands, not the harvest. The Meiji leaders also fostered new industries by providing subsidies to industrial investors. They created a new educational system with an emphasis on applied science, which was good for industries like weapons, shipbuilding, tea, silk, and the national drink sake. The educational system was modeled after American schools but with an emphasis on the Japanese virtues of family, community, and loyalty to the emperor. They also sent many Japanese students abroad to study at Western schools.

The Meiji used their strong military background to create the new and improved Imperial army in 1871, well equipped with the most modern of weapons. It also was compulsory for every Japanese male to serve three years when he came of age.

Japanese culture and society also went through changes. At first, women were allowed to seek an education—which was very daring for Japanese culture—but later with the Civil Code of 1898 they were put back into the context of the family. Japanese society changed from primarily an agricultural society to an industrial one. Finally, the Japanese adopted Western and American fashions and styles, leaving traditional Japanese dress behind.

Ready to Join the Imperialist Club

Japanese culture altered a great deal with its Westernization. By the beginning of the twentieth century, it was heavily influenced by Western art and literature, although it emulated many different time periods of Western culture at once. There was also a movement to retain Japanese culture. In 1889, the Tokyo School of Fine Arts was founded to promote traditional Japanese styles. Japan also exported some culture, including Japanese gardens and traditional arts and crafts.

With the Meiji Restoration, Japan was ready to join the club of the Western powers. The problem was that they lacked the resources to keep up with the imperialist pace. Japan needed to expand. So in 1874, Japanese forces seized control of the Ryuku Islands. Then in 1876, they forced Korea to open ports to Japanese trade. Finally, in 1894, the Japanese humbled China by destroying the Chinese fleet and capturing the Manchurian city of Port Arthur.

Japan needed to defeat a Western or partially Western nation. In 1904, the Japanese attacked Port Arthur, which was by this time Russian territory, since they had taken it from China in 1898. Japan then mopped up a Russian army in Manchuria. As a result, the Russians sent their Baltic fleet to teach the Japanese a lesson. Of course, Japan was the teacher and the Russian fleet was destroyed at the Battle of Tsushima. The Russians were forced into the Treaty of Portsmouth, which gave the Liaodong Peninsula to Japan. Japan was now a member of the club. In 1910, Japan annexed Korea, but suspicion between the United States and Japan started to grow as interests in the Pacific came into conflict.

The Least You Need to Know

- Imperialist polices of the nineteenth century created competition between the European nations.
- The majority of the African continent was dominated by European powers before the beginning of the twentieth century.
- British imperial policies in India created an Indian nationalist movement led by Gandhi.
- The Qing dynasty in China declined because of the imperialist policies of the Western nations.
- Japan westernized itself in reaction to the imperialism of South Asia.

The Twentieth Century and Beyond

The beginning of World War I was the end of European dominance. The nationalism that began in Europe eventually spread around the world and helped to end Europe's imperialist supremacy. The United States and the Soviet Union fought a Cold War to fill the void left by the European supremacy. In the end the United States came out on top; for how long is another question.

The global trading network that developed in the previous period expanded, and its influence can be seen in the phenomenon of globalization. With globalization has come some problems, including substantial environmental issues. In addition, globalization has often brought cultural traditions into question. Fundamentalist religious movements have been a reaction against that trend.

The War to End All Wars

In This Chapter

- The causes of World War I
- August 1914
- Trench warfare
- The Russian Revolution
- The coming of the Americans
- The end of the "War to End All Wars"

World War I was a watershed event in world history. It marked the beginning of the end of European imperial dominance of the world. The war also created the right environment for a shift in power in the West. The long-term causes of the war were some of the "isms" of the nineteenth century, including industrialism, nationalism, and imperialism, but there were more immediate causes as well.

The Seeds of War

The Balkan Peninsula had gained gradual autonomy from Austria-Hungary beginning in the late nineteenth century. By 1878, Greece, Serbia, Romania, and Montenegro were all independent nations, but other states remained under the influence of the European powers. Bulgaria was a Russian protectorate; Bosnia and Herzegovina were Austria-Hungarian protectorates.

Both Bosnia and Herzegovina were annexed by Austria-Hungary in 1908. This angered the nation of Serbia, which had its own designs in the region. Backed by the Russians, who competed with Austria in the region, the Serbs prepared for war.

Germany stepped in to back Austria-Hungary, so the Russians backed down and so, necessarily, did the Serbs. Tensions subsided for the moment in the Balkans, but various wars during 1912 and 1913 caused tensions to rise again.

> **NOTABLE QUOTABLE**
>
> "Serbia will some day set Europe by the ears, and bring about universal war on the Continent."
>
> —Sir Maurice de Bunsen, British ambassador to Austria (1913)

The Assassination of Franz Ferdinand

In June 1914, the Austrian Archduke Franz Ferdinand—heir to the imperial throne in Austria-Hungary—decided to visit the annexed state of Bosnia. During this official state visit, Gavrio Princep, a 19-year-old member of the Black Hand, a Serbian nationalist group, assassinated both the archduke and his wife while they were riding through the streets of Sarajevo. Tensions in eastern Europe went from hot to boiling in a matter of days.

Austria-Hungary had wanted a reason to crush Serbia for some time, due to competing interests in the state of Bosnia, and the assassination provided it. But Russia was certain to back Serbian interests, so the Austrians again looked to Germany for help. Kaiser Wilhelm of Germany gave the Austrians his full unconditional support, often termed as a "blank check" of support, for an invasion of Serbia. Austria-Hungary sent an ultimatum to Serbia on July 23, 1914, with purposely extreme demands, including suppressing any dissent against Austria, which the Serbians could not meet. Five days later when the demands remained unanswered, Austria-Hungary declared war on Serbia. This had a domino effect on the nations of Europe.

Tensions Boil Over

The first nation to respond to this small regional conflict was Russia. Czar Nicholas II ordered the mobilization of the Russian army. In the political and military world of 1914, mobilization was an act of war. For Russia to partially mobilize to just fight Austria was not plausible. It was all or nothing, meaning that Russia was going to take on Germany also. So when the Russian czar gave the order for full mobilization on July 29, Germany declared war on Russia.

The German declaration of war broadened the conflict from a regional to a continental affair. There were several reasons for this. Germany, led by Alfred von Schlieffen, had a long-standing plan developed for war with Russia and France. France was part of the German plan because they knew that Russia and France had an alliance. The plan recognized that Germany could not survive a two-front war, so it called for an immediate one-two punch by hitting France first and Russia afterward. The plan's success—and Germany's survival—depended on it being implemented immediately, so military necessity quickly outran political caution or restraint.

Germany declared war on France on August 3, then issued an ultimatum to the Belgian government to allow German troops to pass through their borders on the way to France. Belgium was neutral and refused, so German forces invaded Belgium en route to France. At that point on August 4, Great Britain declared war on Germany for violating Belgian neutrality—and because Great Britain had secretly allied itself with France and Russia.

A small conflict had turned into the Great War. On one side were the Allied powers of France, Great Britain, and Russia. On the other side were the Central—or Axis—powers of Germany, Austria-Hungary, and the Ottoman Empire.

 NOTABLE QUOTABLE

The world of peace which has now collapsed with such shattering thunder—did we not all of us have enough of it? Was it not foul in all its comfort? Did it not fester and stink with the decomposition of civilization …. Morally and psychologically I feel the necessity of this catastrophe and that feeling of cleansing, of elevation and liberation which filled me, when what one had thought impossible really happened."

—German writer Thomas Mann (1914)

The Great War

When the Great War started, all of the sides involved were euphoric with nationalism. Most saw the war as a chance for glory and adventure that would be over by Christmas. These feelings were aided by the mass of new media propaganda being cranked out of the government presses of Europe. Hundreds of thousands of men volunteered to fight for their nation's honor. But the Great War did not progress like the propaganda said.

Dig In!

Germany's plan to win the war was a military gamble. They needed to take Paris quickly, as in the Franco-Prussian War, but the plan did not work that way. The German forces moved swiftly at first, but were stopped cold by French and British forces at the First Battle of the Marne, from September 6 to 10.

The German armies kept trying to swing around French forces, but were stopped by a series of trenches protected by barbed wire. These trenches, which developed in response to the new technology of machine guns, stretched from the English Channel to neutral Switzerland. The German forces responded by building their own set of trenches. The western front of the Great War had begun in a thunderclap. Once entrenched, the great armies stayed in relatively the same positions for four long years.

The Eastern Front

The eastern front, where Germany and Austria faced Russia, had more movement. Germany defeated the Russian armies in eastern Germany at the Battle of Tannenberg on August 30 and the Battle of the Masurian Lakes on September 15. The Austrians were not so successful. They were defeated in the region of Galicia and thrown out of Serbia.

As a result, Italy, initially allied with the Central powers, decided to switch sides to the Allied powers in order to gain territory in Austria-Hungary. They then attacked southern Austria in May 1915 with some success. Seeing Austria as the weak link, Germany aided the Austrians in defeating the Russians in Galicia. This put the Russian armies on the verge of collapse on the eastern front. Bulgaria saw its chance to cash in on the war and joined Germany and Austria-Hungary in August 1915.

The Meat Grinder

As the war slowed to a crawl, the casualties rose to incredible numbers. The unprecedented casualty rates had to do with advances in weapons technology and the lack of advances in war strategy. The use of millions of miles of barbed wire, machine-guns, and heavy artillery created a no-man's land between the trenches of the soldiers. No one seemed able to figure out tactics to capture enemy trenches that did not involve sending thousands of men in charges to break the other's lines. These charges were futile despite the bravery of the men involved. From 1914 to 1917, millions of young men were sent to their deaths charging the enemy's trenches. Eventually the war became one of attrition.

NOTABLE QUOTABLE

"They advanced in line after line, dressed as if on parade, and not a man shirked going through the extremely heavy barrage, or facing the machine-gun and rifle fire that wiped them out."

—British Brigadier Rees (July 1916)

The Air War

Above the trenches, another new type of battle was going on. Invented only a decade earlier by the Wright brothers, aircraft were first used in war during the Great War. At first they were used for reconnaissance to track troop movements. Soon pilots dropped bombs on unsuspecting targets. Then things really started to heat up. Pilots started to fire at each other using pistols, then machine guns. Rapidly the air filled with "dogfights" as planes battled for air superiority.

The Germans were quite adept at creating and using airships called *zeppelins* to bomb London and even eastern England. These zeppelins contained hydrogen, which allowed them to float in the sky propelled by a system of controls and propellers. Of course, hydrogen is very flammable, making them very vulnerable to enemy fire. The bombings in England did little damage but did have a psychological effect on the English.

DEFINITION

A **zeppelin** is a rigid, cigar-shaped balloon designed to carry passengers and bombs, named for its inventor, Count Ferdinand von Zeppelin.

The War Spreads

In a matter of time, the regional conflict that turned into a continental conflict finally became a global conflict. The declining Ottoman Empire joined Germany in August 1914, seeing an opportunity to expand its influence in the Balkans.

In response, the Allied powers tried to invade the Ottoman Empire at Gallipoli, southwest of Istanbul, in April 1915. After a disastrous campaign, they were forced to withdraw. Still wanting to create problems for the Ottoman Turks, a British officer, Lawrence of Arabia, was charged with encouraging the local Arab princes to rise up against the Ottoman Empire. In 1918, the British seized control of Egypt from the Turks.

Japan also wanted to get into the war, seeing it as a good opportunity to expand its influence in the Pacific Rim. Unlike the Turks, they picked the right side. The Japanese allied themselves with the British and the Allied powers. With the backing of the alliance, they seized several German colonial possessions in the Pacific. Australia also did the same and took control of German New Guinea.

The position of the United States on the conflict was a topic of intense interest. The United States maintained a policy of neutrality, but blockades of British and German ports caused problems. The German navy, in a fit of impatience, decided to use its submarine fleet in a campaign of unrestricted submarine warfare. On May 7, 1915, a German submarine sank the *Lusitania*, a passenger vessel, killing over 1,000 civilians, including 100 Americans. This changed the relatively neutral American view of Germany and the Central powers to a very negative one. After the incident, the German navy stopped unrestricted warfare, but the negative image stuck.

A year later the German government became desperate. They were convinced that the British would starve before the United States would respond to the unrestricted warfare on merchant vessels. So the German navy, again, used unrestricted warfare on all ships coming into Britain. It was the wrong call. The United States had enough and entered the war. (The Anglo-American bond is strong even to this day.) By early 1918, American troops had arrived in Europe in large numbers, a significant psychological and military boost for the Allies.

WHAT IN THE WORLD

Just before the German invasion of Belgium, two German naval cruisers shelled French ports in Algeria. These ships were chased by the British navy and escaped to a Turkish port, where the German government sold them to the Turks. The acquisition of these advanced ships convinced the Ottoman Empire to side with the Central powers.

Revolution in Russia

Russia was not prepared for war, which was economically, culturally, politically, and socially disruptive. The czar was not a good political or military leader, and he insisted on having control of both during the war. Also, Russia was not ready or able to equip its troops for the new industrialized warfare. The lack of leadership and preparation led to the deaths of over two million Russian soldiers on the eastern front from 1914 to 1916. The confidence of the Russian people in their government was at an all-time low.

Adding to the complexity of the situation was the figure of Rasputin, a Siberian peasant and holy man who garnered the support of the Russian royal family because he was able to stop the bleeding of the czar's son Alexis, who had hemophilia. The Russian people believed that he had too much influence on the royal family and Russian politics. This resentment eventually resulted in Rasputin's assassination, in December 1916. Finally, the Russian economy, which had suffered before the Great War, suffered even more once the war commenced.

The March Revolution

The Russian Revolution began with the March Revolution, which started in March 1917 when the women of Petrograd, the Russian capital, went on strike, citing lack of bread and long work hours. The strike escalated on March 8, 1917, when 10,000 women marched on the capital. This unrest spread to all the industries and there was a general strike. The czar ordered his palace soldiers to break up the striking protestors, but instead they joined the women. The Duma, which had been dissolved by the czar, met and on March 12, created a provisional government, forcing Czar Nicholas to step down on March 15.

In the span of a week, Russia went from an autocracy to a democracy. Alexander Kerensky emerged to lead the Russian nation, and one of his first decisions was to continue the war on the eastern front. That was a big mistake. A group of Soviet councils made of workers and soldiers and influenced by socialism opposed the war. They were the key to a larger takeover.

Red October

The Marxist Party had many factions across Europe during the early twentieth century. One faction was the Russian Social Democrats, led by Vladmir Ilyich Ulianov, better known as Lenin. Lenin always believed there should be a violent overthrow of the Russian government. He was exiled to Switzerland for his extreme views from 1900 to 1917.

In April 1917, German leaders, thinking his subversive ideology would be detrimental to the Russian war effort, shipped him back to Russia in secret. Once in Russia, Lenin and his Marxist followers, called Bolsheviks, took over the socialist-leaning *soviets* by promising to end the war and give the factories to the workers, the land to the peasants, and power to the soviets.

DEFINITION

A **soviet** was a council of representatives made up of workers and soldiers.

By October 1917, the Bolsheviks held a slight majority in the soviets in Petrograd. Impatient for change, Lenin gave Leon Trotsky the go-ahead to start another revolution. On November 6, 1917, Bolshevik forces seized the Winter Palace where the provisional government met.

Once in control, Lenin turned the power of the government over to the Congress of the Soviets, but the real power resided in the Council of People's Commissars dominated by Lenin. As a result, the Bolsheviks changed their name to communists and the Russian nation to the Soviet Union. Trying to keep some of his promises, Lenin immediately made diplomatic maneuvers to end the war for the Soviet Union. On March 3, 1918, the Soviets signed the Treaty of Brest-Litovsk with Germany in which it gave up eastern Poland, Ukraine, Finland, and the Baltic provinces to Germany.

The Reds vs. the Whites

The Bolshevik takeover of Russia did not go unopposed. Civil war raged across the Russian landscape. Those who opposed the communist revolution were czar loyalists, liberals, anti-Lenin socialists, and the Allied powers. The Russian opposition formed the White Army, supported by the Allied powers with supplies and a small number of soldier advisors. But the communists, or Red Army, fought the White Army fiercely. As a result, they were able to take control of the Ukraine, Georgia, Russian Armenia, and Azerbaijan from the White Army. The Red Army also ended the threat of a royal returning to the throne by murdering the czar and his family on July 16, 1918.

In due time, Lenin and the communists took control of the former Russian Empire. Some of this was due to the leadership of Trotsky, who organized their forces and instituted a draft to aid in the civil war effort. Additionally, Lenin had a clear goal—centralize the state under government control—while the White Army had no goals other than to fight the communists. The communists also used the Cheka, or secret police, to root out sympathizers to the White Army cause. Finally, the people of Russia saw the White Army as anti-nationalists, since they were aligned with the foreign armies of the Allied powers. So by 1921, the Red Army had prevailed and the civil war for control was over. Russia was officially a communist nation.

The Final Years of the Great War

The last year of the war was difficult for all the nations involved, especially the Allied powers. The Battle of the Somme did not go well for the Allied powers; in fact, the British lost over 21,000 men on the first day of the battle. The Russian Revolution knocked out Russia as an ally. And the Allied powers suffered numerous other defeats on the Western front. The only glimmer of hope that the Allied powers had was the coming of the Americans.

One Last Try

The Germans recognized the coming of the Americans as a turning point in the war. They knew that, for Germany to win the war, they needed to mount a major offensive before the Americans reached the shores of Europe in vast numbers. So the leader of German military operations, Erich von Ludendorff, devised a plan for an offensive.

Starting in March 1918, the Germans renewed the offensive at the Second Battle of the Marne. By July 18, the German forces were completely halted by Allied forces using the new military technology of tanks. With the failed offensive, the war was over for Germany. The trickle of fresh American troops had turned into a flood, with two million people reaching Europe's shores.

WHAT IN THE WORLD

Over 300,000 African Americans served in the U.S. Army during World War I in segregated units. Some units fought alongside French regiments. Because of their distinguished service with the French, 171 African Americans were awarded the French Legion of Honor.

German Revolutions

Seeing the writing on the wall in September 1918, General Ludendorff demanded that the German government sue for peace. They tried to negotiate with the Allies, but to no avail. The Allied powers did not want to make peace with the unreformed government of Germany. As a result, the Germans began to reform the government in a more liberal mold. But the reform process was slow and the German people grew impatient.

On November 3, German sailors at the port of Kiel mutinied. This inspired other soldiers and workers to make sovietlike councils. A revolution appeared to be brewing, so on November 9, Kaiser William II fled the country (he understood what happened to despots during revolutions). Quickly, the Social Democrat party formed under Fredrich Ebert to take a lead in creating a democratic republic called the Weimar Republic. This satisfied the Allied powers, and on November 11, an armistice was signed to end hostilities on the western front.

Turmoil and revolution did not stop in Germany with the armistice. The German Communist Party tried to seize power from the democratic republic in December 1918. This violent revolution was put down, but it resulted in a widespread fear of communism in the German middle class. This was an important factor for the rise of the Nazi party in the 1930s.

Peace at Last?

With the armistice, a peace settlement needed to be arranged. U.S. President Woodrow Wilson had been discussing a basis for a peace settlement before the end of the war, which he called the Fourteen Points. Wilson called for open peace agreements rather than secret diplomacy. He also wanted to reduce the armaments of all of the nations. For the people of Europe, Wilson wanted self-determination. Finally, to ensure that everyone would follow these points, he wanted to see the creation of a general association of nations called the League of Nations.

Paris Peace Conference

In January 1919, at the Paris Peace Conference, Wilson, with his Fourteen Points and 26 representatives, met to discuss the arrangements for peace. It became painfully obvious to Wilson when he arrived that secret agreements had already been made before the end of the war. In addition, the European nations had many different goals for the talks. David Lloyd George of Great Britain just wanted Germany to pay for the cost of the war, while Georges Clemenceau of France wanted Germany stripped of weapons, reparations for the war, and the creation of a buffer zone in the Rhineland.

Wilson, George, and Clemenceau made the most important decisions of the conference; other major European nations like Italy were not involved in the decision making. Russian delegates refused to be a part of the process, and Germany was not even invited to attend. One of the important decisions reached was the creation of the League of Nations on January 25, 1919. Sadly, Wilson could only get the creation of the league arranged after agreeing to territorial changes that compromised his Fourteen Points. Wilson was not the only leader who compromised. Clemenceau gave up the idea of a buffer zone in the Rhineland under the condition that if Germany attacked France in the future, then Great Britain and the United States would come to France's aid.

The Treaty of Versailles

The treaty to end World War I was in reality five separate treaties with the defeated nations of Germany, Austria, Hungary, Bulgaria, and the Ottoman Empire. The most important was the Treaty of Versailles, which was signed by Germany on June 28, 1919. Germany agreed that it was responsible for the war and had to pay reparations. In addition, Germany reduced its army and navy and eliminated its air force. The treaty also took territory from Germany, including Alsace and Lorraine, which were returned to France, and part of eastern Germany, which was given to the new nation of Poland. Finally, Germany agreed to create a demilitarized zone on the German and French border.

The end result served to humiliate an already beaten nation. It was a mistake that would come back to haunt Europe.

A New Map

At the end of the Great War, a new map of Europe and the Middle East had to be drawn. Germany and Russia had lost a lot of territory that went to enlarge or create other nations. The Austro-Hungarian Empire disappeared, giving rise to the independent nations of Austria, Hungary, Czechoslovakia, and Yugoslavia. Other new nations appeared, including Finland, Latvia, Estonia, Lithuania, and Poland. But the complex mixture of ethnic groups in eastern Europe made the drawing of nations without problems next to impossible. The seeds of more ethnic conflicts were sown with redrawn boundaries.

Also, the Ottoman Empire was broken up. Independent Arab states created from regions that supported the Allies included Lebanon, Syria, Iraq, and Palestine.

They did not retain their independence long. France took control of Lebanon and Syria, while Britain took control of Iraq and Palestine as mandates that were governed on the behalf of the League of Nations.

Real Result of the Great War

What were the real results of the Great War beyond the obvious political changes? First, the war undermined the idea of progress and nationalism. Both concepts had ushered the nations of Europe into the nightmare of World War I. Industrial progress created the guns and bombs that killed in such merciless numbers. Nationalism incited the passions that made men able to use those guns and bombs.

With millions dead, European global domination began to slip and decline. A generation of men was wiped out. Europe was weak economically and physically. The centralized power of European governments increased in response to the policy of total war. Once centralized, it remained as such into the twenty-first century. Finally, those who survived the war were left looking for answers and security. Some found those answers and security in more revolutions.

During World War I, there were some significant social changes in the nations involved. The social status of women changed, at least temporarily. There were many new job opportunities open to women as millions of working men went to war. This increase in economic status led to many women gaining the right to vote.

With the advent of the Great War came the beginnings of policies that would create "total war," which involved the entire nation, not just the soldier in the field. The power of the people, economy, civil liberties, and information were all given over to the national government to coordinate the war effort, so the entire society was involved and affected by the war. Not only that, government took control of people's lives to a much greater degree than ever before and has not relinquished that control without political struggle.

Of course, in the aftermath, no one believed that any nation would willingly start another horrific war like the Great War. The need for peaceful rather than military solutions to political problems was felt by all the people and nations that witnessed the devastation firsthand. So to most, the Great War became "the war to end all wars." Little did they know that more was in store for Europe and the world.

The Least You Need to Know

- Industrialism, nationalism, and imperialism set the stage for a world war.
- The assassination of Archduke Ferdinand by a Serbian nationalist was the immediate cause for the war to end all wars.
- The Russian Revolution, caused by Russia's involvement in the war, ended with a communist takeover.
- The U.S. entry in the war tipped the scales in favor of the Allies.
- The Treaty of Versailles caused resentment among the nations of Europe, especially Germany.

A Time of Uncertainty

In This Chapter

- Problems in Europe
- The Depression and its effects
- The rise of totalitarian regimes in Europe
- Political developments around the world
- Cultural trends

The period after World War I was not a time of peace and prosperity—rather, it was a time of uncertainty in politics and culture. European dominance on the world stage was declining and the nations of the world were left searching for meaning in its place.

Problems with Peace?

The provisions of the Treaty of Versailles, which secured the peace after World War I, were one cause for uncertainty. The treaty caused many border disputes in eastern Europe. The League of Nations, created to foster peace and cooperation, was ineffective, partially because President Wilson was unable to convince the United States Senate to join. The Senate even refused to ratify the Treaty of Versailles to officially end the war with Germany. Not until 1921 did the United States sign a separate treaty with Germany. Regardless of the ineffectual nature of the League of Nations, it did create a standard for future international cooperation in the twentieth century.

WHAT IN THE WORLD

As if things hadn't been bad enough for the world population after the horrors of World War I, from 1918 to 1919 a Spanish influenza pandemic killed an estimated 50 to 100 million people worldwide. No region of the world was left untouched. The disease even spread to the Arctic and remote islands of the Pacific. This great medical holocaust easily compares with the Black Death of the Middle Ages.

Germany was also dissatisfied with the terms of the peace. France had insisted on harsh terms and strict enforcement, which put Germany in an economically tough spot. The German government needed to pay $33 billion in war reparations by April 1921. A year after the deadline, the German government announced to France that it could not pay. In response, the French sent troops to occupy the Ruhr Valley— Germany's chief industrial and mining center—intending to collect reparations from the operation of the mines. Of course, the German workers of the Ruhr Valley did not care for this and went on strike. In order to pay the workers to return to work, the German government printed more paper currency. This was a bad move by the German government; inflation skyrocketed and the German mark became next to worthless.

To correct this situation, in August 1924, U.S. financier Charles Dawes suggested that the amount of the reparations and the annual payments be reduced. The Dawes Plan also granted a $200 million loan to the German government to help it recover economically. This loan brought American investments to Germany and for a time, from 1924 to 1929, the nation of Germany enjoyed some economic stability.

To improve their deteriorated relations, Germany and France drafted the Treaty of Locarno in 1925, aided by the cooperative relationship between the foreign ministers of Germany and France, Gustav Streseman and Aristide Briand. This treaty guaranteed the western borders of France and Belgium and paved the way for Germany to join the League of Nations. Many viewed this treaty as a new era of peace in Europe.

The Kellogg-Briand Pact, drafted in 1928, also reassured many that a new era of peace had begun. Signed by 63 nations, this pact renounced war as an instrument of national policy and called upon the countries that signed it to reduce their military forces. Of course, there was no way to enforce the pact, and few countries wanted to risk national security by reducing their armed forces, so in the end it was a fairly worthless agreement. But it made people feel good about peace.

A Bit Depressed

But just when things seemed to be going well, the Great Depression, which lasted most of the 1930s, dragged America, Europe, and the world into economic and social despair. Many factors created this economic disaster; the individual economies of several Western nations suffered economic downturns during the late 1920s. But the major contributing event was the U.S. stock market crash of October 1929.

When the U.S market crashed, American investors withdrew their money from European markets. As a result, by 1931, industrial production had slowed considerably, causing unemployment to rise. And as unemployment rose, consumer demand fell, since no one had money to spend. A vicious cycle took hold. By far the worst year was 1932, with 25 percent of British workers and 40 percent of German workers out of work. The governments of the West scrambled to make things better, but the traditional economic solutions did not work. Governments took control of economies, creating even stronger central governments. Communism also became popular; after all, Marx had predicted that capitalism would fall from overproduction.

There were also many political changes, some of which led to another world war. In Germany, the Weimar Republic, the democratic government created after World War I, did not cope well with the Depression. President Paul von Hindenburg did not have the leadership qualities to end unemployment and inflation. Eventually, his inabilities pushed middle-class Germans into supporting parties that were anti-republic.

At the beginning of the Depression, France was the strongest nation on the European continent. The French economy only experienced a light economic depression around 1932. But the French government changed six times in two years, which suggested some problems. By 1936, a coalition of communists, socialists, and radicals formed the Popular Front government and rose to power by promising workers a 40-hour work week, vacations, and collective bargaining abilities. They never did solve the problem of the Depression, but in reality they didn't really have to. It worked its way out of the French economy.

Great Britain, like Germany, experienced many problems because of the Depression. The ruling Labour Party was unable to find an economic solution and fell from power in 1931. The Conservatives were able to lead Great Britain through the worst stages of the Depression.

English economist John Maynard Keynes suggested that government should create a variety of public works projects; pumping wages into the private sector would create a larger demand for products, which would pull a nation out of economic depression.

The Conservatives in Britain largely ignored Keynes, but the policy caught on with President Franklin Roosevelt in the United States.

When Roosevelt was elected president in 1932, he had his work cut out for him: in 1933, more than 15 million workers were unemployed. Using Keynesian economics, Roosevelt conceived the New Deal, which created many public works projects. Additionally, he began the U.S. welfare system in 1935 with the Social Security Act, which guaranteed pensions and unemployment insurance to all Americans. Despite these changes, in 1938 there were still more than 11 million American workers unemployed. Roosevelt had not been able to solve the economic problem of the Depression.

The Rise of Short Men Who Mean Business

By 1939 in Europe, only France and Great Britain remained democratic nations; most of the other European countries fell into nationalistic dictatorships and totalitarianism. Totalitarian governments controlled the political, economic, social, intellectual, and cultural lives of the people. They wanted everyone's hearts and minds. To do this, totalitarian governments used propaganda and modern communications. Usually, these governments had a single leader or party in control. No competition was permitted. These leaders believed that they understood the collective will of the people, so they could bypass individual liberties for the benefit of the people.

Mussolini and Fascism in Italy

The Italian Fascist state started its development in the 1920s. Benito Mussolini preached the gospel of the glory of the state over the individual, strong centralized government, and the state suppression of opposition, playing on the middle-class fears of a communist takeover of Italy. He created a political group called the League of Combat to spread his message. In 1920, Mussolini formed the Blackshirts, who not only vocalized his message but made it physical, attacking various offices and newspapers of socialist parties. When his original message was not enough, Mussolini used the lack of territory in the peace settlement of World War I as a rallying cry.

By 1922, Mussolini had enough support to make demands for power. He threatened to march on Rome with his Blackshirts if he was not given a leadership role in the Italian government. The king of Italy, Victor Emmanuel III, gave in to his demands and made Mussolini the prime minister of Italy. With political power in hand, Mussolini created a dictatorship and outlawed all political parties except, of course, the Fascists. Then he used the secret police and mass media to control the Italian people. Mussolini even created a Boy Scout–type group to promote Fascist values of discipline and war in the young people. His power over Italy was assured for the decades of the 1920s and 1930s.

> **WHAT IN THE WORLD**
>
> Mussolini was not the best student when he was in school. He was a rebellious student who was once expelled for stabbing a fellow pupil. Mussolini did end up graduating, and later went back to school for a short while, this time as an elementary school teacher.

The Rise of Stalin

After World War I, Lenin saw the decline of the *war-communism* system he had created in Russia. In 1920 and 1922, famine hit the Soviets, with more than five million people dying as a result. Industry collapsed, too. So in March 1921, Lenin started the New Economic Policy, or NEP, a modified version of the capitalist system. Peasants and small businesses could sell openly under the NEP. The economy of the Soviets stabilized; economic disaster had been stopped.

> **DEFINITION**
>
> **War-communism** was a policy developed by Russian communists during World War I in which the government controlled the banks and most industries, seized the grain of the peasants, and centralized government administration.

When Lenin died in 1924, there was a struggle for political power. Trotsky, who had helped the revolution so much, wanted to end Lenin's NEP in lieu of rapid industrialization and spreading communism to the world. Another group led by Joseph Stalin wanted to focus on domestic needs and thought that rapid industrialization was not the answer. In the end, Stalin, who as party general secretary appointed regional and local party officials, gained control of the party. In 1929, he established a dictatorship and expelled Trotsky from the party.

Trotsky had many difficult years after he fell out of favor in Soviet Russia. At the end of his life, he lived in exile in Mexico City. But Stalin, paranoid of Trotsky's political aspirations, sent several assassins to kill Trotsky. On August 20, 1940, one assassin finally succeeded in passing Trotsky's bodyguards and struck him in the head with an ice axe. Trotsky died the next day of a brain hemorrhage.

With dictatorial powers in hand, Stalin ended the NEP in favor of his Five-Year Plans. These economic goals for five-year periods were created to gradually transform the Soviet Union from an agricultural to an industrial nation. The first of Stalin's Five-Year Plans called for capital equipment. As a result, steel and oil production increased. But Stalin's first plan cost the Soviet Union. Living conditions in the cities declined and wages decreased more than 40 percent. Also, the brutality of the collectivization of the farms, another part of the plan, was disheartening to the Soviet people. During this period, 26 million small farms were turned into 250,000 collectivized farms. People were forced off of their small farms, resulting in a famine during the years of 1932 and 1933 in which more than 10 million peasant farmers died. Stalin also purged the party of old Bolsheviks; more than eight million people were arrested and sent to Siberia or executed. It was not the best of times for the Soviet Union.

WHAT IN THE WORLD

Joseph Stalin's real name was Joseph Dzhugashvilli. He adopted the name Stalin because it means "Man of Steel." Stalin wanted his name to show his frame of mind.

Authoritarian Governments in Eastern Europe

Other authoritarian states emerged in eastern Europe in the countries of Austria, Poland, Yugoslavia, Romania, Bulgaria, and Hungary. Why? Because the parliamentary systems failed to work. There was no tradition of democracy among the illiterate peasants of these regions, and the middle classes feared communism and were willing to support authoritarian governments to prevent it. So during the 1920s and 1930s, these states came into being and tried to maintain the old order.

General Franco in Spain

The same pattern also occurred in Spain. Popular with the people, General Francisco Franco led a revolution against the democratic government of Spain in 1936. The result was a Spanish civil war. Germany and Italy supported Franco in his military endeavors to control Spain, while the Spanish republican government was helped by the Soviet Union. In the end, General Franco captured Madrid, the capital of Spain, in 1939 and established a dictatorship. Franco supported the old order of Spain, so he remained a favorite with large landowners and businesses, who didn't seem to mind losing civil liberties.

The Rise of Hitler

Germany also saw the rise of a totalitarian regime under Adolph Hitler during the 1930s. Hitler was born in Austria in 1889 and later moved to Vienna to live as an artist. His artwork was rejected by the Vienna Academy of Arts, and his attention turned to politics. During his stay in Vienna, Hitler developed his basic ideas of politics, racism, anti-Semitism, extreme nationalism, propaganda, and terror.

After serving as a corporal in World War I in 1919, he joined the German Worker's Party. By 1921, Hitler was in control of the party and renamed it the National Socialist German Worker's Party, or Nazi Party for short. In 1923, he organized an uprising against the government in Munich called the Beer Hall Putsch.

The revolt was put down and Hitler was put in prison for a time, during which he wrote a thousand-page book on his views called *Mein Kampf*, or *My Struggle*. Drawing on Social Darwinism, Hitler believed that superior nations had the right to gain living space just as superior individuals had the right to acquire leadership over others. He also put forth his anti-communist, anti-Semitic, and nationalist ideas, including the Final Solution, which called for the extermination of the Jewish race so that the Aryan race could be perfected.

The Rise of the Nazis

Regardless of Hitler's scary potential, the German authorities freed him. Hitler then spent the last of the 1920s and early 1930s leading the Nazi Party to power by legal means. By 1932, the Nazi Party had expanded to all of Germany and was the largest party in the Reichstag.

When the Depression came to Germany, Hitler used it to acquire more popularity through promises of nationalism and militarism. Eventually, the German elite started to look to the Nazis to save Germany from economic disaster, while the middle class looked to the Nazis to save Germany from the communists.

In 1933, President Hindenburg agreed to allow Hitler to become German chancellor. After Hindenburg's death, Hitler dropped the title of chancellor, created a new German totalitarian government, and adopted the title most associated with him: the *führer*, or leader. With the Enabling Act of 1933, the German government was allowed to ignore the constitution and its guaranteed freedoms for four years. With this Hitler had a legal basis for his political actions.

Hitler Takes Total Control

Once Hitler was appointed dictator of Germany, a totalitarian state emerged. The Nazi Party purged all German institutions of Jews and democratic elements. Opposition to the Nazis was dealt with harshly, and opponents were placed in concentration camps. Trade unions and political parties were dissolved. Public officials and soldiers were required to take an oath of loyalty to Hitler as their *führer*.

Hitler wanted more than just control over Nazi Germany. He envisioned Germany as the dominant Aryan state that would be the center of an empire like that of ancient Rome. Thus, Hitler gave Nazi Germany the title the Third Reich, believing that it followed third in line after Charlemagne's Holy Roman Empire of the ninth century and the German empire of the nineteenth century.

To end the Depression in Germany, Hitler created massive public works projects and started to rearm the German military. His economic policies were a success and by 1937 only a few Germans remained unemployed. Because Hitler turned the economy around, the German people accepted his extreme nationalism. Churches, universities, and schools were brought under Nazi control. Mass public demonstrations and spectacles were put on by the Nazis as a show of power. The Hitler Youth taught Nazi ideals to young Germans. Women were encouraged to be wives and mothers and not work, while men were warriors who had to breed to create a pure Aryan race.

NOTABLE QUOTABLE

I was a little shocked at the faces, especially those of the women, when Hitler finally appeared on the balcony for a moment. … They looked up at him as if he were a Messiah, their faces transformed into something positively inhuman.

—*Berlin Diary,* William Shirer (1934)

At the heart of Hitler's extreme nationalism was anti-Semitism. In 1935, new racial laws were enacted called the Nuremburg Laws, excluding Jews from citizenship and requiring all Jews to be registered and labeled with the government. Then on November 9, 1938, on the night known as Kristallnacht, or Night of Shattered Glass, Nazis burned synagogues and businesses across Germany and Austria. In addition, 30,000 Jewish men were sent to *concentration camps*. Afterward, Jews were barred from public buildings and transportation and they were not allowed to work in the retail industry. Finally, Jews were strongly urged to leave the country. This was just the beginning of the persecution of the Jews in Germany.

To keep power, Hitler used terror methods. Hitler's bodyguards, known as the SS or Guard Squadrons, kept a close eye on all German institutions for Hitler. Heinrich Himmler, the commander of the SS, controlled the secret and regular police. During the war, he also oversaw the use of concentration camps, execution squads, and death camps.

> **DEFINITION**
>
> **Concentration camps** are camps where minority groups, political prisoners, and prisoners of war are detained under very harsh and brutal conditions. During World War II, the Nazis used these camps to try to exterminate the minority Jewish population of Europe.

Turmoil in the Middle East

During World War I, Great Britain supported the Arab nationalist movement throughout the Middle East. After the war, France and Great Britain created mandates of former territories of the Ottoman Empire. The mandates were supervised by the League of Nations. Great Britain had been given the right to govern Iraq and Jordan, while France had the right to Syria and Lebanon. But the European powers never respected Arab nationalism or the people's will when drawing up the lines in the sand.

End of the Ottomans

Beginning in the eighteenth century, the Ottoman Empire lost territory and power in the Middle East. As a result, in 1876 Turkish reformers took control of the government. They adopted a constitution and legislative assembly to create a democratic state. Finally Sultan Abdulhamid II, wanting to remain in power, stepped in and suspended the constitutional reforms.

In due time, a group called the Young Turks organized politically and restored the constitution in 1908. They then deposed the sultan in 1909. Allied with Germany during the war, the Turks committed genocide on the Christian Armenians in the empire. By 1918, they had killed more than one million Armenians.

After the war, the Ottoman Empire came to an end, with France and Great Britain dividing a majority of the empire's territories. The Greeks saw a chance for expansion and invaded the region of Turkey, but Colonel Mustafa Kemal organized the remnants of the Ottoman army and drove the Greeks from Turkey. Afterward he declared the former Ottoman territory of Turkey to be the Turkish Republic. He was promptly elected its first president.

Kemal became known as Ataturk, or "Father Turk." He pushed for the modernization of Turkey and put the democratic system in its place. Opposition to his rule and policies was suppressed. Ataturk instituted public education using a European model and made his people adopt European names. Like Stalin, he developed a five-year industrialization plan.

Ataturk especially wanted a strictly secular state, so he tried to break the power of the Islamic religion by forbidding Islamic men from wearing a fez and Islamic women from wearing a veil. He also enacted new laws that gave women rights, including voting. Ataturk permitted all Turkish citizens the right to convert to other religions. So with Ataturk came some good things, but also some questionable things.

Arab Nationalism

In the 1920s, Ibn Saud emerged as a leader to unite the population of the Arabian Peninsula. He created the kingdom of Saudi Arabia in 1932. At first, Saudi Arabia's source of income was tourism, in the form of pilgrimages to Mecca and Medina. In the 1930s with the search for oil by U.S. businesses, there was a shift, which became a complete change in 1938 when Standard Oil found oil in the Persian Gulf. The oil industry brought an economic boom to Saudi Arabia that increased the stability and power of Ibn Saud.

The Arab nationalists did have another problem besides that of the European powers. In 1917 with the Balfour Declaration, the British declared their support for the creation of a Palestinian homeland for the Jews. The problem with the declaration was that 98 percent of the population of Palestine was Muslim. During the 1930s, Jews began to migrate to Palestine, creating tensions in the region. By 1939, almost 500,000 Jews had come to Palestine. Conflict was inevitable between the Jewish and Muslim populations.

Introducing Iran

In the region of Persia, the Qajar dynasty had ruled from 1794 to 1921, but had not been very successful at solving many of the problems that Persia faced. With the discovery of oil in 1908, foreigners flocked to Persia for economic gain. Then in 1921, Reza Khan led a military uprising against the dynasty and took control of Persia. He proclaimed himself the shah, or king, and used his power to try to modernize Persia, Western-style.

The Shah wanted educational, military, and governmental institutions to fit the Western mold. As a result, he forbade women to wear a veil in public, although he tolerated other Islamic beliefs. In 1935, Persia became known as the nation of Iran. As time went by, the shah allied Iran closely with Nazi Germany to rid himself of the influence of Great Britain and the Soviet Union. During World War II, British troops occupied Iran because of that fact. The shah resigned in protest of the occupation and his son Mohammad Reza Pahlavi took the title of shah.

Making Progress in India

The European colonial system stood firm in most of the world after World War I. Some African states thought they might gain independence from the European nations, but most black Africans had their dreams dashed when Germany's colonies were given as mandates to Great Britain and France. There were small independence movements across Africa, but they were not organized enough to be successful until after World War II.

Unlike Africa, the Indian independence movement gained steam after World War I. Gandhi had been active in the nationalist movement before World War I. His form of nonviolent protest and civil disobedience attracted a great deal of attention to the Indian nationalist cause. Gandhi was arrested several times and spent several years in prison. After World War I, the British government was willing to give the Indian nationalists some concessions. With the Government of India Acts, Indians were given a greater role in the governing process, with two houses of parliament in which two thirds of the members could be elected. In addition, more than five million Indians were extended the right to vote.

NOTABLE QUOTABLE

Non-violence for me is not a mere experiment. It is part of my life. ... For me it is both a means and an end and I am more than ever convinced that in the complex situation that faces India, there is no other way of gaining real freedom.

—Mahatma Gandhi (1933)

For Gandhi, released from prison in 1930, the Government of India Act was not enough. So in protest against the salt tax, which forbade Indians from harvesting their own salt, Gandhi undertook his "Salt March" to the sea, where he picked up a pinch of salt and was promptly arrested by British authorities and put in prison again. To some it appeared the Indian nationalist movement had come to an end. But Jawaharlal Nehru, son of Motilal Nehru, former leader of the Indian National Congress, stepped forward to lead the movement. Like Gandhi, he was an intellectual who studied law in Great Britain. Unlike Gandhi, Nehru's leadership and movement was secular and modern, while Gandhi's had been religious and traditional.

The Indian nationalist movement was now divided between religious and secular and also Muslim and Hindu, making the situation very complex. In 1930, the Muslim League called for a separate state from India in the northwest of the country called Pakistan. Conflicts between Hindus and Muslims grew.

Political Developments in Asia

During the early twentieth century, communism lacked appeal to the people of Asia, mostly because Asia was more agricultural than industrial. So in 1919, the Communist International, or Comintern for short, started to train people to spread revolutionary ideas from its base in Moscow. By the late 1920s, Asia had become well versed in communist ideology and many saw that it could work with an agriculturally based nation. As a result, in Vietnam, Ho Chi Minh—who was educated in the West and trained in Moscow—organized a movement that was a combination of nationalism and communism to fight for independence from the French.

Political Developments in China

The communist movement also made an impact in China. In 1921, the Chinese Communist Party, or CCP, was founded in Shanghai. This party joined forces with the Nationalist Party of Sun Yat-sen in 1923, and they worked together to drive warlords and imperialists from China. In 1925, Sun Yat-sen died, and his successor, Chiang Kai-shek, did not like the idea of working with communists. So in April 1927, Chiang ordered the Shanghai Massacre, in which the CCP was attacked and put on the run. Afterward, Chiang was able to form a Chinese republic with the capital at Nanjing.

After the Shanghai Massacre, most of the CCP went into hiding. One CCP member, Mao Zedong, led a group of party members who had fled to the Jiangxi Province. Mao believed that peasants could lead a revolution in China rather than workers. By 1931, inspired by his leadership and ideas, most of the members of the CCP assembled around Mao. In 1933, Chiang sent troops to confront this threat.

At first surrounded, the People's Liberation Army broke Chiang's lines and, with 90,000 members, began the 6,000-mile Long March to reach the last surviving Communist base in north China. Without sufficient supplies, the Long March killed a majority of the army; by the end, only 9,000 members of the army were left alive. Mao was one of the survivors and emerged as sole leader of the CCP.

After the communist escape to north China, Chiang focused his attention on creating a republican government. Land reform and the modernization of industry were high on his agenda. Chiang tried to combine traditional Confucian values with Western innovations, calling it the New Life Movement. He was able to improve the highway and railroad systems, national banks, and educational system. In contrast with his efforts for reform, Chiang censored free expression, which alienated intellectuals and political moderates. He also had a huge problem: Japan was occupying Chinese territory in Manchuria and appeared to be ready to strike at the Chinese capital.

Militarism in Japan

During the 1930s, militarism was on the rise in Japan. The nation had become prosperous during the Meiji Restoration. *Zaibatsu*, or large corporations, controlled the Japanese economy. With the aid of government, they also controlled much of Japanese life. But the Depression that affected Europe had come to Japan and led to an economic downturn. Many workers wanted to return to the traditional ways, while others wanted to dominate Asia. These two movements eventually combined.

Japan needed raw materials and foreign markets for its growing industrial economy. Militants pushed for the seizure of the territories of Formosa, Korea, and southern Manchuria. Eventually this expansion led to a conflict of interest between the United States and Japan in the Pacific Rim. By 1938, the militant faction completely dominated the Japanese government. They put Japan on wartime status and instituted a draft. Additionally, the militants disbanded labor unions and placed all industries under government control. Finally, the military leaders tried to purge Western values from Japanese culture.

The Banana Republics

During the nineteenth century, most of the Latin American nations had gained their independence. By the twentieth century, their economies were based on the export of foods and raw materials to the industrialized nations of the West. During the 1920s, the United States replaced Great Britain as the largest investor in Latin America, financing and running the export production companies. In some cases, because of their incredible economic influence, these American investors guided Latin American governmental policies. The term "banana republics" came from this period of economic control.

As a result of the heavy-handedness of U.S. investors, Latin Americans began to view the United States as imperialist. They weren't far from the mark, as the majority of the profits went to benefit U.S. industries and political power. In addition, when popular will threatened its interests, the United States intervened in Latin American domestic politics, sometimes militarily.

When the Great Depression hit the United States, the economies of the Latin American nations slowed with the end of exports of cash crops to America. Most of the nations, which had some form of republican government at the beginning of the twentieth century, were then taken over by *oligarchies* controlled by large landowners or military leaders.

DEFINITION

An **oligarchy** is a government ruled by only an elite and powerful few.

Cultural Changes in the 1920s and 1930s

In the 1920s and 1930s, several mass cultural trends affected the majority of the world. With the discovery of the wireless radio waves by Marconi in the early twentieth century, radio became a source of news and entertainment for the public. Motion pictures, invented in the 1890s, also became an important media source throughout industrialized culture. By 1939, a majority of the industrialized world was attending at least one film a week. Of course, people had more time to listen to the radio and see movies with the eight-hour workday and weekends off. In addition, the public went to more sporting events and traveled more with the use of trains, buses, and cars.

After the slaughter of World War I, the trends in art and literature tended to gravitate toward despair and uncertainty. Abstract expressionism became more popular, with a fascination with the absurd and the unconscious; the psychological ideas of Sigmund Freud seemed to spur it on. A movement called Dadaism took hold of the artistic world with its view that life had no purpose and was insane. Surrealism pioneered by Salvador Dali also gained popularity, with its reality beyond the material world. Trends in literature after World War I also seemed to deal with the harshness and confusion of existence, with James Joyce, F. Scott Fitzgerald, and Hermann Hesse all writing popular works with that theme.

The Least You Need to Know

- The terms of the Treaty of Versailles caused tensions in western and eastern Europe.
- The Great Depression of the 1930s affected nations to varying degrees.
- Many totalitarian states were created during the 1920s and 1930s in response to economic and social issues.
- Japan became a militaristic state during the 1930s, bringing it into conflict with the United States.
- Mass culture was influenced by the radio and motion pictures, while art and literature exhibited despair and uncertainty in the wake of World War I.

World War II and the End of European Dominance

In This Chapter

- Hitler and the roots of World War II
- The policy of appeasement
- Blitzkrieg
- Japan in the Pacific
- The Allies turn the tide
- The bitter end of World War II

During the early 1930s, the rise of Nazi Germany led by Adolf Hitler began the final act of European dominance. As the European powers practiced appeasement with Germany, Hitler and his Axis allies of Italy and Japan prepared for war in Europe and the Pacific. World War II started in Europe with the invasion of Poland in 1939 and in the Pacific with the attack on Pearl Harbor in 1941.

The Axis powers experienced initial success against the Allies, but in 1942 the tide started to turn against the Axis powers. The Big Three Allied nations—Great Britain, the United States, and the Soviet Union—mobilized their superior resources for the war effort.

In the end the Allies defeated the Axis powers, leaving Europe in a broken state. It was then, in 1945, that the United States and the Soviet Union replaced Europe in dominating the world stage. As a result, tensions arose between the two rival nations, and the Cold War began.

Hitler and World War II

World War II was directly brought about by the influence of one man: Adolf Hitler. His views on the superiority of the Aryan race and his goal of creating a great German civilization made the acquisition of territory one of his policy priorities. But Hitler knew that this acquisition of territory had to come in baby steps.

Hitler's first step was the rebuilding of the German military, disregarding the military restrictions the Treaty of Versailles placed on Germany at the end of World War I. Hitler announced that Germany was creating an air force on March 9, 1935. Seven days later, he instituted a military draft to enlarge the army. In addition, he sent German troops into the demilitarized zone of the Rhineland.

With these violations of the Versailles treaty and Germany's military incursion, France had the right to use military force to expel German troops, but it did not. Great Britain preferred to follow a policy of *appeasement* with Hitler. No one wanted another war except Hitler.

DEFINITION

The policy of **appeasement** involved giving in to the reasonable demands of unsatisfied nations of Europe (meaning Germany) in hopes of gaining mutual trust and respect.

Hitler's next step was to form new alliances. In 1936, Germany and Fascist Italy reached an agreement based on common political and economic interests, creating the Rome-Berlin Axis. Germany struck another alliance with Japan called the Anti-Comintern Pact, based on their mutual distrust of communism. These agreements created the alliance of nations called the Axis powers.

The next step for Hitler was to acquire the *lebensraum*, or "living space," his new German Empire would require. In 1937, he united Germany with his native land of Austria, rattling his saber and threatening to invade Austria if the Austrian chancellor did not give political power to the Austrian Nazi party. But once the Austrian Nazi party was in power, they invited the German troops to occupy Austria. On March 13, 1938, Germany had officially annexed Austria as part of the Third Reich.

Of course, the annexation of Austria was only a first step. On September 15, 1938, Germany demanded that Czechoslovakia surrender the territory of the Sudetenland in northwest Czechoslovakia, which was inhabited by mostly Germans. A quick conference was convened in Munich with Britain, Germany, France, and Italy attending. At the end of the conference, Czechoslovakia was carved up without its consent to suit Hitler's demands, while Neville Chamberlain, the British prime minister, declared that Europe had satisfied Hitler and secured "peace in our time." Hitler sensed the fear behind the appeasement policy of the British and French and made another bold move. In March 1939, German forces invaded and took control of Bohemia and Moravia in western Czechoslovakia. The British appeasement policy was no brake on Hitler's ambitions.

Hitler was not done; he demanded that the Polish port of Danzig be turned over to Germany. In reality, Hitler was concocting a reason to invade Poland. At that point, the British made a stand and pledged to protect Poland in the event of an invasion. Then France and Great Britain started to negotiate with the Soviet Union to create some type of alliance against Germany.

Little did the British and French know that the Soviets had their own negotiations going on with Germany. On August 24, 1939, Germany and the Soviet Union signed the Molotov-Ribbentrop Pact, a Nazi-Soviet nonaggression treaty in which they promised not to attack one another. During the secret negotiations, Hitler offered Stalin control of eastern Poland and the Baltic states if he would stand by during a German invasion of Poland. When Hitler announced the nonaggression pact in late August, the world was shocked and dismayed. The treaty had given Hitler the freedom to attack Poland. On September 1, 1939, German forces invaded Poland on the pretense of a Polish attack. In response, on September 3, Great Britain and France declared war on Germany. World War II had started.

Japan Turns Very Imperialist

Germany was not the only country inciting conflict with the rest of the world. Japan wanted to create a new order in east Asia, which included Japan, Manchuria, and China.

In September 1931, Japan seized the remainder of Manchuria with the pretense of a Chinese attack on the Japanese railway on Mukden. The League of Nations condemned this action, but did little to stop it. In response, Japan withdrew from the league and continued to acquire bits and pieces of territory in northern China. Chiang Kai-shek was desperate to avoid a conflict with Japan, but eventually was forced to ally with communist forces to form a united front against the Japanese. The front did not work together well, and in July 1937 they clashed with Japanese forces south of Beijing. The Japanese seized the Chinese capital of Nanjing.

With the Anti-Comintern Pact, Japan had envisioned conquering Soviet Siberia with the Nazis and dividing the spoils, but the Nazi-Soviet nonaggression pact forced Japan to look to Southeast Asia, which had traditionally been controlled by the imperialist policies of Britain, France, and the United States.

Japan started by invading and conquering French Indochina. The United States placed economic sanctions on Japan, which threatened Japan's ambitions because they needed U.S. oil and scrap iron to fuel their armies. So the Japanese began to develop a plan to shock the United States and Europe into a quick submission.

Hitler Gets Some Quick Licks In

In Europe, Hitler's war for "living space" was going very well. Using a military strategy called the "blitzkrieg," or lightning war, German tank divisions with the aid of air support were able to defeat the Polish armies in a matter of four weeks. On September 28, 1939, Germany and the Soviet Union, as spelled out in their treaty, divided the territory of Poland. Spurred on by his success, Hitler ordered the invasion of Denmark and Norway on April 9, 1940, and then on May 10, 1940, the Netherlands, Belgium, and France fell to the German blitzkrieg. Once conquered, the Nazis took direct control of those nations' governments and resources, except in France, where they set up the Vichy government led by Marshall Henri Petain.

Shocked by Hitler's quick victories, Great Britain appealed to the United States for help. The United States had practiced a policy of isolationism for most of its existence, especially during the 1930s with a series of neutrality acts. But the old Anglo-American informal alliance was strong and the United States supplied food, ships, planes, and weapons to the British cause.

The Battle of Britain

Britain was for a time alone in its struggle with Nazi Germany. In August 1940, the German Luftwaffe, or air force, launched a major offensive on the British Isles to soften up the island for a German invasion force. At first, they bombed only air and naval bases, but after a British air raid on Berlin, Hitler ordered the bombing of major British cities.

WHAT IN THE WORLD

One city was off limits to the German Luftwaffe in the bombing of Great Britain: the university city of Oxford. Hitler had such respect for the tradition and learning at the various colleges of Oxford University that he did not want to see it destroyed.

This was Britain's "finest hour," as the British population took the brunt of the German attacks. Because the focus of the air raids was on the cities, the British were able to rebuild their military. By the end of September 1940, with the British military rebounding, Hitler ordered the indefinite postponement of the invasion of Britain.

NOTABLE QUOTABLE

We shall not flag or fail. We shall go on to the end. … We shall fight on the beaches, we shall fight in the fields and in the streets, we shall fight in the hills; we shall never surrender.

—Winston Churchill (1940)

Doesn't Anyone Read History?

Thinking that the British were only able to hang on because of the support of the Soviet Union, in addition to his hatred of communism and the need for "living space," Hitler turned his sights east and planned an invasion of the Soviet Union. Before striking, he sent German forces into Greece and Yugoslavia in April 1941; his Italian allies were not having much success with their invasions of those nations.

Finally the stage was set for Hitler's biggest mistake. On June 22, 1941, German armies invaded Soviet territory. At first, the Germans advanced rapidly, capturing two million Russian soldiers and taking a large amount of territory. By the winter of 1941, the German armies had stopped, but not because of Soviet armies. The heavily mechanized German army was not prepared for the brutal Russian winter. Hitler had made a fatal military mistake, very similar to Napoleon's when he invaded Russia.

Japan Gets in Some Quick Licks, Too

Like Germany, Japan also experienced quick success in the Pacific. On December 7, 1941, a "day that will live in infamy," Japanese aircraft attacked a totally surprised U.S. naval base and fleet at Pearl Harbor. The United States declared war, but the Japanese, having caught the United States flatfooted, were able to take the U.S.-controlled Philippines, Dutch East Indies, British Malaya, and most of Southeast Asia and the Pacific Ocean. These territories under Japanese control were now called the Great East-Asia Co-Prosperity Sphere. The Japanese entered these territories as liberators, but treated the countries like conquered lands.

The Japanese hope with the attack of Pearl Harbor was to destroy the U.S. Pacific fleet and shock the United States into quick compliance with the shift of power in the Pacific. This was a miscalculation. American opinion quickly unified against Japanese aggression and the United States joined Great Britain and nationalist China in an effort to defeat Japan in the Pacific. Four days later, in response to the U.S. declaration of war on Japan, Hitler declared war on the United States. Truly it had become a global war.

1942, and Things Don't Look Too Good

At the beginning of 1942, the Allied nations that remained were the United States, Great Britain, and the Soviet Union (strange bedfellows indeed). But rather than focus on political differences, they agreed to stress military operations to end the Axis threat. In 1943, they also agreed that the only surrender they would accept was an unconditional one. They meant business.

The Tide Turns

In the European theater in 1942, things did not appear to be going well for the Allies. In North Africa, German forces led by the "Desert Fox," General Erwin Rommel, broke through British defenses in Egypt and were moving toward Alexandria, and a new German offensive captured the Soviet Crimea. But British forces stopped Rommel's forces at the Battle of El Alamein. Then in November 1942, U.S. and British troops invaded Vichy French North Africa, forcing German and Italian troops to surrender in Africa and Rommel to return to Germany. When superior German forces attacked the key city of Stalingrad, they were surrounded by a Russian counteroffensive. As a result, the entire German 6th Army, Hitler's best of the best, surrendered. The tide had turned in Europe.

In the Pacific theater, 1942 was also a key turning point. In the Battle of the Coral Sea on May 7 and 8, U.S. naval forces stopped a Japanese invasion fleet headed for Australia. Then on June 4 at the Battle of Midway Island, the U.S. naval fleet encountered and destroyed four Japanese aircraft carriers, establishing naval superiority in the Pacific. With naval superiority, General Douglas MacArthur and U.S. forces moved in on south China and Burma, while a combination of U.S. naval and ground forces advanced from island to island toward Japan, a strategy sometimes referred to as island hopping. The tide had also turned in the Pacific.

The Final Years of World War II

At the beginning of 1943, the Axis powers were on their heels and fighting a defensive war. In September 1943, the Allies invaded Italy, seeing it as the weak link in Axis-controlled Europe. Hitler, knowing this was true, had sent German forces to occupy Italy and support Mussolini since the Allies conquered the island of Sicily. The Italian capital of Rome fell to the Allies on June 4, 1944. Two days later, on D-Day, the Allied forces landed on the beaches of Normandy, France, fighting the German occupying forces for a foothold in western Europe. Paris was liberated by the Allies by August 1944. The end of Nazi Germany seemed close at hand.

During the winter of 1944, the Germans made one last offensive to try to push the Allies off the continent. They chose the Ardennes Forest as the site of the major offensive. The resulting Battle of the Bulge, however, went in the Allies' favor. Nazi Germany had no hope of winning the war, but Hitler pushed his people to continue. Continuing air raids by the Allies crippled the German infrastructure. This was apparent in March 1945 when the Allies crossed the Rhine River and advanced into Germany. By April, they had crossed the Elbe River and were closing in on the German capital of Berlin.

The war was not going well for Germany on the eastern front, either. After the Soviets won at the Battle of Stalingrad, they advanced toward Germany at a rapid pace. At the Battle of Kursk in July 1943, the Soviets destroyed the notion of German superiority in mechanized warfare in the largest tank battle of World War II. By the end of 1943 the Soviets reoccupied the Ukraine, and moved into the Baltic states in 1944. In January 1945, Soviet armies entered Warsaw while also sweeping through Hungary, Romania, and Bulgaria. By April 1945, Soviet troops were closing in on Berlin, too.

Victory Around the World

Toward the end of the war, Hitler remained in a protective bunker in Berlin. As time passed, he became more delusional about the predicament that the nation of Germany was in. Finally, with most of Germany in shambles around him, on April 30, 1945, Hitler committed suicide with his long-time mistress. Two days earlier, his Italian ally, Mussolini, was killed by Italian resistance fighters. Without Hitler to bark orders and threaten lives, the German will to continue the war faltered. On May 7, 1945, Germany surrendered to the Allies on what is referred to as Victory in Europe Day (V-E Day).

Japan also suffered many setbacks from the island-hopping campaign. But the invasion of Japan itself was something that scared U.S. military planners and President Harry Truman. Instead, on August 6, 1945, the U.S. Air Force dropped the first-ever atomic bomb, named "Little Boy," on the Japanese city of Hiroshima, killing more than 100,000 civilians. When Japan did not respond with an unconditional surrender, the U.S responded three days later by dropping another atomic bomb, "Fat Man," on the Japanese city of Nagasaki, killing more than 75,000 civilians. Japan surrendered unconditionally on August 14, 1945, referred to as Victory over Japan Day (V-J Day).

Unthinkable Acts

When the war came to a close, the Nazi atrocities surfaced to the world. In an effort to make "living space" for the Germans, Slavic people had been forcibly moved from their traditional homes. Under the direction of the leader of the SS, Heinrich Himmler, one million Poles were moved from northern to southern Poland. Additionally, more than seven million foreign workers were placed in labor camps and forced to work in German agriculture and industry.

But of course, the single largest Nazi atrocity was the Holocaust. Hitler had detailed his anti-Semitic views in his volume *Mein Kampf,* and once he became leader of Germany, he put them to practice. Using the SS to execute his "Final Solution," Hitler waged a war of genocide, termed the Holocaust, on the Jewish population. At first, strike forces of mobile killing units executed Jews in Polish villages and buried them in mass graves. Finding that inefficient, by 1942, all Jews in the nations that Germany conquered were being shipped to extermination centers built in Poland.

At the end of the war, the SS had killed more than five million Jews in camps while also murdering more than 10 million Jews, gypsies, Catholics, and Africans with SS death squads. These staggering numbers became even larger with the addition of more than eight million Slavic and Soviet prisoners who died in German labor camps.

NOTABLE QUOTABLE

I picked my way over corpse after corpse in the gloom until I heard one voice that rose above the gentle, undulating moaning. I found a girl, she was a living skeleton, impossible to gauge her age for she had practically no hair left on her head and her face was a yellow parchment sheet with two holes in it for eyes.

—BBC war correspondent Richard Dimbleby at Bergen-Belsen concentration camp (1945)

The Japanese also committed atrocities in the name of war. With the program Asia for Asiatics, they forced the conquered people to serve in local military units and public works projects. Coupling the forced labor with food shortages (food was shipped to Japan for the war effort), more than one million civilians died in Vietnam alone. After their conquest of Nanzing, China, in 1937, Japanese soldiers spent several days killing and raping the population of the city. Numbers have never been finalized for atrocities in the other nations. Additionally, more than one million Allied POWs and local workers died on forced labor projects for the Japanese government.

WHAT IN THE WORLD

Not only Germany, Japan, and the Soviet Union violated human rights before and during World War II. The United States also had its own episode. During the war, for "security reasons," over 100,000 Japanese Americans were removed from their businesses and homes to internment camps surrounded by fences and barbed wire. They were allowed to return to their homes after the war, but many lost their livelihoods as a result.

The Big Three and Lots of Meetings

During the final years of World War II, the Big Three (Great Britain, the United States, and the Soviet Union) met at three conferences to talk war and postwar strategy. At the Tehran Conference in November 1943, the Big Three seemed to get along quite well, agreeing that the Soviets would liberate eastern Europe while the United States and Britain would free western Europe.

The Yalta Conference

At the Yalta Conference in April 1945, the relationship between the three started to go south (or, in this case, east). With Germany's defeat imminent, Stalin, who was very suspicious of the United States and Britain, wanted to create a buffer zone between the Soviet Union and western Europe. That zone was eastern Europe. President Franklin Roosevelt wanted self-determination for these nations. He also wanted the Soviet Union to pitch in against the Japanese. In return for helping with Japan, Stalin wanted the Sakhalin and Kuril islands (Japanese territories), two warm-water ports, and railroads in Manchuria. Roosevelt agreed, hoping that this agreement would lead to self-determination in eastern Europe. He also hoped that Stalin would agree to his idea of the United Nations. In the end, both Stalin and British Prime Minister Winston Churchill backed the creation of the United Nations, but self-determination in eastern Europe was still up in the air.

The Potsdam Conference

Four months later at the Potsdam Conference in July 1945, the differences in the Big Three became very evident. President Truman (Roosevelt died on April 12) and Churchill demanded free democratic elections in the nations of eastern Europe; Stalin refused and, since Soviet troops occupied those regions, he could back it up. Soon a cloud of mistrust came between the West and the Soviet Union. It became a war of words and ideologies with global capitalist imperialism versus worldwide communist expansion. It crystallized further in March 1946 when Churchill gave his "iron curtain" speech. Stalin saw the speech as a call to war. The whole world was bitterly divided into two camps.

The Impact of World War II

The impact of World War II was immeasurable. It affected the twentieth century like no other event. More than 17 million men had died in combat, while 20 to 60 million civilians died. Europe was completely shattered, with very little of the continent unscathed. No longer were the European nations in control of the world with imperial policies. The United States and the Soviet Union were in command and soon were locked in a cold war of ideologies that dominated the world consciousness until the end of the twentieth century.

The Least You Need to Know

- Hitler's beliefs in Aryan superiority led to World II and the Holocaust.
- The Axis powers experienced initial success against the Allies, but in 1942 the tide turned against them.
- Toward the end of the war, the Big Three—Great Britain, the United States, and the Soviet Union—squabbled over the fate of eastern Europe.
- The war changed the global balance of power with the imperialist policies of the European nations being replaced by the Cold War policies of the United States and Soviet Union.

The Cold War

In This Chapter

- The beginning of the Cold War
- The Cuban Missile Crisis
- Responses in Eastern and Western Europe
- The Cold War gets frigid
- The thawing of relations

At the end of World War II, the United States and the Soviet Union emerged as ideological rivals in Europe and the world. The process of the United States and the Soviet Union moving from allies to enemies started in 1945 when Stalin refused to remove Soviet occupation troops from Eastern Europe. The United States wanted self-determination for these and the rest of the nations in Europe. The Soviet Union under Stalin wanted a buffer zone between the Soviet Union and Western Europe. As a result, the Soviet armies stayed and tensions grew between the nations. The tensions between the nations were called the Cold War.

Plans and Doctrines

Harry Truman was an unknown senator from Missouri who had little experience in foreign affairs, so not much was expected from Franklin Roosevelt's selection for vice president. But after only 82 days, he became president of the United States when Roosevelt died in office. Truman had met Roosevelt only twice before.

President Truman responded to the tension between the United States and the Soviet Union with the Truman Doctrine in 1946, stating that the United States would provide money to any country that was threatened by communist expansion. By 1947 it became apparent to the Soviets that the United States had adopted a policy of containment to keep communism within the existing boundaries of the Soviet Union and Eastern Europe.

After World War II, the rebuilding of Europe was a concern for the United States. The Marshall Plan, enacted in June 1947, was meant to rebuild Europe into a stable, prosperous region, with the belief that communist revolution only occurred in economically unstable nations. Aid totaling $13 billion was offered to the nations of Europe to rebuild, but the Soviet Union and its Eastern European *satellite states* refused to participate. The Soviets responded to the Marshall Plan with their own plan to aid Eastern Europe in 1949. It was called the Council for Mutual Assistance, or COMECON, but it ended in failure because the Soviet Union could not afford to bankroll it.

DEFINITION

A **satellite state** is a small state that is economically and/or politically dependent on a larger, more powerful state. Generally, satellite states adjust their policies based on the desires of the larger state.

The Problem in Germany

At the end of World War II, territory in the defeated nation of Germany was divided by the United States, Great Britain, France, and the Soviet Union into four allied zones. The capital of Berlin, located in the middle of the Soviet zone, was also divided into four zones. In 1948, the United States, Great Britain, and France made plans to unify their respective zones into the nation of West Germany. Threatened by this plan, the Soviet Union responded by blockading Berlin of all food and supplies. As a result, the United States and Great Britain airlifted supplies to Berlin, dropping 1 million tons of supplies into the city. Eventually, the Soviet Union realized the futility of its actions and lifted the blockade in May 1949. The Berlin Airlift was a success.

In September 1949, the Federal Republic of Germany, referred to as West Germany, was created. Its capital was the city of Bonn. The Soviet Union also set up a nation from its occupied zone of Germany, creating in October 1949 the German Democratic Republic. Its capital was East Berlin.

NOTABLE QUOTABLE

Let us not be deceived—we are today in the midst of a cold war.

—Bernard Baruch, United States presidential advisor (1947)

Under Pressure

The Cold War tensions between the United States and the Soviet Union continued to rise through the late 1940s and 1950s. In 1949, the Chinese communists took control of the government of China. The United States perceived this as part of the monolithic, Soviet-led spread of communism. Also in 1949, the Soviet Union tested its first hydrogen bomb, sparking an arms race. By 1952, both the United States and the Soviet Union had developed the hydrogen bomb. In the mid-1950s, the superpowers built intercontinental ballistic missiles with which to deliver and drop atomic weapons on their enemies. The superpowers then adopted the military strategy of Mutual Assured Destruction, or MAD, based on the assumption that neither nation would attack because both nations would be destroyed as a result. It was a no-win war that no superpower was willing to start.

The arms race became a space race in 1957, when the Soviet Union launched *Sputnik*, the first man-made satellite. From there, the superpowers raced to put the first man in space, and then the first man on the moon.

The superpowers also created a series of military alliances to protect their interests around the world. In April 1949, an agreement of mutual protection and cooperation was made among the nations of Belgium, Luxembourg, France, the Netherlands, Great Britain, Italy, Denmark, Norway, Portugal, Iceland, Canada, West Germany, Turkey, and the United States called the North Atlantic Treaty Organization, or NATO. In response, the Soviet Union created a similar organization in 1955 called the Warsaw Pact, which included the nations of Albania, Bulgaria, Czechoslovakia, East Germany, Hungary, Poland, and Romania.

Other treaty organizations were created with the idea of isolating the communist nations of Eastern Europe, the Soviet Union, and China. The Southeast Treaty Organization, or SEATO, was an agreement between the United States, Great Britain, France, Pakistan, Thailand, the Philippines, Australia, and New Zealand. CENTO included Turkey, Iraq, Iran, Pakistan, Great Britain, and the United States. By the end of the Cold War era, the United States had allied itself with over 40 different nations globally.

Satellite Conflicts

Although the Cold War was not a direct conflict between the two superpowers, it was a conflict nonetheless. These political and military conflicts ensued as the superpowers competed for spheres of influence in satellite nations of central Europe, Latin America, and Southeast and east Asia.

Another Brick in the Wall?

With the West Germans enjoying the many freedoms of democracy, it was natural that East Germans would want to migrate to the West. The problem was that they could not. The communist governments were particularly insistent on making the people stay in the country. As a result, barbed wire fences and border guards were placed to keep people in some of the communist nations.

In August 1961, Nikita Kruschev, the Soviet leader at the time, ordered that a wall be built in East Berlin to separate it from West Berlin and to help prevent East Germans from escaping. Of course, this gesture was not truly needed. There were plenty of guards, guns, and barbed wire to separate East from West Berlin. But it did add to the Cold War tensions between the United States and the Soviet Union, leading up to the Cuban Missile Crisis.

The Cuban Missile Crisis

The Cold War between the Soviets and the Americans almost became hot with the Cuban Missile Crisis. In 1959, Fidel Castro overthrew the Cuban dictator Fulgencio Batista and set up a communist regime in Cuba. President John F. Kennedy, worried about a communist regime so close to American shores, approved a secret plan to support Cuban exiles in an invasion of Cuba at the Bay of Pigs, to overthrow the communist Castro. This plan failed disastrously when the United States pulled air support at the last minute, but it angered Castro enough to seek help from the Soviet Union.

The Soviet Union started to send arms and advisors to Cuba after the Bay of Pigs incident, and in 1962 Kruschev sent nuclear missiles to the island nation in response to the United States placing nuclear missiles in Turkey (a U.S. ally). In October 1962, Kennedy got wind of the Cuban missiles through a U.S. U2 spy plane and also discovered that more missiles were being sent. In response he ordered a U.S. naval blockade of Cuba, which caused some very tense moments as each superpower threatened nuclear war.

Finally, in this game of nuclear chicken, Kruschev blinked. He ordered the Soviet ships to return and removed the nuclear missiles from Cuba. From that point, the superpowers saw the need for open communication between Washington and Moscow. In 1963 they installed the red phone, a direct line between the nuclear superpowers.

NOTABLE QUOTABLE

We're eyeball to eyeball and I think the other fellow just blinked.

—U.S. Secretary of State Dean Rusk (October 24, 1962)

Domino Theory and Vietnam

The U.S. policy of containment was apparent in the Korean War from 1950 to 1953. The United States led a small United Nations military force to stop communist North Korea, which was supported by the Soviet Union and later the People's Republic of China, from taking over democratic South Korea. The war ended in an uneasy stalemate and finally an armistice creating a military demarcation line between North and South Korea that continues to exist today.

In 1964, President Lyndon Johnson sent U.S. troops to Vietnam to prevent the communist takeover of South Vietnam by North Vietnam. Johnson believed that if South Vietnam fell to communism, other nations of Southeast Asia would soon follow. He also thought that the Soviet Union and China were together coordinating a communist takeover in Southeast Asia starting with Vietnam. This was Johnson's domino theory.

In the Vietnam War, U.S. troops ended up fighting a defensive war in South Vietnam against North Vietnamese troops and the Viet Cong, who were South Vietnamese communist sympathizers. With a strong antiwar movement emerging in the United States, the war dragged on for U.S. forces. In 1968, the North Vietnamese and Viet Cong attacked U.S. forces across South Vietnam in the Tet Offensive. Although militarily a failure, the Tet Offensive galvanized U.S. public opinion against the Vietnam War. In 1973, U.S. President Nixon agreed to withdraw U.S. forces from the region and by 1975, South Vietnam fell to North Vietnamese forces.

In the end, the domino theory that Johnson used in defense of U.S. involvement in South Vietnam turned out to be wrong. China and the Soviet Union did not have strong enough relations to coordinate the spread of communism in Asia. In fact, the

North Vietnamese communist movement was a nationalist movement. Ho Chi Minh even compared himself to George Washington and other American freedom fighters. Communism did not spread to the rest of Southeast Asia after Vietnam.

Behind the Curtain

In the late 1940s, Winston Churchill used the term "iron curtain" to denote the division between Western and Eastern Europe. This division was enhanced in 1948 when the Soviet Union took control of the governments of Eastern Europe to ensure that they remained communist. With Soviet direction, the governments of East Germany, Bulgaria, Romania, Poland, and Hungary created five-year plans similar to those of the Soviets. These plans emphasized heavy industry rather than consumer goods, collectivized agriculture, and eliminated all noncommunist parties. But the Soviet-guided plans were used to exploit the Eastern European nations, so the communist systems created in these countries did not have deep roots.

The lack of conviction became apparent beginning in the 1950s. When the Soviet Union made it known that independence from Soviet directives was not an option, the people of Eastern Europe protested, with mixed results. In 1956, the Polish protested the situation and the Polish communist party responded with reforms. The secretary of the Polish communist party decided to pursue an independent domestic path in Poland but continue to be loyal to the Warsaw Pact.

In Hungary, the protests persuaded Imre Nagy, the political leader of Hungary, to declare that Hungary was a free nation on November 1, 1956. He also promised free elections that would include other noncommunist parties. The Soviets did not care for that type of talk; on November 4, 1956, the Soviet army invaded Hungary and took control of Budapest, the Hungarian capital. Nagy was captured and later executed.

In Czechoslovakia there was also a call for change. In January 1968, Alexander Dubcek was elected as first secretary of the communist party of Czechoslovakia. He made reforms to satisfy the Czech people, including freedom of speech, press, and travel. Dubcek also promised to democratize the political system. This time of reform was referred to as the "Prague Spring," but it was too much to bear for the Soviets, and a Soviet army moved in and crushed the reform movement.

Take Me to the Other Side

The end of World War II and the ascension of the United States and Soviet Union as the two superpowers had dethroned the European nations as world powers. But compared with the other side of the curtain in Eastern Europe, the people of Western Europe were enjoying economic prosperity and democratic freedoms.

Eventually this economic freedom and prosperity led to unity in Western Europe. In 1957, France, West Germany, Belgium, the Netherlands, Luxembourg, and Italy signed the Rome Treaty. The treaty created the European Economic Community (EEC) or Common Market. The EEC was a free-trade area benefiting the member nations economically, and it became one of the largest exporters of finished goods and purchasers of raw materials.

The EEC gained members as time went by. In 1973, Great Britain, Ireland, and Denmark joined, followed by Spain, Portugal, and Greece in 1986. Finally in 1995, Austria, Finland, and Sweden joined the economic club, by which time the EEC had transformed into the beginning of another treaty, the Treaty of European Union.

Enacted in 1994, the goal of the EU was to create a common currency, end any trade barriers between the European nations, and create a sizeable economic entity. They accomplished those goals on January 1, 2002, by instituting a common currency, the euro. The EU process was Europe becoming free of old Cold War politics. Eastern Europe did the same, but by another route.

Thawing and Freezing

In the 1970s, the relationship between the United States and the Soviet Union improved considerably. As a result, the United States started to sell excess stores of American grain to the Soviet Union, which needed it. But the thaw in relations went frigid in 1979 with the Soviet invasion of the nation of Afghanistan. *Détente* officially ended when U.S President Jimmy Carter stopped grain shipments to the Soviet Union.

DEFINITION

Détente refers to the lessening of tensions between nations due to treaties or trade agreements.

The tension between the countries again increased when U.S. President Ronald Reagan was in the Oval Office. Reagan considered the Soviet Union an "evil empire" and said so to the American public. He also sent aid to Afghan rebels that were fighting the Soviet army. Finally, in a televised presidential address, Reagan announced his intention to create the Strategic Defense Initiative, or SDI, a missile defense program also called "Star Wars" that would destroy incoming Soviet nuclear missiles in space while allowing U.S. nuclear missiles to reach the Soviet Union. To the Soviets, it appeared that another arms race in space had started.

WHAT IN THE WORLD

By the early 1980s, the United States and the Soviet Union had more than 12,000 intercontinental ballistic missiles (ICBMs) pointed at each other. The superpowers had the power to not only destroy each other with a nuclear exchange, but the rest of the world, too. Actually, they had enough missiles to destroy the world seven times over.

Tensions between the Soviet Union and the United States escalated a great deal during the early 1980s. Most of the nations of the world were aligned with one or the other while the rest of the world held its collective breath.

Tensions were high when Mikhail Gorbachev came to power in the Soviet Union in 1985. But unlike his predecessors, Gorbachev was a progressive communist. In 1987, with his guidance, the United States and Soviet Union came to an agreement to eliminate intermediate-range nuclear weapons. This agreement was good for both of the superpowers. It gave Gorbachev time to work on much-needed Soviet economic reforms, termed *glasnost* and *perestroika*, and the United States to change its status as one of the largest debtor nations.

As part of his economic reforms, Gorbachev stopped providing economic support to the communist countries of Eastern Europe. As a result, a democratic reform movement swept through Eastern Europe in 1989, symbolized by the fall of the Berlin Wall. By October 3, 1990, East and West Germany had reunited as one country. It wasn't long before the Soviets themselves were swept into the democratic reform movement. Gorbachev, in his effort to provide economic reform for his country, had opened the door to more freedoms. Once the freedoms flowed into the communist nations, they could not be stopped. By 1991, the Soviet Union was officially dissolved into a multitude of republics. The communism of the Soviet Union and Eastern Europe was gone. In just a few years, the Cold War had simply melted away.

A New Economy in the West

After the end of the world wars, a new society emerged in the West. With new technologies built on the successes of industrialization, Western civilization transformed from the industrial to the computer age. Change accelerated after World War II, with communication and transportation innovations such as television, computers, and cheap air transportation, all creating a more complex and mobile society.

The middle class, which before the world wars was composed of factory managers and shopkeepers, turned within a matter of decades into technicians and tech managers. Industrial or working classes also declined as Western industry was outsourced to other developing nations. With advances in agriculture, the numbers of farmers decreased drastically, too. While these decreases continued into the twenty-first century, the white-collar class increased, filling the ranks of service-oriented businesses (corporations and banks) that spread throughout the Western world. The West turned into a consumer society depending on other nations to supply it with consumer goods while it focused on service industries.

The status of women changed considerably after the mid-twentieth century. Women had acquired voting rights during the early twentieth century and entered the workforce in more numbers after World War II. Despite the spike in birthrates during the "baby boom," the size of families in the West decreased dramatically during the latter half of the twentieth century. Finally during the late 1960s, there was a renewed interest in feminism, or women's liberation. More and more women started to fight inequalities in the workplace and the home. By the end of the twentieth century, women had started to make real progress toward equality of the sexes.

NOTABLE QUOTABLE

And even today woman is heavily handicapped, though her situation is beginning to change. Almost nowhere is her legal status the same as man's, and frequently it is much to her disadvantage. Even when her rights are legally recognized in the abstract, long-standing custom prevents their full expression.

—*The Second Sex,* Simone de Beauvoir (1949)

After World War II, higher education opened up for most of Western society. Universities and colleges allowed for larger class sizes to bring in more students. This meant that professors provided less attention to each individual student. As a result, discontent was high among the student population by the 1960s. Additionally, a wave of student radicalism swept through the universities. There were several causes for this movement, including protests over the Vietnam War and calls for reform in the universities. Some students believed that the universities did not respond to student needs or to the realities of the modern world. The Paris demonstrations of 1968 were the high-water mark for the European student protest movement. With reform, this movement lost steam and faded by the late 1970s. Some of these student protestors became the middle-class professionals that populated the corporations of the West. With the opening of higher education, the Western nations established their lead role in the development of the computer age.

The Least You Need to Know

- At the end of World War II, the United States and the Soviet Union emerged as the two superpowers of the world.
- The tensions that resulted from different ideologies and actions resulted in the era known as the Cold War.
- Most of the nations of the world aligned with one of the superpowers during the Cold War.
- The Cold War ended when the Soviet Union, beset with economic problems, experienced a democratic revolution.
- The Western world moved from the industrial to the computer age, with significant and rapid changes in society as a result.

Out from the Shadows

27

In This Chapter

* The rise of the Third World
* Patterns of decolonization
* Middle East and Africa
* Asia and Latin America
* The former Soviet Union

After World War II, the developing world—also referred to by its Cold War classification, the Third World—emerged to take a larger role in world politics. These nations from Latin America, Asia, Africa, and the Middle East were not as economically and politically advanced as the Western nations. Most of this backwardness originated from the colonial and imperial policies that had once dominated these nations.

The Rise of the Third World

Some steps had been taken to decolonize territories under Western control after World War I. Britain and France had taken control of most of the former German territories, but found administration difficult at best. World War I had weakened the nations of Western Europe. As a result, they were simply unable to keep control of large imperial empires.

At the end of World War II, decolonization became the prevailing trend throughout Asia, the Middle East, and Africa. What was weakened by World War I was outmoded and destroyed by World War II. For the Western European nations, the reality was that they were no longer able to exert imperial control over faraway territories whose citizens were becoming more and more educated and nationalistic themselves. As a result, from the 1940s to 1970s, dozens of new nations were established after being freed from the dominion of their imperial mother country.

There were no set patterns to decolonization; the causes, means, and results varied from country to country. But some basic factors did help to determine whether a new, decolonized nation succeeded. Did the new nation have a tradition of self-government under imperial rule? Did the nation have to fight for independence? Were there different ethnic, cultural, or religious groups in the new nation? What natural resources did the new nation have to establish its economy? What position did the new nation take in the Cold War? The Middle East responded to these questions in several ways.

The Middle East

After World War II, several general trends influenced the politics of the Middle East:

- The development of petroleum resources
- Cold War political rivalries in the region
- The Arab-Israeli conflict
- The conflict between modernization and traditional Islamic culture
- The tradition of authoritarian government in the region

Walk Like an Egyptian

Egypt became an independent republic in 1952. In 1954, Colonel Gamal Abdel Nasser took control and created an authoritarian government. Nasser was an advocate of modernization and pan-Arabism. He tried to create a United Arab Republic that would link all of the Arab nations together in a commonwealth. Although he failed at that, he was successful in modernizing Egypt. To bankroll this modernization, Nasser nationalized foreign corporations and industries. In addition, he courted the Soviet Union enough that it sent advisors and engineers to help construct the Aswan Dam. Later, however, when the Soviet Union tried to influence Egyptian politics, Nasser expelled them. These bold nationalist actions were not Nasser's last. He also declared ownership of the Suez Canal, which angered France, Britain, and Israel. These countries tried to regain control of the canal but were forced to withdraw by the Cold War superpowers.

When Nasser died in 1970, he was succeeded by Anwar el-Sadat. Unlike his predecessor, Sadat drew Egypt closer to the United States, and became the first Arab leader to recognize the nation of Israel in 1978. As a result, Sadat was assassinated by Islamic terrorists in 1981. From that point, Egypt was ruled by Hosni Mubarak, a secular authoritarian who served as president.

The Papyrus Revolution

Egyptian objection to Mubarak's autocratic rule started in January 2011 when thousands of people took to the streets to protest poverty and corruption in the government. These were the first protests on such a large scale to be seen in Egypt since the 1970s. The government responded by blocking Twitter, Facebook, email, and text messaging, all methods used by protestors to coordinate their actions. But the protests continued in Cairo and other major Egyptian cities.

The Egyptian military was called in to take over security of the country from the police. This move was welcomed by the protestors. The United States, wanting to see democratic reforms in Egypt, announced they would review the aid given to Egypt (Egypt is the second-largest recipient of U.S. aid). Finally, after a long silence, President Mubarak appeared on state television to announce that while he would reform his government by dismissing corrupt officials, he would not resign.

Protestors reacted violently to Mubarak's announcement. The continued protests initiated a process of social and political reform, beginning with Mubarak's announcements that concessions would be made. President Mubarak resigned 18 days after the protests started. This revolution has paved the way for democratic reforms in Egypt and the Middle East.

The Nation of Israel

With the Balfour Declaration after World War I, the British declared their intention to create an independent Jewish nation in Palestine. During the 1920s and 1930s, they kept this decision low-key, to avoid Arab unrest in the region.

After World War II and the Holocaust, the British, backed by the United States and United Nations, revisited the question of a Jewish nation. In May 1948, the nation of Israel was created out of territory from Palestine, displacing millions of Palestinian Arabs. This upset the Arab community, who quickly invaded the territory but were summarily defeated. In 1964, the displaced Palestinian Arabs gained leadership and a voice with the establishment of the Palestinian Liberation Organization (PLO) led by Yasser Arafat. This organization was controversial because of its combination of terrorist and political tactics in seeking its goals, which included the destruction of the nation of Israel and the return of its territories to Palestinian Arabs.

WHAT IN THE WORLD

Albert Einstein was very active in the discussions regarding the creation of Israel. In 1952, when the president of Israel died, the Israeli government asked Einstein if he would take the powerful political position. Einstein declined, but was honored to have been asked.

The Arab nations of the Middle East fought frequently against Israel, most notably in the Six-Day War in 1967 and the Yom Kippur War in 1973. In each war, the well-trained and armed Israeli army defeated the Arab nations quickly and decisively. Afterward, Israel acquired territory from the Arab nations to enhance its own borders. Responding to these defeats, the PLO terrorism continued in the Israeli nation and abroad. The most infamous attack abroad involved the assassination of members of the Israeli Summer Olympic team in 1972 in West Germany.

By the end of the 1970s, many Arab nations started to understand the political reality of the situation. Israel was in the region to stay. Anwar el-Sadat of Egypt, at the urging of President Jimmy Carter, was the first Arab leader to recognize the nation of Israel. Other Arab states followed Egypt's lead, but this was not the end of problems for Israel.

The Israelis had to constantly deal with terrorist attacks, demonstrations, and protests within its borders from the Palestinian population that lived in Palestine but worked in Israel. Israel, which as a democracy was committed to human rights, often used force against Palestinian civilians. Through the 1990s, despite peace agreements between the Palestinians and Israelis, tensions were high and continue to be so. This ensured that Israel's relationships with the other Arab nations remained delicate at best.

NOTABLE QUOTABLE

We are embarking on a course that will greatly endanger any hope of a peaceful alliance with forces who could be our allies in the Middle East. Hundreds of thousands of Arabs who will be evicted from Palestine … will grow to hate us.

—Aharon Zisling, Israeli minister (1948)

Traditional Authoritarianism

In Iran and Iraq, old ways of traditional authoritarian governments emerged by the twenty-first century. During the 1920s, Iran had been ruled by the secular Pahlavi shahs. The last shah of Iran ruled from 1941 to 1979. The shahs, with the help of opportunistic British industry, used Iran's oil resources to industrialize and modernize the nation. The shah discouraged traditional Islamic culture and encouraged the Westernization of the nation. Thus Iran made a natural ally to the United States during the rule of the shah. But not all Iranian people were as convinced of cooperative policies with the British and the United States. The Iranian Prime Minister Mohammad Mosaddeq was one who disliked the pro-Western trend in the shah's policies. When he acted on his convictions, the British and the United States sponsored an Iranian pro-shah force to remove him from power. This Western action would later be a rallying cry for the Islamic Revolution of 1979.

Ironically, the shah, in his attempt to Westernize, also stepped on many human rights and repressed all opposition. In response, in 1979, the Shiite cleric Ayatollah Khomeini organized a group of loyal followers and took control of the country. The Islamic Revolution changed Iran into a decidedly anti-Western nation. The theocracy that Khomeini created remains in power today, despite a devastating war with neighboring Iraq from 1980 to 1988. The sixth and current president of Iran, Mahmoud Ahmadinejad, continues to guide Iran on its authoritarian and anti-Western stance.

Iraq came under the control of the dictator Saddam Hussein in 1979. Once supported by the United States in his opposition to neighboring Iran, Hussein repressed his people in his quest to retain power in Iraq. In 1990, he invaded Kuwait in hopes of gaining more control over the price of oil in the region. A coalition of nations led by the United States pushed Hussein out of Kuwait in the First Gulf War in 1991. The UN then placed trade sanctions on Iraq to force Hussein to follow the cease-fire agreement at the end of the war.

In 2003, the United States and member nations of NATO invaded Iraq and toppled Hussein's dictatorship because of noncompliance with the peace agreement, human rights violations, and bad intelligence, which suggested that Iraq possessed weapons of mass destruction (WMD). Saddam Hussein was executed after a trial by the Iraqi people in 2006. The nation of Iraq was occupied by U.S. forces who supported the creation and development of an Iraqi democratic republic until 2010, when they were withdrawn under the Obama administration. It remains to be seen whether this will work in Iraq. The mistrust and conflicts between Sunni and Shiite Muslims is intense, as it is with the Kurdish ethnic minority in northern Iraq.

The Others

The other nations of the Middle East responded to decolonization in a more moderate fashion. Syria, Lebanon, Saudi Arabia, Kuwait, and Jordan all tried to walk the uneasy balance between traditional and secular authoritarianism while following the general trends of decolonization that shaped the Middle East. They have emerged as powerful political players with many economic and political resources that influence regional and international politics very successfully.

African Independence

After World War II, European colonial rule in Africa quickly came to an end. During the 1950s and 1960s, most of the African nations had gained independence. The first nation to do so was the Gold Coast in 1957. After becoming free of British rule, the Gold Coast changed its name to Ghana. Others soon followed. By 1960, there were 17 new, independent nations in Africa. Eleven more were founded from 1961 to 1965.

Challenges in Africa

The new African nations had a diverse background and future. A movement for African unity, Pan-Africanism, became popular on the continent, leading to the creation of the Organization of African Unity (OAU) in 1963. This organization represented the diverse economic views of 32 African nations.

But the Pan-African movement and OAU had a tough job. Although gaining independence, the nations of Africa faced many challenges in the late twentieth and early twenty-first centuries:

- Reliance on a single export crop
- The lack of technology and manufactured goods
- Little foundation for an industrial economy
- Population and urban growth
- AIDS epidemic
- Lack of infrastructure
- Large gap between the rich and the poor
- Corruption and oppressive military regimes

- Warring tribal and ethnic groups
- Little concept of nationhood due to indiscriminate borders created by the Berlin Conference of 1884

WHAT IN THE WORLD

Some of the African nations, in an effort to inspire a sense of nationhood among their people, took names from African history. The Gold Coast and the French Sudan were declared to be Ghana and Mali, while Southern Rhodesia was named Zimbabwe after the Bantu cultural center.

Change in African Society and Culture

The list of challenges the African nations face is long, but there is hope. Some dictatorships have given way to democratic governments, although this has sometimes resulted in civil war. Another reason for hope comes from the example of leadership by Nelson Mandela.

Nelson Mandela was a leader in the African National Congress (ANC), which worked to end apartheid in South Africa beginning in the 1950s. In 1962, Mandela was arrested for protesting and calling for armed resistance against apartheid laws. From prison, Mandela continued to be a voice and symbol of protest against apartheid. Released from prison in 1990, he became a political leader in South Africa when apartheid was coming to an end. When South Africa had its first truly free democratic elections in 1993, Mandela was elected South Africa's first black president.

With independence during the 1950s and 1960s, the new African nations experienced cultural and societal changes. There was tension between the traditional or country culture of Africa and Western ways and urban culture. Many in Africa wanted to Westernize because they equated it with modernization, which would be economically beneficial. The tension between the two groups was evident in African art and literature, where there appears to be a balance of tradition and the West. That balance is still being sought out by African culture and society.

An Imperial-Free Asia

Among the decolonized nations of the world, Asia was the most successful at creating economic prosperity and stable governments. There was also cooperation among the nations, with the Association of Southeast Asia Nations (ASEAN) founded in 1967.

But regardless of these developments, Asia has experienced growing pains, sometimes magnified by the Cold War. The Philippines received its freedom from the United States in 1946 and others followed from that point.

Indian and Pakistani Independence

The people of the Indian subcontinent gained their independence from Britain quickly, with conflicts and riots between Hindus and Muslims speeding up the process. On August 15, 1947, the nations of India and Pakistan were created: Pakistan for the Muslim population, India for the Hindus. With this partitioning, the religious populations caught on the wrong sides of the border had to flee in a chaotic and devastating diaspora. At least a million lives were lost. In addition, Mohandas Gandhi, a leader in the Indian nationalist movement, was assassinated in January 1948 by a Hindu extremist who was opposed to his stance on tolerance between the religious traditions.

Despite their rough starts, both nations made it into the twenty-first century. Pakistan has become a modern Islamic republic and power in the region. However, it has an unstable authoritarian form of government that has been repressive. India has become a democratic nation and a regional political power and global economic power. These nations have always been at odds, fighting three wars since 1947 because of the nature of their religious and political differences. Tension has been especially high over Kashmir, a disputed border territory. Unfortunately, both nations have nuclear weapons, making the tensions and their consequences even more difficult.

Developments in Southeast Asia

After the Indian subcontinent was freed, Britain also granted freedom to its colonial possessions in Southeast Asia, including Burma in 1948, Malaysia in 1957, and Singapore in 1965. The Dutch East Indies, or Indonesia, gained its freedom in 1949 from the Netherlands. At the Geneva Conference of 1954, the French colonial possessions of Laos, Cambodia, and Vietnam were also granted independence. Finally, in 1997 Hong Kong was returned to mainland China by the British.

Sadly, with these countries' independence, military or authoritarian governments soon followed and became the trend throughout Southeast Asia. These governments value conformity and tradition over freedom and human rights. As a result, they have been oppressive to different ethnic, religious, and political groups.

Modern Japan

After World War II, with the aid of the United States, Japan modernized quickly. By the 1960s, it had become a regional economic power. By the 1980s, Japan was a global economic power, with the world's third most productive economy and one of the world's highest per capita incomes. This amazing comeback from devastation was partly due to the fact that the United States viewed it as an anchor in its Cold War policy in Asia and spent a lot of time and money investing in creating a democratic capitalist nation.

Modeled after the British constitutional monarchy, Japan became a parliamentary democracy, with the Japanese emperor retaining only a symbolic role in the government. During the 1990s, the Japanese economy experienced a serious downturn that put into question the traditional Japanese values of family and conformity. As a result, the younger Japanese generations have a desire for greater gender equality and individual voice.

On March 11, 2011, the coast of Japan was rocked by a 9.0 magnitude earthquake. This quake, which was the most powerful ever recorded, set off a series of tsunami waves that devastated the coast, causing massive casualties and the destruction of Japanese infrastructure, including several nuclear power plants. Hundreds of thousands of Japanese residents were displaced by the destruction of the tsunami waves, with its cost estimated at over $300 billion. The total effect of this disaster, the most expensive in world history, on the social, economic, and cultural life of Japan has yet to be seen, but indications suggest a deep setback for Japan.

The "Little Tigers" and North Korea

Much like Japan, Taiwan and South Korea emerged as economically prosperous and free nations. At first, Taiwan and South Korea both had authoritarian governments. Taiwan was dominated by the Nationalist Party and Chiang Kai-shek until his death in 1975, when Taiwan began to move rapidly toward a democratic and free society.

South Korea had an authoritarian form of government until 1989, when free elections were held. Afterward, the South Korean economy expanded rapidly, becoming one of the leading nations in the information age. Because of their economic strength, both South Korea and Taiwan became known as "little tigers," with the big "tiger" being the Japanese economy.

Unfortunately, North Korea has not advanced as much as South Korea and Taiwan because its dictator, Kim Il Sung, created a communist and oppressive regime that stifled economic prosperity and human rights. These practices have continued to this day under his son and successor, Kim Jong-Il, who has already named his youngest son, Jong-un, as heir apparent.

Communist China

The People's Republic of China was established in 1949 by Mao Zedong and the Chinese Communist Party (CCP). It was the most populous nation to become communist to date. Like the other nations of east Asia, China worked to modernize. Mao led the country from 1949 to 1976, creating an authoritarian government that was able to carry out social, economic, and industrial reform in the country. But Mao's reforms (the Great Leap Forward and the Cultural Revolution), launched to modernize and remove capitalist influences in China, were oppressive against dissenters.

Even after Mao's death, this trend continued in China. When the events in Eastern Europe inspired Chinese students in May 1989 to protest for human rights, the government refused and sent the military into Tiananmen Square to disperse the students by force. So although China is modernized and actively becoming a large part of the global economy, the Chinese government's human rights violations are still an issue to be dealt with in the twenty-first century.

Latin America

The Latin American nations before World War II had been independent for close to 100 years. During the 1930s, with the Great Depression, most of the states' economies moved away from the export of raw materials and the import of finished goods. The new problem that faced these nations was that they were dependent on Western industrial nations for their technology in industry. In addition, they had a problem finding markets for the new finished goods that they were producing.

By the 1960s, these frustrations resulted in the return to the export-import type of economies that had dominated Latin America before World War II. And like before, the nations of Latin America encouraged multinational corporations to take over agriculture and industry. So by the early 1980s, Latin America was again dependent on the industrialized West.

When the West experienced economic difficulties during the 1980s, the Latin American nations that depended so much on the West fell apart. The Latin American people believed these economic problems were caused by governments having too much control and peasants not growing enough food for consumption. So there was a general movement from authoritarian governments to democracies during the 1980s and 1990s. Still, resistance to democratic rule was seen in groups like the leftist Sendero Luminoso in Peru that attempted to disrupt free elections in 1990. The country of El Salvador remained under the control of the military. But in Nicaragua, which was no longer under the Sandinistas, the people elected its first president, Violeta Chamorro. In Mexico in 2000, the oppressive PRI lost its majority status with the election of Vicente Fox of the PAN party as president. But there were also challenges to democracy in Columbia and Venezuela. Hopefully the trend toward democratization of Latin America will continue; but in order for democracy to advance, the economic issues of the region need to be solved.

Since the inception of the Monroe Doctrine and the Roosevelt Corollary, the United States has taken a heavy-handed approach with Latin American nations, with frequent political and military interventions. The Latin American nations started to resist this intervention after World War II, when Latin America went through significant cultural changes, mostly due to a population explosion that increased the size of the cities and magnified urban problems. In addition, the economic gap between the rich and the poor grew wider.

In 1948, the Latin American nations formed the Organization of American States (OAS), which called for an end to U.S. involvement in Central and South America. Of course, U.S. involvement did not end. With the Cold War, U.S. involvement actually intensified, with the United States supplying more money and aid to anti-communist nations, including repressive dictatorships and authoritarian governments.

At the beginning of the twenty-first century, there are still many challenges for Latin America. The region's economy is still dependent on the export of bananas, coffee, and cotton. The Latin American nations are dependent on the West—especially the United States—economically and politically. The divide between the rich and the poor continues to grow. Because of the economic problems associated with the lack of industry and population growth, the international drug trade took root in Latin America. Unstable governments, especially Bolivia, Peru, and Colombia, permitted the manufacture and export of cocaine and marijuana to the world, including the United States. This drug trafficking and the power it bestows upon a criminal element has continued into the twenty-first century despite U.S. preventative measures.

The Walls Come Tumbling Down

During the late 1980s and early 1990s, the communist governments of the Soviet Union and Eastern Europe had serious economic challenges to overcome. As a result, the communist ideology of the governments was overturned and replaced with governments that were self-deterministic and democratic.

The Reign of Gorbachev

When Mikhail Gorbachev became the leader of the Soviet Union in 1985, he believed that only radical reforms would help solve the economic problems of the country. He introduced policies of *perestroika* (restructuring), which launched a limited market economy to the Soviets, as well as *glasnost* (openness), to encourage journalistic and political freedom. In 1988, guided by some economic success, Gorbachev also initiated democratic political reforms that created a new Soviet parliament called the Congress of People's Deputies. This democratic reform was followed by the legalization of noncommunist parties. In addition, in March 1990, Gorbachev was elected the first and also last president of the Soviet Union.

With Gorbachev's reform movement, ethnic tensions in the Soviet Union surfaced. Nationalist movements formed in the different Soviet republics. From 1988 to 1990, there were many calls for independence from these nationalist movements in the Soviet republics. Communist conservatives in the Soviet Union decided that they had enough of Gorbachev and democratic reforms. They seized power and arrested Gorbachev on August 19, 1991, but Boris Yeltsin, the president of the Russian Republic, resisted this group and was able to regain control for Gorbachev. By 1991, the Soviet republics' continued calls for independence were successful. Gorbachev relented and the Soviet Union ceased to exist. Gorbachev then resigned from power on December 25, 1991, and gave up his responsibilities to Yeltsin.

NOTABLE QUOTABLE

Society now has liberty; it has been emancipated politically and spiritually. And that is the main achievement that we have not fully comprehended because we have not yet learned how to use that liberty.

—Mikhail Gorbachev, 1991

Yeltsin and Putin

When Boris Yeltsin took office in 1991, he introduced a complete free-market economy to the Russian Republic as quickly as possible. Despite his well-meaning intentions, this introduction brought economic hardships to the republic, leading to the rise of organized crime and corruption. In addition, Yeltsin used brutal military force against the Chechens to force them to remain with the Russian Republic. By the end of 1999, his rule of the Russian Republic was ineffective. As a result, he resigned and was replaced by Vladimir Putin.

Vladimir Putin took office vowing to set the region of Chechnya straight. He also promised reforms to help strengthen the Russian economy. These reforms included the introduction of free purchase and sale of land and tax cuts. Putin also made numerous attempts to join the World Trade Organization (WTO) in order to aid the sagging Russian economy. He remained president of Russia until 2008, both trying to integrate Russia with the European community and to remain a world power.

Medvedev ... and Putin?

In 2008, the Russian people elected Dmitry Medvedev to be the new Russian president. Medvedev was Russia's first leader to have no links either to the former Soviet Communist party or secret services. But Medvedev was very close to Putin. He campaigned as Putin's protégé and continued Putin's policies as soon as he won the election. Medvedev pledged to continue to develop civil and economic freedom in Russia into the twenty-first century. Yet with former president Putin now the prime minister of Russia (a newly created role that holds as much power as the president), questions have been asked as to who really holds power in Russia. With Putin's poor human rights record and repressive, anti-democratic policies and Medvedev appearing to follow in his footsteps, it remains to be seen what Russia's role will be in the twenty-first century.

The Least You Need to Know

- After World War II, many former colonies around the world were granted independence.
- The newly independent nations developed differently according to the economic, cultural, and political environment.

- These nations have a variety of economic and political challenges including the development of stable governments and economies in a competitive globalized twenty-first century.

- The Soviet Union has broken up into many independent states with the Russian nation becoming the political leader.

- It is yet to be seen whether the democratic reforms of the former Soviet Union will remain intact.

Where Do We Go from Here?

In This Chapter

- Technological challenges
- Environmental challenges
- Globalization
- Terrorism and extremism
- Responses to challenges

The world community will face many challenges in the twenty-first century. These include technological and environmental challenges, in addition to the economic and cultural problems associated with globalization. Several organizations are trying to confront these challenges, including the United Nations, NATO, the European Union, and other nongovernmental groups. The solution to these problems would be more easily reached if the world community learned to settle many of its disputes peacefully. But sadly, with the rise of extremism and terrorism, this goal appears to be far away.

Challenges for the Future

As the world continues into the twenty-first century, it is not without a little fear and trepidation. The twentieth century, which started with a great deal of promise and progress, became one of the bloodiest centuries in human history. In addition, changes on the world stage are happening so quickly that it's hard to understand or keep up. With that in focus, there are a few major challenges at the beginning of the twenty-first century that the world community will need to address.

Technology (No, I Am Not a Luddite!)

Modern transportation and technology have changed the world. The world has access to jumbo jets, the Internet, satellites, television, fax machines, and cell phones. The exploration of space has led to some of these changes. Satellites transmit information to the world through radios, television, and telecommunications. Space probes have even increased our knowledge of our solar system, galaxy, and universe.

The exploration of space began in the twentieth century. In 1957, the Soviet Union launched the first satellite, Sputnik. Later, they launched the first manned spaceflight. The United States trailed the Soviet Union in the "space race" but soon overtook them, succeeding in landing astronauts on the moon in 1969. During the 1970s, the Soviet Union and the United States jointly worked on the International Space Station. In 1990, the United States and European nations jointly launched the Hubble Telescope that allows scientists to observe objects in the farthest reaches of the universe where "no man has gone before."

Entertainment has long been a source of technological advancement in the world. The film industry started by Thomas Edison created exciting new forms of entertainment by the 1920s. The public's desire for entertainment allowed radios into many homes by midcentury. These were supplanted by the television as the main source of entertainment by the late 1950s.

During the late 1960s, computers were linked together in a communication network called the ARPANET. This developed into the Internet by the early 1990s. Alongside the evolution of the Internet was the development of computers, which started quite large (room size!). By the late 1970s, with the development of transistors and microchips, the computer became smaller and more personal for work and entertainment. Currently, the Internet accessed by personal computers (PCs) has become the leading source of entertainment, allowing access to digitized television programs, movies, and music. In addition, the Internet allows people to participate in electronic communication which includes email and social networking Internet sites like Facebook and Twitter. As the world continues into the twenty-first century, more of its citizens will be linked through computers and the Internet.

WHAT IN THE WORLD

Most people believe that multimedia communication is more easily controlled and manipulated than the printed word. But a potential drawback to this type of communication is that it limits the imagination.

Medical technology has advanced the way doctors treat diseases and perform surgery; because of this, people are able to live longer and healthier lives. The changes in medical technology have also raised some new concerns. For example, genetic engineering allows scientists to alter the genetic information of cells to produce new variations. But what if the new cell variations are deadly? Or what if someone were to misuse this new technology? Additionally, the use of antibiotics in animals and humans has created "supergerms" that are very resistant to available antibiotics. Finally, issues over stem-cell research and human cloning have become the center of intense debates between the scientific and religious communities.

The agricultural *Green Revolution*, using fertilizers and pesticides to grow new crops, has promised big rewards to the world community. It once was thought that these new and better crops were the solution to problems created by the world's growing population, with all its mouths to feed. But many nations cannot afford to supply their farmers with the fertilizers, and the pesticides have created environmental problems, including the contamination of water supplies.

DEFINITION

The **Green Revolution** is the development of types of rice, corn, and other grains that have better yields per acre than traditional crops.

The technological revolution brought about the development of nuclear, biological, and chemical weapons. With the end of the Cold War, the threat of nuclear war diminished to some degree, but there is a fear that *rogue nations* or even terrorists may acquire nuclear weapons. The same problem exists with biological and chemical weapons. Many governments have made agreements to limit the research, production, and use of these types of weapons, but rogue nations and terrorists have not.

DEFINITION

A **rogue nation** is one that acts outside the boundaries of international law and diplomacy.

The Environment

In 1962, the American scientist Rachel Carson published a book called *Silent Spring* in which she warned the world about the dangers of pesticide use on crops. Carson documented evidence that the chemicals used to kill insects were also killing birds, fish, and other animals. She also warned that humans, too, could be affected by pesticide residue on or in food. Her stark warnings led to the emergence of a new field of science called ecology, which is the study of the relationships between living things and the environment. The world community started to become aware of dangers to the environment.

One danger to the environment is overpopulation. The world's resources cannot sustain such a large number of people. As a result of this overpopulation, many areas of the world have been overdeveloped and deforested. Deforestation is when forests or jungles are cut down to provide space for farmland and building development, destroying animal and plant habitats. Tropical rainforests are the biggest concern with this type of clear cutting. They support more than 50 percent of the world's plants and animals. In addition, rainforests are vital in the process of removing carbon dioxide from the air and returning oxygen to it. Rainforests are the lungs of the world. They help the earth breathe.

Chemical waste is another danger to the world's environment. Chlorofluorocarbons (CFCs) found in gases used in aerosol cans and Freon in refrigerators and air conditioners have destroyed a portion of the ozone layer. This thin layer of gas protects the earth from the sun's ultraviolet rays. Scientists believe that the buildup of carbon dioxide in the world's atmosphere is creating a greenhouse effect. As a result, the temperature of the earth is steadily increasing and melting the polar ice caps. Finally, acid rain, which comes from sulfur being released from factories and mixing with moisture in the air, has browned and killed thousands of acres of forests in North America and Europe.

Several major ecological disasters in the past two decades have contributed to the destruction of the environment. In 1986, an explosion and fire at a nuclear reactor at Chernobyl in the Soviet Union spread a radioactive cloud over thousands of square miles. In 1989, the oil tanker *Exxon Valdez* ran aground, causing a massive oil spill that did serious harm to the Alaskan environment.

With the environmental challenges brought to the attention of the world community, the nations of the world have worked to improve the situation. In 1987, representatives from 46 countries met in Montreal to draft the Montreal Protocol to limit CFCs. In 1992, the Earth Summit in Rio de Janeiro looked at environmental challenges and proposed solutions. Finally, in 1997, the major nations of the world met at Kyoto, Japan, to draft the Kyoto Protocol to limit the production of greenhouse gases. This protocol that has to be followed voluntarily by nations has not received widespread support.

NOTABLE QUOTABLE

Even the most ardent environmentalist doesn't really want to stop pollution. If he thinks about it, and doesn't just talk about it, he wants to have the *right amount* of pollution. We can't really *afford* to eliminate it—not without abandoning all of the benefits of technology that we not only enjoy but on which we depend.

—*No Such Thing as a Free Lunch,* Milton Friedman (1975)

Globalization

The end of World War II was the beginning of globalization. A globalized economy is one in which the production, distribution, and sale of goods take place on the world market. There is some question as to whether this is a new phenomenon or an old variation of imperialism in a new package. Organizations like the World Trade Organization (WTO), North American Free Trade Association (NAFTA), and the European Union (EU) have tried to capitalize on this global economy, but not without criticism. At times the WTO has placed commercial interests above environmental concerns. These organizations have also been criticized for being exclusive and arbitrary in leaving out some nations.

There are other problems with globalization, such as the enormous gap between the rich and the poor. The rich, industrialized countries that make up the West have many advantages, including well-organized infrastructures, advanced technologies, and good educational systems. Developing nations are poorer and are located mainly in Africa, Asia, and Latin America, all of which experienced colonialism and imperialism. These countries were exploited in the past for raw materials and did not experience industrialization like the West during the nineteenth century. These nations are mostly agricultural nations with little technological and educational innovation. The possibility of being exploited by the West is still a factor, even if imperialism has withered away.

NOTABLE QUOTABLE

The central challenge we face today is to ensure that globalization becomes a positive force for all the world's people, instead of leaving billions behind in squalor.

—United Nations Secretary-General Kofi Annan (2000)

Populations and Migrations

A problem that these developing nations have is population growth. In comparison to the nations of the West, they have experienced the bulk of the world's growth in population, now estimated at more than six billion people. Many of those people have moved to the urbanized areas of the world where living conditions are poor. Additionally, these cities are developing faster than the environment can support. Hunger, starvation, sanitation, and disease are serious concerns. Nearly eight million people die of starvation annually, most of them in the developing nations. In addition, the lack of food and other resources to support life in these nations results in conflicts. For example, in the Sudan in the 1980s, a civil war was fought in which the prevention of the import of food was used as a tactic of war. As a result, more than one million people died of starvation in the Sudan. During the 1950s and 1960s, shortages in labor prompted Western European countries to look for workers from other areas, such as southern Europe, Africa, the Middle East, and Asia. These "guest workers" received low wages and were the subject of frequent discrimination, especially toward the end of the twentieth century when their services were not needed as much.

Countries of east Asia experienced a high growth in population. By the 1980s, South Korea had the highest population density in the world. Population pressure caused many South Koreans to migrate to other countries in the Pacific Rim. The Japanese addressed the population issue by promoting birth control and abortion.

After World War I, in Latin America, population expanded as immigrants came to Argentina and Brazil. Urban growth exploded as many Latin Americans migrated within the continent from the rural to the urban areas in search of employment. These newcomers to cities were often forced to live in slums on the outskirts of the urban centers. Sometimes these slums were incorporated into the cities, improving some of the living conditions.

During the 1920s, workers from Mexico crossed the border into the United States while people from Central America crossed into Mexico. All of these migrants were seeking employment. In the 1940s, the United States cooperated with Mexico to provide workers assistance. Migration from Latin America to the United States has mainly been controlled by the search for employment. But some migrants have reached or attempted to reach the United States to escape political oppression and war. This group includes immigrants from Cuba, Haiti, Nicaragua, and El Salvador. During the 1950s and 1960s, the United States opened its borders to Latin American and Asian immigrants, but by the early twenty-first century this policy had turned into a hotly contested issue.

Divisions of countries and political boundaries have also produced migrations. The larger displacement of a people happened in South Asia from 1947 to 1948. It was at this time that India and Pakistan were partitioned based on Muslim and Hindu populations. This caused a major migration of Muslims to Pakistan and Hindus to India. The first Arab-Israeli War in 1948 also created hundreds of thousands of Palestinian migrant refugees. Refugees from war resulting from boundary changes have also created migrations in central Africa and the European Balkans.

Another pattern of migration is one of movement of South Asians and Arabs to the oil-rich countries of the Middle East. Workers from developed countries, including the United States, have also been involved in this migration based on oil production.

Changing Roles of Women

In the West, differences between the sexes have decreased economically and socially. Women have entered the workforce and university systems in steadily increasing numbers. Many laws have been passed to institute equality in every way imaginable for women. Women in the developing nations do not have it quite as good.

Throughout the twentieth century, Latin American women kept their traditional roles. Women were not allowed to vote until 1929, when Ecuador became the first Latin American nation to grant women's suffrage. By the early twenty-first century, women in Latin America control some small businesses and are sometimes active in politics, but there are more steps to be made.

Women's suffrage has been written into the constitutions of the new African nations. The active participation of women in the African independence movements of the twentieth century has resulted in more opportunities for women to hold political office. Many of the African nations have also granted more opportunities for women in education and employment. Despite these advances, early marriages—traditional for African cultures—continue to trap women in old roles.

In the Middle East and Asia, many cultural and religious traditions continue to foster systems of inequality for women. Most women are still treated as subordinate to their husbands or fathers. In addition, education, property rights, and employment are still male centered and male dominated. Thus, women in developing countries have a much longer road to travel to gain equality with men.

Terrorism and Extremism

The world is facing political problems in terrorism and other forms of extremism. There are many different dictatorships and one-party governments in power around the world. Many of these governments practice extreme ideologies that do not permit public discourse. As a result, the world has experienced many regional, ethnic, and religious conflicts.

The Eastern European nation of Yugoslavia was torn apart by ethnic divisions during the 1990s. Hundreds of thousands of Africans have been killed because of ethnic differences. Religious differences in the region of Palestine have brought Israelis and Palestinians into conflict. Massive terrorist attacks like that on September 11, 2001, demonstrate the advanced ability of terrorists and their tactics. To combat these groups, nations have worked together to cooperate on responses and security. The United States has been able to use this cooperation in its "War on Terror" to bring many extremists to justice, including Osama bin Laden, the leader of al-Qaida, who was killed by U.S. Navy Seals in a secluded compound in Pakistan in 2011.

Solutions, Anyone?

With all of the challenges that face the world—including environmental, political, and social concerns—it appears that the twenty-first century could be a tough one if measures are not taken. But whose responsibility is it to take these measures?

The United Nations, NATO, and the European Union

Several organizations have stepped up to take on the challenges that face the world. The United Nations (UN) was created after World War II with two main goals: to maintain peace and to advance human rights. The General Assembly of the UN consists of representatives from the majority of the nations of the world. It discusses and recommends solutions to issues the world faces today. The secretary-general of the UN executes and supervises the administration of UN mandates.

The most important group in the UN is the Security Council, made up of five permanent members—the United States, Russia, Great Britain, France, and China—and ten other members selected to serve for limited terms. The Security Council works to settle international disputes, sometimes with the use of peacekeeping forces. Three of the UN's specialized agencies have important functions in maintaining human rights. They are the United Nations Educational, Scientific, and Cultural

Organization (UNESCO); the United Nations International Children's Emergency Fund (UNICEF); and the World Health Organization (WHO). These agencies address economic and social problems related to human rights.

Another group, the North Atlantic Treaty Organization (NATO), works to stabilize regions of the world with military force. The role of NATO is evolving from its original Cold War purpose. New members from Eastern Europe have joined, and the United States has a less prominent role. Whether this organization will have military objectives like those of the past is yet to be seen.

The European Union (EU) is also working to maintain economic stability in Europe. In recent years, its role has changed to include applying economic pressure to obtain human rights for other regions of the world. For example, the nation of Turkey wanted to be a member, but the EU denied its entrance based on human rights violations in the nation.

Think Globally, Act Locally!

Another approach to the challenges of the world has been the emergence of social movements at the grassroots level with ordinary citizens. Local groups have organized to make a difference in their respective communities and have inspired citizens in other locations. In addition, nongovernmental organizations like business and professional organizations, foundations, and religious groups have worked to solve the challenges facing the world. These groups bring awareness to global perspectives and inspire political and diplomatic action.

Even with all of the efforts of the UN, NATO, the EU, and other nongovernmental groups, the world's problems cannot be solved without help. The disputes over political, ethnic, and religious differences must be resolved in a peaceful forum. During the twenty-first century, it is the people's hope that the governments of the world can do that more effectively.

The Least You Need to Know

- The world community will face many technological and environmental challenges in the twenty-first century.
- Economic globalization has many benefits, but might prove to be disadvantageous for developing nations.

- Population growth and migrations of populations still continue to be a source of anxiety.

- Women in Western nations have slowly gained a more equal status with their male counterparts, while other non-Western nations are still working toward equality.

- The UN, NATO, EU, and other nongovernmental groups are trying to tackle the global challenges of the twenty-first century.

- The path of the twenty-first century will be difficult unless the world community learns to solve its disputes peacefully.

Glossary

absolute monarchy   Type of government that arose in Europe during the seventeenth century in which the monarch controlled a nation-state for the greater benefit of the people.

alphabet script   Written communication in which symbols represent speech, sounds, and/or letters.

animism   Belief that life is produced by a spiritual force that is separate from matter; sometimes includes the belief in the existence of spirits and demons that inhabit particular objects.

anti-Semitism   Hostility and discrimination toward the Jewish people.

apartheid   Legal and institutional separation of blacks and whites that existed in South Africa during most of the twentieth century.

authoritarianism   Enforcement of unquestioning obedience to authority without individual freedom; dictatorships characterize this type of rule.

B.C.E.   Newer historical term that replaces B.C. and stands for Before the Common Era.

bureaucracy   Administrative system based on nonelected officials, policies, and procedures.

C.E.   Newer historical term that replaces A.D. and stands for Common Era.

caste system   System in which people obtain their rank in the society from their birth parents; change of rank or class in this system is very difficult.

city-state   Form of political organization in which a city-based ruler controls the surrounding countryside.

civilization   Society that has developed systematic agriculture to produce a food surplus in addition to an elite and merchant class.

colonization New settlement of people linked to the parent country through trade and government control.

Columbian Exchange Exchange of goods, plants, animals, and also diseases between Europe and the Americas that happened after Columbus's discovery of the New World.

communism Economic theory that advocates the ownership of property by the community as a whole.

conservative Policies that support tradition and stability; during the early nineteenth century, conservatives believed in obedience to political authority and the importance of organized religion.

coup d'état French term used to designate a sudden, violent, and forcible overthrow of a government by a small group of people with military or political authority.

cultural diffusion Exchange of culture between societies.

culture Ideas, customs, language, and skills of a society that are transmitted through time.

cuneiform Wedge-shaped writing produced on clay tablets; developed by the Sumerians.

democracy Government by the people, either directly or by elected representatives.

détente Lessening of tensions between nations due to treaties or trade agreements.

dynasty Family of rulers who pass on the right to rule within the family.

empire Government that controls several different territories and people.

empiricism Belief that sensory experience through observations and experiments is the only source of human knowledge.

enlightened monarchs Rulers who used the principles of the Enlightenment during their rule while also maintaining their absolute powers.

Enlightenment Intellectual movement centered in Europe during the eighteenth century that featured the application of scientific methods to the study of society; belief that rational laws and reason can describe society.

environmentalism Use of policies to solve environmental problems such as pollution, shortage of natural resources, and population growth.

epic poem Long poem that details the deeds of heroes.

fascism   Government led by a dictator that glorifies the state above the individual.

feudalism   Economic, political, and social system in which land, worked by peasants who are bound to it, is held by a lord in exchange for military service to an overlord.

filial piety   Duty of family members to lower their needs and desires to those of the male head of the family or ruler.

globalization   Interconnectedness of the nations of the world in communication, commerce, culture, and politics.

Green Revolution   Development of types of rice, corn, and other grains that have better yields per acre than traditional crops.

gunpowder empires   Empires formed by unifying different regions through conquest based on the superior use of firearms.

Holocaust   The genocide of approximately six million European Jews during World War II by Nazi Germany.

hominids   Humans or humanlike creatures that walk upright.

humanism   System of thought with man at the center; man is the sum of all things.

iconoclasm   Policies that oppose the religious use of images and advocate the destruction of such images.

ideographic script   Written script in which a graphic symbol represents an idea, concept, or object without expressing that sound that forms its name.

imperialism   Extension of political and cultural power over many different regions.

Industrial Revolution   Technological revolution starting in England in the mid-eighteenth century in which newly invented machines were used in production leading to population, agricultural, and commercial growth.

Inquisition   General tribunal used to discover and confront heresy in the Roman Catholic Church during the late Middle Ages.

liberalism   Intellectual movement based on the ideas of the Enlightenment, with several loosely assembled tenets: people were to be free as possible from government restraint; government was to be used to protect the civil liberties of the people; emphasis on the use of representative assemblies in which voting and office should be limited to men of property; the rule of constitutions.

Marxism   Intellectual movement developed by Karl Marx in the nineteenth century in which history was defined as a class struggle between groups without power and groups controlling the means of production.

mercantilism   Economic policy that many European governments pursued during the eighteenth and nineteenth centuries in which nations tried to export more valuable goods than they imported. Theoretically the pursuit of this policy makes a nation rich and powerful by keeping the economic resources in the country.

Middle Passage   Voyages of African slaves from Africa to the Americas that occurred from the sixteenth to eighteenth centuries.

migration   Movement of people from one region to another.

militarism   Dependence on military strength to obtain political objectives.

modernism   Artistic and literary movement during the late nineteenth and early twentieth centuries in which artists intentionally moved away from all previous artistic styles.

monotheism   Religious worship of a single god.

nationalism   Belief that a nation should be made of people who have a common language, traditions, religions, and customs.

Neolithic Revolution   Period of time in which systematic agriculture and the domestication of animals occurred; varies from 8000 to 5000 B.C.E., depending on region.

nomads   Herding societies that move from place to place in search of better pastureland.

Old Regime   Social system of eighteenth century France that consisted of three estates: clergy, nobility, and middle/lower class.

oligarchy   Government ruled by an elite and powerful few.

Pax Mongolia   Period of time in which transregional trade and commerce was renewed under the watch of Mongolian armies.

Pax Romana   Period of 200 years of relative peace in Roman history.

polis   Greek city-state that included the city and the surrounding countryside which it controlled and used for farming.

polytheistic   Religious worship of many different gods.

realism   Artistic movement of the mid-nineteenth century that sought to portray life as it really was.

Reformation   Religious movement of the sixteenth century originating with Martin Luther that demanded the reform of the Roman Catholic Church. The Reformation resulted in the division of the Church.

Renaissance   Cultural and political movement that began in Italy during the fifteenth century. The development of literature and art was more secular than that of the Middle Ages.

republic   Government in which leader acquires consent of the governed through voting.

rogue nation   Nation that acts outside the boundaries of international law and diplomacy.

Romanticism   Artistic and literary movement of nineteenth-century Europe, expressing the belief that emotion is key to understanding human experience.

satellite state   Small state that is economically and/or politically dependent on a larger, more powerful state. A satellite state adjusts its policies based on the desires of the larger state.

Scientific Revolution   Intellectual movement of seventeenth-century Europe that used empiricism to develop wider scientific and theoretical generalizations.

secularism   Intellectual movement that rejects the use of religion or religious consideration.

Silk Road   Trading routes that connected European, Indian, and Chinese civilizations, transmitting both goods and ideas.

socialism   Political movement that started in Europe during the nineteenth century, promoting state control of the means of production to create equality in society.

sultanate   Region ruled by the authority and office of a strictly Islamic monarch.

terrorism   Use of force or threats to demoralize or intimidate in order to obtain political objectives.

theocrat   Ruler who claims to have the sanction of a god or gods in directing a government. The ruler's commands have a powerful effect if the religion is culturally important.

Ptolemaic system   Belief advanced by the second-century Greek mathematician that Earth was a fixed point and the celestial bodies orbited around it.

total war   Warfare that involves the mobilization of an entire nation, including its civilian population.

triangular trade network   Network that emerged during sixteenth through the nineteenth centuries in which manufactured goods were traded in Africa for slaves; slaves were shipped to the Americas, where they were exchanged for sugar, tobacco, and raw cotton; and those products were then shipped to Europe to be made into finished goods, which went back to the colonies or to Africa.

Westernization   Process in which a nation adopts the culture and institutions that typify the West.

Zionism   Movement that argued that the Jewish people must return to the region of Palestine.

The Major Events of World History

4 million B.C.E.—The emergence of Australopithecus from Africa.

1.5 million B.C.E.—The development of *Homo erectus.*

200,000 B.C.E.—The evolution of *Homo sapiens sapiens.*

10,000 B.C.E.—End of the ice ages.

10,000 B.C.E.—Beginning of the Neolithic Revolution.

5000 B.C.E.—Beginning of the river valley civilizations.

3500–1800 B.C.E.—The rise and fall of Sumerian civilization.

3100 B.C.E.—The rise of the kingdom of Egypt.

1500 B.C.E.—The Shang dynasty in China emerges.

1500 B.C.E.—The beginning of the Vedic Age in India.

1400 B.C.E.—The height of the kingdom of Mycenae.

1028 B.C.E.—The beginning of the Zhou dynasty in China.

1000 B.C.E.—The early developments of Hinduism.

800 B.C.E.—The end of the Greek dark ages; the rise of the Greek city-states.

470 B.C.E.—The city-state of Athens at the height of its cultural and political power.

431–404 B.C.E.—The Peloponnesian Wars; the decline of the Greek city-states.

402–201 B.C.E.—The warring states period in China.

338–323 B.C.E.—The rise of Macedonia and Alexander the Great; the beginning of Hellenistic culture.

264–146 B.C.E.—The Punic Wars.

322–184 B.C.E.—The Mauryan Empire rules in India.

221–202 B.C.E.—The Qin dynasty rules in China; the beginning of the Great Wall.

202 B.C.E.–220 C.E.—The Han dynasty rules in China.

30 B.C.E.–202 C.E.—The Kushan rule in India.

27 C.E.—The rise of Augustus Caesar; the end of the Roman republic.

30—The execution of Jesus of Nazareth; the beginning of Christianity.

180—The death of Marcus Aurelius; the end of Pax Romana.

220–589—Period of nomadic invasions and disorder in China.

312–337—The rule of Emperor Constantine; the division of the Roman Empire into East and West; official toleration of Christianity.

319–540—Gupta rule in India.

450—The beginning of the Hun invasions of India.

476—The official date of the fall of Roman Empire; last Roman emperor deposed.

527–565—The rule of Emperor Justinian over the Byzantine Empire.

570–632—The life of Muhammad; the origins of Islam.

589–618—The Sui dynasty rules in China.

618–907—The Tang dynasty rules in China.

634–750—The emergence of Islamic culture as first global civilization.

661–750—The Umayyads rule the Islamic Empire.

668—The kingdom of Korea becomes independent of China.

711—The first Islamic incursions into India.

718—Islamic forces defeated at the walls of Constantinople.

750—The Abbasids rule the Islamic Empire.

777—The development of independent Islamic kingdoms in North Africa.

800—Charlemagne crowned Holy Roman Emperor.

800–1000—The Viking Age.

800–1100—The rise of the feudal system in Europe.

855—The emergence of the principality of Kiev.

864—Cyril and Methodius spread Christianity to Slavs of eastern Europe.

960–1127—The Song dynasty rules in China.

968—The rise of the Toltecs in Mesoamerica.

980–1015—The conversion of principality of Russia to Eastern Orthodox Christianity.

1000—Ghana Empire in Africa at height of power.

1000–1300—The High Middle Ages in Europe; the spread of universities.

1054—Official schism between eastern and western Christian churches.

1055—Seljuk Turks conquer Abbasid caliphate.

1066—Norman conquest of Anglo-Saxon England.

1096–1099—First Christian Crusade.

1100—The invention of gunpowder in China.

1150—The decline of Toltecs in Mesoamerica.

1185–1333—Kamakuru Shogunate rules in Japan.

1200—The rise of the Mali Empire in Africa.

1206—The Delhi sultanate rules in India.

1231–1392—Mongol rule in Korea.

1236—The beginning of Mongol rule in Russia.

1258—The beginning of Mongol rule in Middle East; the end of Abbasid caliphate.

1265—The first meeting of English Parliament.

1279–1368—Mongol rule in China.

1281—The beginning of the Ottoman Empire.

1300—Islam spreads into Southeast Asia.

1320–1350—The Black Death spreads from Asia into Europe.

1325—The beginnings of the Aztec Empire.

1330—Europeans begin to use cannon in warfare.

1338–1453—The Hundred Years' War.

1350—The beginnings of the Inca Empire.

1368—The establishment of the Ming dynasty in China.

1390—Ming dynasty ends overseas trade.

1392–1910—The Yi dynasty rules in Korea.

1434–1498—Era of Prince Henry the Navigator and Portuguese exploration.

1439—The nation of Portugal obtains the Azores.

1440—The start of European involvement in African slave trade.

1453—The Ottoman Turks conquer the Byzantine Empire.

1471–1493—The height of the Inca power in South America.

1492—Columbus expedition to America.

1500–1600—European commercial revolution.

1501–1510—The Safavid dynasty conquers Iran.

1509—The Spanish establish colonies on American mainland.

1510—Portugal conquers Goa and Malacca.

1517–1541—Martin Luther and Protestant Reformation.

1519–1521—Magellan circumnavigates the world.

1519–1521—Cortés conquers the Aztec Empire.

1520–1566—The rule of Suleiman the Magnificent.

1526—The beginning of Mughal rule in India.

1533—Pizarro conquers the Inca Empire.

1550–1700—The Scientific Revolution.

1552—The beginning of Russian colonization of central Asia and Siberia.

1570—The establishment of Portuguese colony of Angola.

1571—The Battle of Lepanto.

1590—Hideyoshi unites Japanese.

1591—The decline of the Songhai in Africa.

1600—The beginning of Dutch and English commerce in India.

1603—Tokugawa Shogunate rules in Japan.

1607–1608—The beginning of English and French colonial activity in North America.

1640—The beginning of isolationist policies in Japan.

1641—The development of Dutch colonies in Indonesia.

1644—The beginning of the Qing rule in China.

1652—The establishment of the Dutch colony of South Africa.

1658—The beginning of the decline of the Mughal Empire in India.

1682–1699—The Ottoman Turks driven from eastern Europe.

1689–1725—The rule of Peter the Great in Russia.

1713—The establishment of the Bourbon dynasty in Spain.

1722—The fall of the Safavid dynasty in Iran.

1756–1763—The Seven Years' War in Europe; the French and Indian War in North America.

1763—England obtains "New France" in North America.

1764—British East India Company dominates Bengal in India.

1770—The invention of the steam engine and the beginning of the Industrial Revolution.

1772–1795—Poland is partitioned.

1776–1783—The American Revolution.

1781—Indian revolts against Spanish in New Grenada and Peru.

1788—The establishment of colonies in Australia.

1789–1815—The French Revolution and the rise and fall of Napoleon.

1792—Slave uprisings against the French in Haiti.

1805–1849—The rule of Muhammad Ali in Egypt.

1808–1825—Independence movement in Latin America.

1815—The English gain territories in southern Africa.

1822—Brazil declares independence from Portugal.

1823—The development of the Monroe Doctrine.

1826—The establishment of colonies in New Zealand.

1830—Democratic uprisings in Europe.

1838—The Ottoman Turks and British agree to trade treaty.

1839–1841—The Opium Wars.

1846–1848—The Mexican-American War.

1848—Democratic uprising in Europe again.

1850—Karl Marx and the development of Marxist doctrine.

1850–1864—The Taiping Rebellion.

1853—The Perry expedition to Japan.

1854–1856—The Crimean War.

1858—English parliament controls India.

1861—The abolishment of serfdom in Russia.

1861–1865—The American Civil War.

1864—The beginning of German unification.

1868–1912—Meiji Restoration in Japan.

1871—The Franco-Prussian War.

1878—The Treaty of San Stefano.

1880–1900—The "Scramble for Africa."

1885–1914—The industrialization of Russia.

1885—The beginning of the Indian National Congress in India.

1894–1895—The Sino-Japanese War.

1895—The Cubans revolt against Spanish rule.

1898—The beginning of the Marxist Party in Russia.

1898—The Spanish-America War.

1898–1901—The Boxer Rebellion.

1901—The establishment of the commonwealth of Australia.

1903—The beginning of construction of the Panama Canal.

1904–1905—The Russo-Japanese War.

1905–1906—The first Russian Revolution and limited reforms.

1908—The uprising of the Young Turks.

1910—Japan dominates Korea.

1910–1920—The Mexican Revolution.

1911–1912—The end of the Qing dynasty in China; the beginning of revolutionary period in China.

1912—The beginning of the African National Congress party in South Africa.

1914–1918—World War I and the end of European dominance.

1916—Arab revolts against Ottoman rule.

1917—The United States enters World War I on side of Allied Powers.

1917—The beginning of the Russian Red Revolution.

1917—The Balfour Declaration promises territory in Palestine to Jews.

1919—The Treaty of Versailles; the establishment of the League of Nations.

1919—The establishment of the first Pan-African Nationalist Congress.

1920—The Treaty of Sèvres.

1921—The beginning of the Chinese Communist party.

1927—The beginning of the rule of Stalin and Five-Year Plans.

1929–1933—The Great Depression.

1930–1945—The Vargas regime rules in Brazil.

1931—Japan invades Chinese Manchuria.

1931–1947—Gandhi leads nonviolent resistance to British rule in India.

1933—Hitler and Nazis rise to power in Germany.

1933–1939—Franklin Roosevelt and New Deal programs.

1935—Italian forces conquer Ethiopia; Germany begins rearmament.

1937—Japan invades mainland China.

1939—Nazi-Soviet Pact partitions Poland.

1939–1945—World War II.

1941—Japanese attack on Pearl Harbor and the United States enters World War II.

1945—The United States drops atomic bombs on Hiroshima and Nagasaki.

1945—The establishment of the United Nations.

1945—Ho Chi Minh and communists declare independence in Vietnam.

1946–1950—The decolonization of Asia and Africa.

1946–1989—The Cold War.

1947—The establishment of the Marshall Plan in Europe.

1947—India and Pakistan gain independence.

1948—The division of Korea into North and South Korea.

1948—The establishment of the nation of Israel and the first Arab-Israeli conflict.

1949—The beginning of the North Atlantic Treaty Organization (NATO).

1949—The communists are victorious in China.

1950–1953—The Korean War.

1955—The Warsaw Pact.

1957—The beginning of the European Economic Community.

1957—Ghana becomes one of the first independent African nations.

1959—The beginning of the rule of Castro in Cuba.

1962—Algeria declares independence from France.

1965–1973—The Vietnam War.

1965–1968—The Cultural Revolution in China.

1972—The rise of Organization of Petroleum Exporting Countries (OPEC).

1975—The communists unite North and South Vietnam.

1975–1988—Democracy spreads throughout Latin America.

1976—The death of Mao Zedong.

1979—The Iranian Revolution and the Iranian hostage crisis.

1980–1988—The Iran-Iraq War.

1985–1989—Gorbachev reforms communist system in Soviet Union.

1989—South Africa reforms policy of apartheid.

1989—Democratic reforms in eastern Europe.

1990—East and West Germany are unified under one government.

1990–1991—The first Persian Gulf War.

1991—The decline of the Soviet Union.

1992—The establishment of the European Union.

1994—Nelson Mandela elected president in South Africa.

2001—Terrorist attacks of September 11.

2001—The United States overthrows Taliban government in Afghanistan.

2003—The beginning of the second Persian Gulf war in Iraq.

2004—Vladimir Putin wins a second term in Russian presidential election.

2004—Abuses of American prison of Abu Ghraib revealed.

2004—Palestinian president Yasser Arafat dies.

2004—Massive earthquake creates tsunami that decimates Indian Ocean region, killing 200,000.

2005—Long-ruling and popular Pope John Paul II dies.

2005—Mahmoud Ahmadinejad elected president of Iran.

2005—Hurricane Katrina devastates Gulf Coast region of U.S.

2005—Earthquake kills more than 70,000 people in Pakistani Kashmir.

2006—Three Gorges Dam in China completed.

2006—North Korea announces that it has tested a nuclear weapon.

2006—Former Iraqi dictator Saddam Hussein is hanged in Baghdad.

2008—Fidel Castro resigns for health reasons; his brother succeeds him.

2008—Dmitry Medvedev elected president of Russia.

2008—Barack Obama becomes the first African American to be elected president of the United States.

2008—Series of bank collapses cause world economic crisis.

2010—Haiti devastated by earthquake, causing over 230,000 deaths.

2010—Massive oil spill in Gulf Coast of U.S. paralyzes region.

2010—President Obama signs into law reforms to control the U.S. financial sector.

2011—Japan devastated by tsunamis caused by earthquake off coast, displacing and killing hundreds of thousands.

2011—Osama Bin Laden killed by U.S. forces in Pakistan.

Important People, Places, and Things to Know

Whether you are reading this book for pleasure or taking the Advanced Placement World History Exam, the following historical people, places, terms, and events are vital to your knowledge and understanding of world history.

Foundations of Civilizations (Prehistory– 500 C.E.)

Mesopotamia	Fertile Crescent	Sumerians
Cuneiform	Akkadians	Persians
Hammurabi	Hittites	Assyrians
Chaldeans	Menes	Nile River
Egyptians	Pharaoh	Amenhotep IV
Polytheism	Mummification	Phoenicia
Alphabet	Coinage	Canaan
Hebrews	Torah	Judaism
Monotheism	Indus River	Harappa
Mohenjo-Daro	Hinduism	Reincarnation
Karma	Buddhism	Diocletian
Four Noble Truths	Mauryan Empire	Gupta dynasty
Caste system	Asoka	Huang River
Shang	Zhou	Qin
Han	Yin and Yang	Constantine

Confucius	Daoism	Legalism
Athens	Sparta	Homer
Democracy	Peloponnesian War	Hippocrates
Alexander the Great	Hellenistic Era	Tiber River
The Republic	Julius Caesar	Augustus
Pax Romana	Christianity	Pope
Germanic Tribes	Siddhartha Gautama	

After the Classics (500–1600 C.E.)

Kush	King Ezana	Islam
Swahili	Ghana	Mali
Songhai	Mansa Musa	Maya
Yucatan Peninsula	Aztecs	Incas
Andes	Quipu	Feudalism
Manorialism	Vikings	Franks
William I	Charlemagne	Toltec
Joan of Arc	Black Death	Scholasticism
Dante	Renaissance	Humanism
Saladin	Song dynasty	Silk Road
Neo-Confucianism	Yuan dynasty	Heian Japan
Shogun	Khmer Empire	Angkor Wat
Genghis Khan	Pax Mongolia	Tatars
Bantu migrations	Great Zimbabwe	Axum
Hundred Years' War	Timur-i-Lang	Anasazi

The World Shrinks (1450–1750)

Scientific Revolution	Enlightenment	Prince Henry
Christopher Columbus	Exploration	Baroque
The Reformation	Martin Luther	Henry VIII
The Thirty Years' War	Frederick the Great	Shogunate
The Glorious Revolution	Ottoman Empire	Ming dynasty
Qing dynasty	Ashikaga Shogunate	Tokugawa
Delhi sultanate	Mughal Empire	New Spain
The Middle Passage	Columbian Exchange	Hernán Cortés
Francisco Pizarro	Jamestown	
Massachusetts Bay colony	French and Indian War	
Atlantic slave trade	British East India Company	
Dutch West India Company		

Western Domination (1750–1914)

Louis XIV	Peter the Great	Nationalism
Jean-Jacques Rousseau	Catherine the Great	George III
George Washington	Thomas Jefferson	Louis XVI
Napoleon Bonaparte	Karl Marx	Czar Nicholas
Abraham Lincoln	Simón Bolívar	Miguel Hidalgo
Otto von Bismarck	King William I	World War I
Nikolai Lenin	The Napoleonic Wars	Imperialism
The French Revolution	The American Revolution	Romanticism
Frederick Douglass	Charles Darwin	
The Boxer Rebellion	The Russo-Japanese War	
Sepoy Rebellion	Scramble for Africa	
Oliver Cromwell	Sino-Japanese War	

The Twentieth Century and Beyond (1914–present)

Franklin Roosevelt	The Great Depression	Adolf Hitler
Joseph Stalin	Mohandas Gandhi	Mao Zedong
Harry Truman	Nikita Khrushchev	Ronald Reagan
John F. Kennedy	Martin Luther King Jr.	Ho Chi Minh
Jawaharlal Nehru	Indira Ghandi	Corazon Aquino
Nelson Mandela	Mikhail Gorbachev	The Cold War
Boris Yeltsin	George Bush Sr.	World War II
The League of Nations	The United Nations	Yasser Arafat
The Third World	The Balfour Declaration	Benito Mussolini
Iranian Revolution	African National Congress	Holocaust
Barack Obama	Osama Bin Laden	The Gulf Wars
Vladimir Putin	9/11	

Go Deep: Further Readings in World History

Appendix

D

General World History

Barzun, Jacques. *From Dawn to Decadence: 1500 to the Present.*

Bentley, Jerry. *Old World Encounters: Cross-Cultural Contacts and Exchanges in Pre-Modern Times; Shapes of World History in Twentieth-Century Scholarship.*

Bentley, Jerry, and Herbert Ziegler. *Traditions and Encounters: A Global Perspective on the Past.*

Braudel, Fernand. *A History of Civilizations.*

Bulliet, Richard. *The Earth and Its Peoples: A Global History.*

Christian, David. *Maps of Time.*

Curtin, Philip. *Cross-Cultural Trade in World History.*

Dawson, Christopher. *The Age of the Gods; Progress and Religion; The Making of Europe.*

Diamond, Jared. *Guns, Germs, and Steel: The Fates of Human Societies.*

Hall, John, and John Kirk. *History of the World: Earliest Times to the Present Day.*

Hodgson, Marshall. *Rethinking World History.*

Keegan, John. *A History of Warfare.*

McNeill, William H. *A World History; The Pursuit of Power; Plagues and Peoples.*

Pacey, Arnold. *Technology in World Civilization.*

Pomeranz, K., and S. Topik. *The World That Trade Created: Society, Culture, and the World Economy; The Great Divergence: Europe, China and the Making of the Modern World.*

Roberts, J. M. *The New Penguin History of the World.*

Singer, Peter. *One World: The Ethics of Globalization.*

Spengler, Oswald. *The Decline of the West.*

Stavrianos, L.S. *Global Rift: The Third World Comes of Age; A Global History.*

Toynbee, Arnold. *A Study of History.*

Wells, H. G. *The Outline of History.*

Wolff, Eric. *Europe and the People Without History.*

Europe

Blair, Peter Hunter. *An Introduction to Anglo-Saxon England.*

Davies, Norman. *Europe: A History.*

Durant, Will. *The Renaissance.*

Freeman, Charles. *Egypt, Greece, and Rome: Civilizations of the Ancient Mediterranean.*

Headrick, Daniel R. *The Tools of Empire: Technology & European Imperialism in the 19th Century; Tentacles of Progress: Technology Transfer in the Age of Imperialism.*

Lawrence, James. *The Rise and Fall of the British Empire.*

Riasanovsky, Nicholas. *A History of Russia.*

The Americas

Bushnell, David, and Neil Macauley. *Emergence of Latin America in the Nineteenth Century.*

Conrad, Geoffrey, and Arthur Demerest. *Religion and Empire: The Dynamics of Aztec and Inca Expansionism.*

Davies, Nigel. *The Aztec Empire.*

Eltis, David. *The Rise of African Slavery in the Americas.*

Hyslop, J. *The Inca Road System.*

Josephy, Jr., Alvin. *The Indian Heritage of America.*

Klein, Herbert. *The Atlantic Slave Trade.*

Skidmore, Thomas E., and Peter H. Smith. *Modern Latin America.*

Stanley, J., and Barbara Stein. *The Colonial Heritage of Latin America.*

Asia

Borthwick, Mark. *Pacific Century: The Emergence of Modern Pacific Asia.*

Cortazzi, Hugh. *The Japanese Achievement.*

Fairbanks, John, and Merle Goldman. *China: A New History.*

Frank, Andre. *ReORIENT: Global Economy in the Asian Age.*

Grousset, Rene. *The Empire of the Steppes: A History of Central Asia.*

Huang, Ray. *China: A Macro History.*

Lu, David J. *Japan: A Documentary History.*

Mason, R. H. P., and J. G. Caiger. *A History of Japan.*

Osborne, Milton. *Southeast Asia: An Introductory History.*

Reid, Anthony. *Charting the Shape of Early Modern Southeast Asia.*

Murphey, Rhoads. *A History of Asia.*

Roberts, J.A.G. *A Concise History of China.*

Wolpert, Stanley. *A New History of India.*

Africa

Davidson, Basil. *Africa in History; African Civilizations Revisited.*

Inikori, J. E. *Forced Migration: The Impact of the Export Slave Trade on African Societies.*

Manning, Patrick. *Slavery and African Life.*

Mazrui, Ali A. *The Africans: A Reader* and *The Africans*.

Newman, James L. *The Peopling of Africa: A Geographic Interpretation*.

Oliver, Roland, and J. D. Fage, *A Short History of Africa*.

Reader, John. *Africa: A Biography of the Continent*.

Shillington, Kevin. *History of Africa*.

The Middle East

Hitti, Philip. *History of the Arabs*.

Hodgson, Marshall. *Adventure of Islam: Conscience and History in a World Civilization*.

Lewis, Bernard. *Islam: From the Prophet Muhammad to the Capture of Constantinople*.

Said, Edward. *Orientalism*.

Index